Grammar

Traditionally, there ~~is~~ a disconnect between theoretical linguistics and language teacher training. This book seeks to bridge that gap. Using engaging examples from a wide variety of languages, it provides an innovative overview of linguistic theory and language acquisition research for readers with a background in education and teacher training and without specialist knowledge of the field. The authors draw on a range of research to ground ideas about grammar pedagogy, presenting the notion of Virtual Grammar as an accessible label for unifying the complexity of linguistics. Organised thematically, the book includes helpful 'Case in Point' examples throughout the text, to illustrate specific grammar points, and step-by-step training in linguistic methods, such as how to analyse examples, which educators can apply to their own teaching contexts. Through enriching language teachers' understanding of linguistic features, the book fosters a different perspective on grammar for educators.

TOM RANKIN'S research investigates diverse aspects of language learning, from generative theoretical approaches to the acquisition of syntax to applications of learner corpora for teaching. His work has been published in *Second Language Research* and the *International Journal of Learner Corpus Research*. He is an editor of the journal *Pedagogical Linguistics*.

MELINDA WHONG'S teaching career spans four continents and ranges from primary to higher education. Her academic career has been devoted to bridging the gap between linguistic research and classroom teaching, with previous books including *Universal Grammar and the Second Language Classroom* and *Language Teaching: Linguistic Theory in Practice*.

Grammar

A Linguists' Guide for Language Teachers

TOM RANKIN
Johannes Kepler University Linz

MELINDA WHONG
Hong Kong University of Science and Technology

CAMBRIDGE
UNIVERSITY PRESS

University Printing House, Cambridge CB2 8BS, United Kingdom

One Liberty Plaza, 20th Floor, New York, NY 10006, USA

477 Williamstown Road, Port Melbourne, VIC 3207, Australia

314–321, 3rd Floor, Plot 3, Splendor Forum, Jasola District Centre, New Delhi – 110025, India

79 Anson Road, #06–04/06, Singapore 079906

Cambridge University Press is part of the University of Cambridge.

It furthers the University's mission by disseminating knowledge in the pursuit of education, learning, and research at the highest international levels of excellence.

www.cambridge.org
Information on this title: www.cambridge.org/9781108486026
DOI: 10.1017/9781108623360

© Tom Rankin and Melinda Whong 2020

This publication is in copyright. Subject to statutory exception and to the provisions of relevant collective licensing agreements, no reproduction of any part may take place without the written permission of Cambridge University Press.

First published 2020

Printed in the United Kingdom by TJ International Ltd, Padstow Cornwall

A catalogue record for this publication is available from the British Library.

Library of Congress Cataloging-in-Publication Data
Names: Rankin, Tom (Anglicist), author. | Whong, Melinda, author.
Title: Grammar : a linguists' guide for language teachers / Tom Rankin, Melinda Whong.
Description: 1. | New York : Cambridge University Press, 2020. | Includes index.
Identifiers: LCCN 2020004389 (print) | LCCN 2020004390 (ebook) | ISBN 9781108486026 (hardback) | ISBN 9781108623360 (ebook)
Subjects: LCSH: Grammar, Comparative and general – Study and teaching. | Second language acquisition – Study and teaching. | Linguistics – Terminology. | Language and languages – Terminology.
Classification: LCC P53 .R36 2020 (print) | LCC P53 (ebook) | DDC 415.071–dc23
LC record available at https://lccn.loc.gov/2020004389
LC ebook record available at https://lccn.loc.gov/2020004390

ISBN 978-1-108-48602-6 Hardback
ISBN 978-1-108-73695-4 Paperback

Cambridge University Press has no responsibility for the persistence or accuracy of URLs for external or third-party internet websites referred to in this publication and does not guarantee that any content on such websites is, or will remain, accurate or appropriate.

Contents

1	A Guide to the Linguists' Guide to Grammar	page 1
	1.1 The Linguistic Terrain	4
	1.1.1 Theoretical Approaches to Linguistics	9
	1.1.2 Fields and Subfields	14
	1.2 The Development of Language in the Mind	21
	1.3 Linguistics and Education	26
	1.3.1 Grammatical Concepts	26
	1.3.2 Brief Overview of (European) Language Teaching	32
	1.4 Conclusion: Bring Back Grammar	37
	1.5 Exercises and Questions for Discussion	38
2	Language and Languages	41
	2.1 What Is Language?	43
	2.2 Linguistic Diversity and Diversity in Linguistics	54
	2.3 Languages within Languages	61
	2.3.1 Varieties and Dialects	61
	2.3.2 Language Register	66
	2.3.3 Pidgins and Creoles	70
	2.4 Conclusion: Moving Forward	72
	2.5 Exercises and Questions for Discussion	73
3	Grammar and Grammars	78
	3.1 What Is Grammar?	79
	3.1.1 Prescriptive Grammar and Descriptive Grammar	81
	3.1.2 Pedagogical Grammar	89
	3.1.3 Interlanguage Grammar	96
	3.2 The Use and Abuse of Grammar	100
	3.2.1 Grammatical Viruses	101
	3.3 Virtual Grammar and Language Education	107
	3.4 Conclusion: Making the Most of Grammar	113
	3.5 Exercises and Questions for Discussion	114

4	Language Learning and Acquisition	117
	4.1 Additional Language Learning: Fundamentally Different?	119
	4.2 Landmarks of L2 Grammatical Development	126
	4.2.1 The Beginning	126
	4.2.2 The Middle Stages	130
	4.2.3 The Advanced End-State	133
	4.3 Additional Language Learning: Fundamentally Similar?	136
	4.3.1 The Language Instinct, Virtual Grammar and Language Learning	138
	4.3.2 Language Input	145
	4.4 Can Language Be Learned Later in Life?	153
	4.5 Conclusions: The Same But Different	156
	4.6 Exercises and Questions for Discussion	157
5	Language Education	161
	5.1 What Is Foreign Language Teaching For?	162
	5.2 Nativeness and Foreignness	166
	5.3 Awareness and Ability	172
	5.4 Grammar Acquisition and Grammatical Skills	177
	5.5 Preliminary Conclusion	183
	5.6 Conclusion: Applying Linguistics	183
	5.7 Exercises and Questions for Discussion	188
	References	192
	Index	206

1 A Guide to the Linguists' Guide to Grammar

It's the natural worry of every novice teacher: that question which you have no idea how to answer. I'll never forget the very bright Korean student who brought me every piece of written work containing feedback from me, on which he had highlighted every instance of the use of the English article, along with a log he was keeping of his encounters with correct and incorrect article use, and every explanation of the grammatical properties of articles he could find in the range of pedagogical materials he had collected. After setting out his findings, he was hoping I would explain the dozen or so 'exceptions' in his list of examples that he could not account for. What this experience and this student taught me was that knowing how to approach challenging points of grammar is much more valuable, and appropriate, than expert knowledge of each and every challenging point of grammar that exists. One motivation for this volume is to provide a degree of linguistics training, so that you have the tools to address any challenging question about grammar that you might encounter. I was, in fact, not able to provide ready answers for my Korean student. But as is often the case with students, he provided the way forward himself. By collecting instances of the grammatical phenomenon in question, he had collated a data set which we were able to work through to make sense of the complex properties of articles in English.

We hope that the language-data-based approach we take in this book will achieve our overarching aim: to help you develop a methodology for approaching the complexity of language – and grammar in particular – so that you are better able to facilitate the development of language amongst your learners. A secondary aim is to boost your own knowledge base of language and languages and linguistics, in order to add to your ever-growing expertise as a language teacher. We will, for example, provide insight into the properties of the English article system (see Case in Point 1.1 on Specificity). But alongside grammatical explanations in English, we will be exploring how linguistic properties

1.1 CASE IN POINT: SPECIFICITY

Particular grammatical structures may be made complicated due to 'hidden' grammatical properties. By this we mean features of semantic or grammatical meaning which play a role in regulating usage, but which do not have an obvious marking. Specificity with regard to English articles illustrates this. There is no explicit grammatical form in English noun phrases which overtly indicates specificity. Specific meaning is nonetheless grammatically relevant in English, and cuts across the perhaps more familiar definite/indefinite grammatical distinction. The sentences (i)–(iv) show how definiteness combines with specificity to result in differences in meaning (examples from Lyons, 1999, p. 167).

(i) He didn't see **a car** parked at the door – until two men got out of it and asked for directions. *indefinite / **specific***
(ii) He didn't see **a car** parked at the door – so he knew the visitors hadn't arrived yet. *indefinite / **unspecific***
(iii) I didn't meet **the professor** during my visit to the philosophy department yesterday morning – but I managed to get hold of him in the afternoon. *definite / **specific***
(iv) I didn't meet **the professor** during my visit to the philosophy department yesterday morning – so I began to wonder whether that chair had been filled yet. *definite / **unspecific***

Later, we will see how this sort of meaning is manifested in other languages and is relevant in the acquisition and learning of grammar (see Chapter 3 for more on articles and specificity).

---

are manifested in language in general, and provide examples from across a wide range of languages.

As you see, we are relying on a set of text boxes, each called 'Case in Point', within which we will present language data that illustrate a particular grammatical phenomenon. We will walk you through how these work in this chapter (see Case in Point 1.2, which explains how to read these). You will find that we make use of a large range of languages, most of which are likely to be foreign to you, including some that you are likely to have never heard of. We have done this intentionally in order to widen the scope of your knowledge of languages in the world. However, as we progress you will find that we highlight larger more 'well-known' languages more because we are drawing from published research on language learning and acquisition, and, for better or for worse, it is these languages that have received the most attention in research terms. While we hope you will want to develop your expertise in language, we also recognise that making sense of linguistic data is hard work. For this reason, we have tried to ensure that the general conceptual point being made in the Case in Point is clear in the surrounding narrative that would allow you to skip a Case in Point in your reading as you might find it more useful to examine the Case in Points separately. In fact, we have written this book in such a way that it would be possible to save all the Case in Points to work through separately. The narrative, by contrast, is designed to develop concepts in an accumulative way that might not as readily allow for the reading of chapters in isolation.

One obvious truth about all learners of a 'foreign' language is that they already have full competence in (at least) one other language. Given that one fundamental tenet of education is the value of building on existing knowledge, we take the view that when teaching a 'target' language, one would do well to make as much use of students' existing language knowledge as possible, a point which is not uncontroversial in foreign language teaching, and which we develop more fully in Chapter 5. At the same time, we realise that it is unrealistic that you would have full mastery of all of your students' existing language knowledge, especially if working with a class of multilingual speakers. What this book aims to do is to expose you to a wide range of linguistic phenomena across many languages in order to raise your awareness of what's possible (and not possible) in the grammar of a language. Along the way, you're likely to learn a thing or two about specific languages; but the overriding aim is to equip you with a more sophisticated understanding of how language works. In doing this, we will introduce the notion of Grammatical Concepts as an important aspect of what we will call a Virtual Grammar. We hope that adopting this understanding of grammar will ensure that you have more confidence when you encounter a student who challenges you, like mine did with English articles. But it will also allow you to think in a different way about how to approach grammatical properties of language in your teaching.

As may be clear already, we are linguists with background and some training in teaching. For this reason, our aim is not to make suggestions on *how* you should teach. It is, instead, to provide a better understanding of *what* you are teaching. Like all areas of academic study, within the discipline of linguistics there has been great advancement in our understanding of language. Unfortunately, another feature of academia is that development in one area does not always make its way into another area of study. The fields of Linguistics and Education are two academic areas of study which have developed away from each other in the recent past. We hope to do our small part to address this by exploring the intricacies of grammar through the eyes of the linguist, but with the interests and concerns of the language teacher in mind. We start by presenting a brief overview of the field of linguistics in a way that attempts to provide an outline of the complexity of language.

1.1 THE LINGUISTIC TERRAIN

Linguistics is a relatively young independent academic discipline, though language itself has been a topic of inquiry since antiquity. There is a level of fragmentation in the field of modern linguistics which is, perhaps, not surprising, given the rich complexity of language. The starting (and ending) point of this overview of Linguistics is the reminder that linguists are all trying to understand and explain the same thing: Language. Because the object of study is shared, one would think that the conclusions that linguists come to would also be shared. However, the sheer complexity of language means that there are many different ways to approach the study of language, each with a different emphasis and, concurrently, with different omissions. This has sometimes led to very different conclusions about the nature of language in general, with much discussion of differences in theory, and different analyses of single features of languages even. One unhelpful result is that publications in linguistics rarely provide an accessible source of information for teachers looking for some tips on properties of grammar. We will try to make sense of the terrain underlying the field of linguistics by presenting it as a set of oppositions.

One basic opposition that captures contemporary linguistic approaches to language is the **Form–Function** opposition. Simply put, this contrast compares those who are more interested in the grammatical structures of language with those who care more about how language is used. The former are often called **Formalists** and the latter, **Functionalists**. These opposing interests broadly correspond to a host of additional oppositions, which can sometimes lead to opposite conclusions within linguistics. Because neither approach has been shown to be uncontroversially correct or incorrect, we take the view that all viewpoints are potentially useful – especially within the context of language teaching. Being able to draw from the full range of possibilities in linguistics means a teacher has options,

1.1 The Linguistic Terrain

a valuable position to be in and appropriate in the 'post-methods' era (Kumaravadivelu, 2001).

To help us illustrate the form–function opposition, consider Case in Point 1.2, which illustrates the passive. The point that emerges here, and will be repeated throughout the book, is that languages present myriad variations on the same grammatical concepts. More specifically, similar grammatical, or formal (='form+al') mechanisms can be used for different functional purposes and/or very different formal mechanisms can be used for similar functional purposes. As shown in Case in Point 1.2, while English adds a participial verb when it expresses passive voice, Swahili changes the morpheme, in the form of an affix on the main verb itself. Mastery of these intricate form/function distinctions in a foreign language is what often proves frustratingly difficult.

1.2 CASE IN POINT: PASSIVE

There is a wide range of ways in which languages express a passive variant of active declarative sentences. In English we are well aware of the structure of a passive sentence, as illustrated in the difference between (ia) and (ib).

(i)   a. Bill cooked the food.
     b. The food was cooked (by Bill).
     c. *Was cooked (by Bill).

However, in linguistics we are also interested in how and why certain related versions of sentences are impossible. We may test the limits of grammar by constructing sentences in order to explore the grammar which underlies them. We use conventions such as the asterisk (*) to indicate that such a constructed sentence is not grammatically acceptable, and brackets to indicate optionality, as in (ic). Grouping the three sentences together, by convention, indicates that the three sentences are related as a set, and should be considered in light of each other. In this case (ia) is the active declarative form in English, (ib) shows the passive version, with (ic) illustrating what is needed, grammatically, for the passive form to be grammatical: an overt subject. Without a subject, the passive is ungrammatical. Thus, we can conclude that the object of an active sentence becomes the syntactic subject of a passive sentence.

Other languages present variations on this theme. For instance, the pattern in Swahili is shown in (ii) (Siewierska, 2013).

(ii) a. Hamisi   a-li-pik-a   chakula
       Hamisi   3SG-PST-cook-IND   food
       'Hamisi cooked the/some food.'
   b. chakula   ki-li-pik-**w**-a   (na Hamisi)
      food   3SG-PST-cook-**PASS**-IND   (by Hamisi)
      'The food was cooked (by Hamisi).'

Notice that in (iib), the passive is signalled by the -w- suffix on the verb. This is glossed as **PASS** to indicate the passive grammatical function of the morpheme; in the same way that the mood of the sentence is also grammatically marked in Swahili, IND shows that these are indicative sentences.

Within a data set presented for an English-speaking reader, the first line is the **language data**, using romanised lettering if the language in question relies on a non-romanised writing system. The second line is a **gloss**, giving a literal translation, and showing grammatical functions like PST (past tense) or 3SG (third person singular), with the hyphen used to indicate morpheme boundaries. The third line is the translation into what would be a natural expression of the language data in English.

Notice in the Swahili examples that the morpheme for 3SG agreement changes (from 'a' to 'ki'). This is because agreement in Swahili changes according to noun class (or gender), and in our example *food* is a different noun class than *a person* (see Case in Point 2.5 on Gender and Noun Classification). When we give examples, there are likely to be grammatical points at play which go beyond the topic of the Case in Point. We will normally show these differences in the gloss, but not comment on them, in the interest of focus.

Linguists, whether formalist or functionalist in orientation, will agree that (ic) in Case in Point 1.2 is unacceptable in English. What differs is the understanding of why this is. For a formalist, the explanation lies in the structural constraints on English: (ic) is ungrammatical because it does not include an overt argument in subject position. In (ia), the active form of this declarative sentence contains an argument in the form of a noun phrase in subject position, making it grammatical. For a formalist, structural constraints in English mean that when an active sentence like (ia) is without its subject, another noun phrase must occupy that subject position; this leads to passive formation with the object argument from the active form 'moving' to subject position. The original subject argument is either omitted, or optionally expressed as a prepositional phrase, as in (ib). A formalist will,

1.1 The Linguistic Terrain

unsurprisingly, use a formal explanation for this descriptive pattern. In this way of thinking, passive formation *is caused* by the structural absence of an overt subject.

By contrast, functionalists will explain that (ic) is not possible because of meaning. It is not possible to make sense of (ic) because we don't know what was cooked in that example. A functionalist will explain that English has two ways of expressing action so that either the agent of the action is foregrounded (ia), which is what happens in active declarative sentences; or the so-called theme or patient of the action is foregrounded (ib), as occurs in the passive. Notice that a functionalist description of the active–passive distinction differs from the formalist in that it comes from the perspective of message and function. Like formalists, functionalists are also interested in going beyond description to offer an explanation, looking to a meaning-based explanation for why the active–passive variants exist. A functionalist will see passive formation as driven by the meaning intended by the speaker; the desire by the speaker to emphasise the action over the actor will result in a passive form.

As we can see, our passive example illustrates two completely different explanations for why there are passive and active declarative sentences in language; the two perspectives even use different terminology to explain the same language data. The formalist might describe the active and passive in terms of *arguments*, *noun phrases* and *subject/object positions* in the sentence structure. A functionalist may prefer terms that reflect meaning and function, such as *agent* and *theme*. Yet both are describing the same linguistic phenomenon. This kind of difference is one reason why grammar and linguistics have come to be seen as complex and difficult. Yet surely we can turn this on its head and say instead that this kind of difference means that language teachers have a richer set of options in their arsenal. This form–function distinction means that there are two ways to explain language at the sentence level. Given that each is said to be the 'correct' understanding by one set of linguists, a skilled teacher can decide when best to appeal to one, or even both explanations. The form–function distinction offers the potential that both those learners who seem to relate to 'meaning' explanations and those who are more comfortable with 'structural' explanations will better understand the language they are learning.

Though there are two ways to think about the passive, both are describing the same language data, and both are reasonable perspectives. We also see differences at a different level of abstraction when we compare languages. The same universal functional relationships, for example between verbs and their arguments, can be realised differently, giving rise to different formal patterns on the surface.

1.3 CASE IN POINT: ARGUMENTS AND ALIGNMENT

Languages can be categorised according to the way that they treat subject and object arguments of verbs in terms of agreement or case marking, and certain grammatical generalisations. Here we concentrate on case marking. The alignment pattern for arguments that you are familiar with as an English speaker is a nominative–accusative system in which nominative case is apparent with subject arguments and accusative case with object arguments, though only within the pronoun system.

(i) a. **I** saw **her**.
    1SG.**NOM** saw 3SG.**ACC**
  b. **She** saw **me**.
    3SG.**NOM** saw 1SG.**ACC**

Ergative-absolutive languages align arguments with case differently: objects of transitive verbs carry absolutive case but so do subjects of intransitive verbs, as illustrated in Walpiri, an indigenous Australian language. For example, in (ii), *wawirri* (direct object of a transitive verb) and *kurdu* (subject of an intransitive verb) each appear in the bare form, which linguists refer to as absolutive for these languages. It is the subject of transitive verbs which carry distinct ergative case marking (data from Hale, 1983, in Deal, 2015).

(ii) a. **Kurdu** kapi wanti-mi
    child.**ABS** AUX fall-NONPAST
    'The child will fall.'
  b. Ngarrka-ngku ka **wawirri** panti-rni.
    Man-ERG AUX kangaroo.**ABS** spear-NONPAST
    'The man is spearing the kangaroo.'

(See Case in Point 1.3.) This sort of thing may seem exotic and difficult when one comes to learn grammatical features of a foreign language which instantiates familiar concepts in different ways.

As we will see, distinctions like the case marking patterns illustrated in Case in Point 1.3 are one facet of deeper generalisations which hold true across languages. An important part of the job of the academic linguist is to explain why language works as it does, because explanations are the stuff of linguistic theory. Our discussion of the passive, for example, is not just an illustration of how one feature of English can be described from different angles; it corresponds to differences in theoretical frameworks.

1.1 The Linguistic Terrain

1.1.1 Theoretical Approaches to Linguistics

The need to provide explanations has led to a number of theoretical frameworks in linguistics, with each having a broadly form-based or function-based orientation. The most influential formalist framework is that of the Generativists, while functionalist theories can be combined under the umbrella term, Constructivists. (For full length overviews, see Newmeyer, 1998; Ambridge & Lieven, 2011.)

The establishment of **Generative Linguistics** came in the 1950s and 60s when Noam Chomsky challenged the Behaviourist understanding of child language acquisition, arguing that repetition and reinforcement of language input cannot fully explain the rich complexity of language that children develop (e.g. Chomsky, 1959). In this view, the linguistic input, or 'stimulus', that any one child receives is poor compared to that child's ultimate ability with language. Chomsky's argument was that the **poverty of the stimulus** available to any developing child means that children must possess an in-built blueprint that guides the acquisition of language. Ever since, the formalist approach has been devoted to defining the **Universal Grammar** which underlies all languages. This approach argues that one limited set of universal grammatical constraints allows a speaker to generate an infinite number of sentences. This is possible because all languages abide by this shared set of constraints, which are part of the biological code setting the human species apart from other animals. This '**nativist**' view puts the emphasis for language and language development on the cognitive predisposition of the individual as the explanation for the development of language, with a 'language instinct' constraining what is possible in language. In this approach, what is of interest is so-called **competence**, which is the implicit knowledge of linguistic principles which each speaker possesses. Generative linguists work hard to isolate competence from the many circumstantial influences that affect the production of language such as fatigue, attention, personality – which in this approach are referred to as **performance**. The interesting contribution from a generative perspective is that some areas of competence are highly complex when analysed linguistically, but might not necessarily give rise to performance issues. For example, for any number of performance reasons, one might produce a slip of the tongue when forming the passive. But passive is only one element of intricate systems of grammatical voice which different languages realise differently, and in which we have very subtle competence – at least in our primary language (see Case in Point 1.4).

1.4 CASE IN POINT: VOICE

Passive is one instance of the voice system of a language. Passive voice can be opposed to the active voice. Transitive constructions in the active voice align the actor/agent with the subject and the theme/patient with the object. The passive aligns the theme/patient with the subject and the actor with some other form depending on language (an optional prepositional by-phrase in English, or in an oblique case in other languages).

(i) The boy bent the stick.
(ii) The stick was bent (by the boy).

But this by no means exhausts the limits of voice distinctions. Further ones can be made, and are realised differently in different languages. All such voice alternations define how arguments relate to a verb. For example, middle voice is grammatically marked in Sanskrit to indicate that an action occurs of itself, as in (iii) and (iv) from Polinksy (2001) (see also Case in Point 1.6). The voice system is marked morphologically with different paradigms for active and middle.

(iii) So namati daṇḍam
 he.NOM bends.**ACT** stick.ACC
 'He bends the stick.'

(iv) daṇḍaḥ namate
 stick.NOM bend.**MIDDLE**
 'The stick bends.'

While English does not syntactically mark middle as a separate grammatical category, it does allow middle constructions with certain types of verbs, as in (v).

(v) This stick bends easily. (meaning it is easy for someone to bend this stick)

We see that this meaning can be an inherent part of certain verbs' meaning. Other verbs do not inherently have this sort of meaning, but they may take part in a syntactic middle construction when the context allows, as in (vi) versus (vii).

(vi) *This book reads.
(vii) This book reads well.

1.1 The Linguistic Terrain

The opposite view places the onus for the development of language on the experience of each user and learner of language, recognising the differences that each person will experience in terms of not only linguistic form, but also differences in context and the role that it plays in the development of language. **Usage-based approaches** take a **Constructivist** view, seeing language as constructed by the individual and as such, '**emergent**' in response to the particular input which a learner actually encounters. This view stresses the role of meaning in language. It will point out that language cannot be seen as devoid of meaning, and argues that it is meaning-making that drives the development of language because young children are driven by the need to communicate. While it might seem that this is the same thing as the Behaviourist claims refuted by early generative linguists, in fact significant developments in linguistics and cognitive science now underpin the Constructivist approach, with statistical modelling used to support claims that the frequency of exposure to a specific word can affect development of language, for example. However, the development of technology from eye-tracking to fMRI capability for neuroimaging has led to significant developments in many subfields of linguistics. By permitting exploration of the neuropsychological mechanisms underpinning language, both formal and functional linguistics traditions have been able to find support from cognitive processes for their views of language.

Cognitive psychologists use these psycholinguistic and neurolinguistic techniques to investigate the mental mechanisms underpinning language. There is also the school of **Cognitive Linguistics** whose development lies outside neuroscience. The 'cognitive' part of the cognitive linguistics framework sees the properties of language as intimately tied to general cognition so that lexical and grammatical phenomena reflect conceptual structure. General mental processes such as metaphor and extension play crucial roles in the lexical and grammatical structures of language. Of great use to the language classroom, there is work done within a cognitive linguistics framework that has direct relevance for learning vocabulary. Franz Boers has done very useful work with research findings showing, for example, that teaching the literal meanings of words before their metaphorical meaning leads to significantly more robust learning and retention of learning. See Boers and Lindstromberg (2008) for a volume full of useful applications for the classroom coming from research from cognitive linguistics. In addition to words having literal and metaphorical meanings, you will know that in English the same word can often function as a verb and a noun. In fact, Germanic languages like English have relatively free word formation abilities, or, in linguistic terms, are quite **productive**. Even lexical phenomena like word class changes entail potentially intricate grammatical phenomena, which we do not perhaps immediately think of when it comes to the learning/teaching of vocabulary and the lexical properties of languages (see Case in Point 1.5). But thinking in terms of grammar may provide a productive perspective on types of vocabulary learning too, as indicated by the Cases in Point in this chapter which illustrate how grammatical commonalities often fall out of lexical classes.

1.5 CASE IN POINT: DEVERBAL NOUNS

Deverbal nouns are nouns which are derived from verbs. They may retain different semantic or grammatical properties of their related verbs. This is one instance of the general fact that noun phrases bear a certain relationship to whole clauses, as indicated by (i) and (ii).

(i) It is well-known that **I prefer chocolate cake**.
(ii) **My preference for chocolate cake** is well-known.

The object argument of the verb in (i) maps onto complements of the noun phrase in (ii), with the subject argument becoming the possessive *my*, and the patient NP becoming the prepositional phrase *for chocolate cake*. Verbs may pick out different features of meaning (see also Case in Point 1.6). The realisation of complements of deverbal nouns will differ depending on the features of the verb's meaning which the noun retains, illustrated in (iii) and (iv).

(iii) I discovered Jody hiding in a wine barrel.
    a. The discovery of Jody   was shocking.
    b. *Jody's discovery   was shocking
(iv) Jody discovered a new solution to the theorem.
    a. *The discovery of Jody   was ground-breaking.
    b. Jody's discovery   was ground-breaking.

The meaning of *to discover* includes the process/event of finding something new as well as the resulting state of having some new knowledge. The derived noun *discovery* may emphasise the process/event meaning. In this case, the object of the verb can only be realised as an *of*-phrase, as in the (a) versus (b) contrast in (iii). When the deverbal noun picks out the result meaning, we see the opposite pattern, as in (iv). Here, the genitive form *Jody's* has to be used as it is construed as an agent, the result of whose action was a new discovery.

While the same semantic properties of process versus result are at play across different languages, the way these properties are encoded differs. For example, in Catalan, the way that the 'arguments' of nouns are realised is subtly different compared to English (data from Picallo, 1991). The sentence in (v) is ambiguous, meaning either Pythagoras proved the theory (process/event), or someone proved Pythagoras' theory (result).

(v) la demonstració del teorema de Pitàgores
     the proof of the theory of Pythagoras

Notice, however, that the direct English translation is not ambiguous. As illustrated previously, a post-verb *of*-phrase doesn't encode an agent in English. Catalan realises these arguments in different ways, as in (vi) and (vii).

(vi) la demonstració del teorema de Pitàgores per part d'en Joan.
      the proof of the theory of Pythagoras on the part of Joan
      'Joan's proof of Pythagoras' theory'
(vii) la demonstració d'en Joan del teorema de Pitàgores.
      the proof of Joan of the theory of Pythagoras
      'the proof by Joan of Pythagoras' theory'

The functionalist approach to language which takes meaning and use as its starting point has given rise to another strand of linguistics altogether, **Systemic Functional Linguistics (SFL)**. As a meaning-driven approach, SFL's approach to language is always in relation to the wider context. The establishment of SFL is attributed to Michael Halliday, whose thinking developed out of European approaches rooted in literary studies and semiotics, the latter of which traces directly to the influential early linguist Ferdinand de Saussure who is well known for describing language as a system of signs (see Halliday & Webster, 2009). SFL sees language as a product of metafunctions. **Ideational metafunctions** come out of how we make sense of reality, while **interpersonal metafunctions** derive from how we relate with each other. These metafunctions determine the shape of language. In our example of the passive, we saw that it is the speaker's view of the importance of the action which leads to a passive form instead of an active variant which emphasises the actor. To truly make sense of this example, it is important to go beyond the level of a sentence to the wider textual level. As such, linguistic analysis within SFL draws on another category of metafunction, the **textual metafunction**. For SFL, metafunctions are the broad impulses that drive language, with specific instances of language output affected by the parameters of the larger linguistic context in which it occurs.

As an approach to linguistics, Systemic Functional Linguistics, much like Generative Linguistics or Cognitive Linguistics is interested in the properties of language. Within these broad theoretical approaches there are fields and subfields which are devoted to specific aspects of language.

1.1.2 Fields and Subfields

The fact that fields with subfields of specialised study have developed over time reinforces the point that language is rich and complex. Extending beyond pure linguistics, the field of **sociolinguistics** connects the properties of language, as studied by linguists, with the use of language by people through interaction within a social context. Influential within language education in particular is the work of Dell Hymes who challenged the Chomskyan notion of competence by insisting on the importance of **communicative competence**. For Hymes (1972), what really matters is what speakers need to know in order to be communicatively competent in a speech community. This requires clear understanding of the social and cultural knowledge needed to understand and use linguistic forms in appropriate contexts, and in line with the cultural norms as they exist in a speech community. Given the interest in context, it is not surprising that many sociolinguists find affinity with linguistic approaches which lie more on the functionalist end of the linguistic terrain.

The subfield of **discourse analysis** is interested in features of text, but studies these by exploring the important role that the norms and expectations of the target audience plays in determining features of text. Given that the framing of discourse analysis is around the target audience, when considering a piece of either written or spoken text, the context in which that text is produced is shaped by the attitudes of both those creating and those receiving the text. Thus it is perhaps not surprising that this field of study has overtones of political activism, which in academic discipline terms is often captured in the word *critical*, giving us critical discourse analysis, or as an even more specialised example: critical English for academic purposes (i.e. critical EAP). While discourse analysis is interested in language at the level of texts, another subfield studies the language of interaction which does not necessarily conform to text types. In the field of **pragmatics**, linguists explore the relationship between the pressures that the wider context exerts on particular interactions between individuals. Pragmatics is interested in speech acts, and includes the observation that successful interactions require that people abide by rules that are usually implicit, such as remaining relevant within an interaction, for example.

1.1 The Linguistic Terrain

With emphasis in understanding how speech communities use and shape language, these subfields also tend to align with functionalist theories of language. This is not to say that functionalists are not interested in language at the level of the sentence, phrase or word. But these core linguistic elements are approached from the perspective of the wider context. Because of the interest in context and meaning, it is perhaps not surprising that when functionalists analyse language at the micro level, the tendency is to focus on words. While this interest at the lexical level includes grammatical words such as the past participial forms used in the English passive, for example, there tends to be more interest in the larger category of content-rich words which hold meaning. This corner of the linguistic terrain has given much attention to the ability of people to extend the meanings of words, bringing to attention the vast scale to which our use of words is metaphoric in nature. Formalists are of course also interested in the lexical level, but often this involves a grammatical slant by considering how generalisations across semantic types of words may have grammatical effects (see Case in Point 1.6).

1.6 CASE IN POINT: VERB CLASSES AND ARGUMENT ALTERNATIONS

While different languages mark the relationships between a verb and its arguments in different ways (see Case in Point 1.3), there can also be variation within a language. Arguments of certain verbs can occur in alternative patterns in relatively predictable ways based on elements of shared meaning, a phenomenon known as alternation. Consider the English verbs *break* and *hit*. Each verb is essentially transitive with an agent, a direct object, and an optional instrument argument, as shown in (i) and (ii).

(i) The boy broke the window (with a ball).
(ii) The boy hit the window (with a ball)

The word order similarity hides underlying grammatical differences. As shown in (iii) and (iv), while *break* can occur in an intransitive form as well, *hit* cannot.

(iii) The boy broke the window.
    a. The window broke.
    b. *The boy broke at the window.
(iv) The boy hit the window.
    a. *The window hit.
    b. The boy hit at the window.

The pattern in (iii) is known as an **inchoative** form because the window, in this example, came to be broken. This contrasts with the **causative** pattern in (i) which explicitly captures meaning which indicates that the boy caused the window to be broken. But these are not idiosyncratic properties of two random verbs. In English, *hit* and *break* are members of different verb classes with *break* in a class with *bend, crack, shatter*, etc. and *hit* a in a class alongside *beat, kick, punch*, etc. (see Fillmore, 1970). As shown in these examples, *break*-type verbs take part in the **causative/inchoative alternation** but *hit*-type verbs cannot.

You might have noticed that each set of verbs has a degree of shared meaning. Linguists have gone beyond this intuition to differentiate between manner verbs, which express the manner of an action (*hit* vs *beat* vs *thump*), and result verbs, which encode the result of the action (*break* vs *bend* vs *crack*) (Rappaport Hovav & Levin, 2010).

This semantic principle is not limited to English, but regulates the grammar of verbs cross-linguistically. Kimarang Dusun, spoken in Malaysia, shows verb class effects parallel to English, although obviously implicating the grammatical machinery of Kimarang Dusun (see Kroeger, 2010). More specifically, Kimarang Dusun differentiates between transitive versus intransitive uses of verb roots with a prefix. This paradigm allows productive prefixation to get a verb alternation with *break*-type verbs but not *hit*-type verbs, very much in parallel with the previous causative/inchoative distinction (from Kroeger, 2010, p. 4).

(v)
Root	Gloss	Intransitive	Transitive
babak	shatter	mabak	mamabak
apas	tear (e.g. ear, nose)	gumapas	mangagapas
kinis	tear (e.g. cloth)	kuminis	monginis
putut	break (e.g. rope etc.)	mutut	momutut
tipu	break (e.g. stick etc.)	tumipu	monipu

(vi)
Root	Gloss	Intransitive	Transitive
bobog	beat (w. stick)	*mobog	momobog
duntuk	bump, knock	*dumuntuk	monguduntuk
duntung	punch (w. fist)	*dumuntug	mongoduntung
lapis	slap	*lumapis	mangalapis
sudsur	poke	*sumudsur	monudsur

This paradigm also makes the result/manner distinction apparent in the choice of root. Where the verb root includes the meaning of its argument, *break*-type verbs require expression of the thing that was broken as the result of the action (*putu* versus *tipu*), while *hit*-type verbs encode the manner in the form of the instrument used to carry out the action (*bobog* versus *duntung*).

1.1 The Linguistic Terrain

Work by linguists at the word level has inspired a good amount of work within language education, with Michael Lewis' **Lexical Approach** one example (Lewis, 1993). The commitment to words has led to a view by Lewis in which there is no grammar per se, but instead, each language is a collection of words. The Lexical Approach looks to how words are related as the basis for deciding which words to teach, and in what order. This approach is one of many beneficiaries of the advent of computational search engines. The development of **Corpus Linguistics** takes full advantage of the ability to collect and analyse large samples of language for specific instances at the word and multi-word level. This has seen direct benefit within language education (see Aijmer, 2009; Götz & Mukherjee, 2019). You may already have experience with concordancing in language teaching and learning.

Areas of linguistic study which drill down to a focus on language below text level tend to lead to subfields that have more in common with formalist approaches. With a focus on the mechanics of language at the sentence and phrase level, the core subfield within the formalist approach is **syntax**, the field which is interested in explaining the ordering of phrases and words. This formalist interest in word order is interested not so much in specific words, but instead in broad word classes. Whether the noun happens to be 'murderer' or 'saint', for example, isn't usually going to make a difference in a linguistic analysis by a syntactician. While the difference between 'murderer', as a member of the class of nouns, and the ability 'to murder' as a verb is of interest to the syntactician because of the effect of this difference on the structure of the sentence in which it is used. To give a simple example of the approach taken by syntacticians, we know that in English if a word directly follows the word 'the', it is not going to be a verb. Distribution testing is a relatively simple but powerful syntactic tool. We can see that syntax is made up of syntactic constituents. A **constituent** is a group of words that act as a unit within hierarchical structure. The relevant factor for syntax is not the number of words in a constituent, but instead that it is of the appropriate syntactic type. For example, *she, the girl, the inquisitive young girl with an interest in science*, are all semantically and pragmatically very different, but they are all noun phrases because the most important element in each phrase is a noun. So, they can all occur in a noun-constituent slot in syntax. This practice of **distribution testing** in syntax in which language is analysed in terms of how different classes of words distribute across different sets of examples can be a valuable tool in the language classroom, and a powerful way to approach challenging questions from students, like my student with his data set of English articles.

We can use distribution testing to make sense of other areas of language, including the smallest meaningful grammatical unit of language, the **morpheme**. **Morphology** helps us to understand how words are derived from other words. Adding the affix *-er* to existing words in English is one way to form nouns which mean 'someone who carries out the action', as in the 'murderer' example. Morphemes like this are known as **derivational** morphemes. In addition to studying how words are derived, a morphologist studies the bits of words known as **inflection**, which have a grammatical function in a sentence, such as the 's' on the word 'studies' in this sentence. We have seen in the Cases in Point that languages can package many different grammatical functions into such inflections, such as passive and case. The use of these sorts of grammatical inflection is often particularly difficult for language learners. A distinct sense of foreignness or difficulty may arise when learners are confronted with a language that requires grammatical expression of a function which is a purely optional communicative element in their own language. As shown in Case in Point 1.7, there are languages that require verbal affixes for information which, in English, would be expressed through circumlocution, and only if that information were needed or useful in terms of clarity.

1.7 CASE IN POINT: EVIDENTIALITY

Evidentiality is a grammatical category in many languages, including Korean and Japanese, for example. In the same way that grammatical concepts like tense, definiteness, and gender are grammatical categories (see Cases in Point in later chapters), evidentiality can be expressed through specific grammatical morphemes. For languages which have evidentiality as a grammatical category, statements are grammatically marked to represent the source of the information or the 'evidence', much like a language which has tense as a grammatical category has to grammatically locate statements in time (see Aikhenvald, 2004). As with any grammatical category, evidentials require different levels of expression. A simple evidential system may just require marking of information reported from someone else. A large system may require subtle levels of distinction. This is illustrated on the basis of the Arawak language Tariana, spoken in Brazil (from Aikhenvald, 2004, pp. 2–3).

1.1 The Linguistic Terrain 19

> (i) Juse irida di-manika-**ka**
> José football 3SGNF-play- REC.P.VIS
> 'José has played football (we saw it).'
>
> In (i), the -*ka* ending combines recent past tense (REC.P) and the indication that the statement is based on direct visual evidence (VIS). The grammar will change depending on the source of evidence for the statement: non-visual in (ii), based on an inference in (iii), or based on an assumption from our knowledge in (iv).
>
> (ii) Juse irida di-manika-**mahka**
> José football 3SGNF-play- REC.P.NONVIS
> 'José has played football (we heard it).'
>
> (iii) Juse irida di-manika-**nihka**
> José football 3SGNF-play-REC.P.VIS.INFR
> 'José has played football (we infer it from visual evidence).'
>
> (iv) Juse irida di-manika-**sika**
> José football 3SGNF-play-REC.P.VIS.ASSUM
> 'José has played football (we assume this on the basis of what we already know).'
>
> This inflectional paradigm is likely to seem very exotic to speakers of English. But the functions are of course perfectly expressible by a range of grammatical or lexical means, as shown in the English translations. The crucial difference is that expression of evidentiality is not morphosyntactically required by English, even if it can be expressed by different means where communicatively relevant (as in v and vi).
>
> (v) I heard that José played football.
> (vi) José must have played football... I just saw his kit in the washing.

Below the level of morpheme is the level of the sound, studied within **Phonetics**. One enduring and incredibly useful achievement by linguists dates back to the late 1800s with the establishment of the International Phonetic Alphabet (IPA), which designates a distinct symbol for every linguistic sound found in any and every language of the world. This system captures each sound in terms of the **manner of articulation**, or the way in which the sound is made, combined with the **place of articulation**, or where within the vocal tract the sound is made. For example, in English the difference between the sound /s/, as in *sit* and /z/ as in *zit*, is only to do with whether the vocal chords vibrate, as in /z/, or not, for /s/. This difference, known as

voicing, is solely a difference of manner because the place of articulation doesn't change: in both of these sounds, air rushes through the small gap between the upper and lower dental structures.

While we have emphasised the importance of structures for formal approaches to language, it would be a mistake to say that formalists are not interested in meaning. **Semantics** is the subfield within formal linguistics which explores those aspects of meaning which have direct effects on language structure. It is research from semantics which has shed light on the challenge of articles that so intrigued my Korean-speaking student learning English, with specificity combining with definiteness to influence correct article choice. You may be familiar with other semantic concepts like stative and active. Such terminology is sometimes used in grammar teaching materials to describe differences between the uses of the verb *to be* when we say sentences like *Sue is a doctor* versus *Sue is happy*. What distinguishes meaning in semantics from a lay person's understanding of meaning is that the element of meaning is reflected in the grammar of language in different but systematic ways, which reflect a complex contribution of different elements.

Throughout this book we will be relying on what we will refer to as **grammatical concepts**, which can be thought of as kernels of meaning which have grammatical effects in language. Our argument will be that understanding these sorts of concepts is valuable, even if they are not standardly discussed in the grammatical explanations of the language you teach (see Evidentiality in Case in Point 1.7 for example, and the discussion that follows). They provide a coherent way of thinking about language and cross-linguistic differences which can enrich your perspective on grammar. And as we will see, such grammar-semantics properties are crucial in understanding language acquisition. This will in turn permit you to reflect on learning difficulties and grammar teaching materials from different points of view. In other words, we take the approach that grammar is 'real', as opposed to approaches which see language as only a collection of words. Linguistic properties such as those highlighted in the Cases in Point combined with findings from language acquisition research have persuaded us of the reality of grammar. The reality of grammar extends beyond the encoded actual variants of grammars in specific languages to encompass a Virtual Grammar which defines the grammatically possible in addition to the specific encodings in any one language. By highlighting this conceptual basis of grammar, we hope to help you to develop expertise in language that engages with its complexity and its impacts on learning and acquisition, but in an accessible and useful way.

1.2 The Development of Language in the Mind

In summary then, the linguistic terrain finds the study of everything from how we use language to the smallest features of language structure. The term 'grammar' has an affiliation with the structure of language, and how it works at the sentence or phrase level. This will explain why this book is inclined to the formalist end of the linguistics terrain. However, despite coming from a formalist tradition, we will not be limiting ourselves to traditional formalist approaches for two reasons. As already noted, we think that language teachers would do well to know as much as they can about all approaches in order to have as rich a base of linguistic expertise as possible. The second reason is that advances in the study of language mean that formalists are no longer uninterested in areas of language study which traditionally have been seen as in the domain of functionalists. This is evident when we consider the cognitive mechanisms underlying language learning which are assumed in this linguist's guide to grammar.

1.2 THE DEVELOPMENT OF LANGUAGE IN THE MIND

The formalist exploration of the structural properties of language with its interest in Universal Grammar has meant investigation of specific linguistic properties across a large range of languages. This can be seen as an approach that sees language, and in particular grammar, as something that *exists*, as opposed to an approach that sees language as something that people *do*. Formal linguists who are interested in language development have similarly taken the approach of studying language learning by capturing snapshots of language data from learners at different stages of development. The analysis of language produced (or understood) by a language learner at a given stage of development provides a so-called **property theory** approach to exploring language development because it is based on a methodology that describes the properties of learner language at a moment in time. An inherent weakness of this approach is that it values the understanding of the properties of language over the understanding of the transition from stage to stage.

There is one formalist approach to language development that places transition at the centre of its understanding: the Modular Cognition Framework (MCF) of Sharwood Smith and Truscott (2014) (see also Sharwood Smith, 2017). MCF combines a formalist view of language with a cognitive view of language development. The term **modular** refers to the view that linguists from both sides of the linguistic terrain have come to, that the brain has localised functionality which specialises in particular cognitive functions (Whong et al., 2014). That language is localised has been known for a long time, as illustrated by the loss of language ability as a symptom for victims of stroke while other cognitive functions are not affected. The Modular Cognitive Framework (MCF) takes a strong view of modularity, with a view of the specialised nature of language such that constraints on syntax are particular to syntax and not, for example, relevant to the constraints on the sound system in language. These in-built domains of language are natural features of being human, but the specific linguistic repertoire developed by any single individual is unique, and dependent upon the linguistic experiences that the individual is exposed to.

According to MCF, language knowledge develops in response to input, with, for example, a specific instance of language knowledge becoming stronger and stronger every time it is activated. Brain-imaging research tells us that neurons in the brain respond to stimuli. The electromagnetic response shows itself as 'lighting up' when activated in research. Priming research showing relationships between related words, for example, allows us to explore the relationship between what's happening inside the head in relation to linguistic experience coming from the context. The MCF draws on a cognitive perspective, and presents an understanding of language development which resonates with what research in second language development is clearly demonstrating: that language develops when learners are genuinely engaged in and with the language they are learning. MCF helps us to understand what's happening in terms of cognitive engagement. When exposed to a specific instance of linguistic knowledge, there is **activation** of neurons needed to make sense of the associated form and meaning. From the billions of neurons in the brain, the ones that are activated during linguistic processing experience a little boost from whatever their current **resting level** is to a slightly higher level. When the same neurons are called upon again, the resting levels underlying the linguistic knowledge rise yet again. We can understand 'mastery' of language being the state in which the resting levels of the relevant neurons are at a high enough level that they can be called upon effortlessly. For the language teacher, all this points to value in providing your learners with loads of examples and ample opportunity to practice those aspects of language which you have chosen to focus on.

Notice that in this discussion of 'engagement', we have made no mention of whether engagement with grammar should include explicit explanations of how the grammar works, or implicit exposure to

1.2 The Development of Language in the Mind

the grammar. By emphasising the need for activation, this question is less central to MCF because both explicit 'thinking about' a point of grammar and implicit cognitive working in the mind are accepted as taking place. This is not to say the implicit-explicit question isn't an interesting and important one. Indeed, much research in second language acquisition has been devoted to whether learners 'naturally' **acquire** language along the lines of child language development, or whether the process is wholly dependent on **learning**, understood as a more conscious, deliberate act employed for coming to grips with a range of abilities from learning to play the piano to developing the ability to win tennis matches. While this distinction has inspired debate and controversy, we will follow the lead of the MCF of recognising it when it is useful and relevant, but not getting overly distracted by it.

Most crucially, because activation is the aim, cognitive engagement is what matters, whether through talking about a point of grammar or using some aspect of grammar. Activation of a specific piece of linguistic knowledge raises the resting level of that knowledge. In the MCF approach there are thresholds at which knowledge reaches a level which can then be said to be stable, and will coincide with what we mean when we say we know something. So is developing knowledge just to do with how many times exposure happens? You will not be surprised to know that frequency alone does not provide all the answers. Imagine that you are a Mandarin Chinese speaker on a savannah looking for lions. If your English-speaking guide points and shouts 'lion!' it only makes sense that you will interpret this as the English word for the large animal you have been looking for. It also makes sense that the word *lion* will be boosted in a way that it wouldn't be if it were activated in a decontextualised English as a second language lesson as just one more animal on a list of zoo animals. Just hearing the word will not raise the resting level of the word as much as hearing it alongside a picture of a lion, which itself will not lead to nearly as strong an activation as seeing one out on the savannah. Of course, bringing language to life in the classroom is the constant challenge for the teacher. But the point here is that language, like all types of knowledge, will develop in direct correlation with the extent to which the learner is cognitively engaged in what is being taught. As we know in education generally, it is not good enough for something to be taught; what matters is that learners learn.

An MCF way of thinking is also useful for language educators because it helps to make sense of language learning when a learner already knows a language, or languages. Because knowledge is connected with cognitive prominence through resting levels, no single language has a privileged status per se by virtue of being there first. What gives a language privilege is its resting levels. In other words, the reason why one's mother tongue is dominant is that it is usual for one's mother tongue to be the knowledge that is actively used on a more regular basis, and with a very rich and long history of use by the individual in question. According to MCF, this is true not just for a full language, but for aspects of language. When trying to express something, the expectation is that all available linguistic resources will be drawn upon, regardless of which language they might happen to belong to, unless the difference in resting levels is so strong that 'faint' resources are too weak to be called upon. If, for example, I speak a language that does not grammatically mark tense, but instead uses adverbial phrases like *yesterday* for past, or *soon* for future, I may be inclined to unnecessarily include time adverbials when I speak a language like English that does grammatically mark tense. This is because these lexical entries will enjoy high resting levels as markers of time. This sort of issue is even more likely for other areas of grammar like Aspect, which encodes complex interactions between universal semantic distinctions and the realisation of specific distinctions which vary widely from language to language (see Case in Point 1.8).

This view of cross-language activation aligns with the notion of translanguaging, which captures the experience of the majority of people in today's world, with monolingualism a minority phenomenon. Reliance on resting levels can explain why one has difficulty reaching for words that one doesn't frequently hear or use, in any language. And it explains why language learners often experience 'interference' from the other language(s) that they know, a phenomenon better known by the less negative term **transfer** in second language acquisition research. One recurring theme in this volume is that instead of viewing effects from existing language knowledge as interference, there is value in drawing on that existing language knowledge in a facilitative way. We see the existing knowledge of your learner as a potential source from which to encourage the restructuring of that language knowledge in a way that flexes, adding to the linguistic repertoire.

Combining our approach to language development with our understanding of language itself provides a positive way to approach multilingualism from a cognitive perspective. For example, though language knowledge may be distinct from other types of knowledge, the constraints on, say, syntactic knowledge apply equally across the languages that your learner knows. Knowing the limits of what is

1.8 CASE IN POINT: ASPECT – TELICITY

Tense and aspect are closely related in the sense that they each deal with expression of events in time. Tense locates events in time, illustrated in (i), where the action is located in the present, past, or future by tense changes. Aspect describes the temporal structure of an event, such as describing it as complete, incomplete, ongoing, momentary, etc. In (ii), the event of eating took place in the past, but we can focus on different aspects of the event – completeness versus ongoingness at a past point, etc.

(i) Joe eats / ate / will eat the cake.
(ii) Joe has eaten / was eating / has been eating the cake.

Inherent or lexical aspect is an intrinsic property of verbal predicates. A widely used categorisation scheme sees predicates falling into one of four categories: States (*be intelligent*), Activities (*eat cake*), Accomplishments (*eat a cake*), Achievements (*arrive*). These basic categories are universal as they are cognitively salient for humans depending on whether there is a change of state due to the action and whether the action involves a duration or is instantaneous. However, the way that languages derive lexical aspect can vary.

Telicity is a feature of lexical aspect which refers to whether an event has a natural endpoint (a telic event), or does not have an endpoint (atelic). The nature of objects of verbs contributes to the telicity of a predicate in English activities and accomplishments. A specific or quantified object gives a telic interpretation (iii); a bare object results in atelic interpretation (iv). You can test for a telic interpretation by checking whether you can add a complete time expression such as *in just 5 minutes.*

(iii) Joe ate a cake / three cakes   in just 5 minutes.   *telic*
(iv) Joe ate cake / cakes   *in just 5 minutes. *atelic*

A language like Russian, which does not have article-based distinctions in nouns, marks telicity with verbal morphology. An imperfective verbal form results in an atelic interpretation while a perfective prefix results in a telic interpretation (see Slabakova, 2008, ch. 6).

(v) Maša   jela   tort
    Masha **IMP**.eat-PAST cake
    'Masha was eating cake/Masha used to eat cake.'
(vi) Maša   s-jela   tort
     Masha **PERF**-eat-PAST cake
     'Masha ate the cake.'

possible in language will help you to know the extent of the knowledge that your learners may already possess. As a teacher, your objective is to provide as much opportunity for activation of existing knowledge as possible. With all language-oriented knowledge coexisting, what matters most for language development are activation levels. This view of languages and domains of language all 'available' at once also explains what is known as **interlanguage** (Selinker, 1972). An interlanguage can be seen as a property theory description of the grammar of the individual at any given point in their language development. It is expected that the interlanguage will reflect both the target language which the learner aspires to, and the already existing language(s) that the learner knows. But we'll leave this discussion of interlanguage for further exploration in later chapters, and turn now to the teaching of language.

1.3 LINGUISTICS AND EDUCATION

Given our understanding of how language development happens, all existing language knowledge that the learner already possesses can be seen as a rich resource and even as a glaring omission if not fully exploited in the classroom. As we will see through this book, features of language at an abstract level are shared across all languages. This is not surprising given that the human species has a shared genetic endowment, with the capacity to feel, think, etc. in a way that is not determined by any sociological grouping or geographical boundary. How these abstract linguistic constraints, or Virtual Grammar, are realised in specific languages shows a wonderful range of variation. As a language teacher, your knowledge of the range of what is possible in language can be a valuable resource. As you think about the Cases in Point in this book, whether the specific grammatical feature(s) in question are implicated in the language you teach or not is irrelevant because that feature traces back to a shared linguistic impulse inherent to all of us.

1.3.1 Grammatical Concepts

The Cases in Point illustrate a range of **grammatical concepts**. A grammatical concept is conceptual in the sense that it represents an underlying nugget of meaning which cuts across a range of grammatical differences and commonalities in the languages of the world. It does not refer to a particular 'piece' of grammar, as in a verb-ending,

1.3 Linguistics and Education

case marking, or any specific word-order permutation. In fact, we will see that the same grammatical concept can find structural realisation in a rich range of ways across languages. At the same time, one particular piece of grammatical machinery in a language can implicate different grammatical concepts. And there is rarely a one-to-one mapping between a particular morphosyntactic element and an underlying grammatical concept (see, for example, Case in Point 1.9).

Understanding something of the nature of grammatical concepts and the range of ways grammatical concepts can be mapped onto specific grammatical properties in a language provides a different way of thinking about language learning difficulties, and can equip you with a way to address these difficulties from a fresh perspective. To be clear, we are not saying that you should teach the (sometimes complex!) grammatical properties that we use to illustrate the wonderful capacity amongst the world's languages. Instead, we hope to alter the mindset that exists with regard to grammar and grammar teaching. As linguists, we know that there is a large degree to which the 'rules' typically found in grammar books don't hold. Some aspects of grammar have been studied enough that we can now make a good stab at explaining why this is the case for some rules of thumb (like those applied to articles). But even so, we are not advocating just more or clearer rules. The way that grammar interacts with wider aspects of language means that the traditional paradigm, or rule-based approach to grammar teaching is, in our view, misguided. This is not to claim that the way of thinking advocated in this book is a magic bullet that will automatically solve any learning problems. For a language learner, a learnability problem remains a problem no matter how we as researchers or teachers decide to conceptualise it. The perspective from a grammatical concepts approach should, however, provide a linguistically informed and educationally useful window on the nature of language and language use that can help to facilitate grammar learning in a way that a traditional rule-based orientation cannot.

In each Case in Point, we exemplify some facet of a grammatical concept, showing how it is realised in different languages. English will serve as the point of comparison given that you, as a reader of this volume, are clearly familiar with English. However, an important feature of the Cases in Point and grammatical concepts is to break down notions of the foreignness or strangeness of different languages. The comparison with English is purely practical rather than indicating some privileged position for English. We will see that all languages rely on a shared set of underlying grammatical concepts, but their realisation in different languages diverges from one language to another. We will try to convince you that if the grammar of a foreign language seems unusual or difficult, this is only because of the strength of the familiarity you have with the knowledge you hold. We all have access to a Virtual Grammar, in the sense that the distinctions that grammar encodes are inherent to being human and are accessible to all of us. However, the way that individual languages encode the distinctions may seem strange or unnecessarily elaborate from the familiar perspective of our entrenched and highly activated grammatical system. We break this down by exploring the virtual realm of grammar: the *possible* expression of grammatical properties rather than just the actualised properties of an individual language.

Let's consider the case of genericity as a grammatical concept. This will serve as an example to illustrate some of the issues, and it further illustrates how to read Cases in Point. Genericity plays a role in a range of grammatical constructions in different languages. Grammatical concepts are often considered in terms of how they relate to other concepts (e.g. genericity versus existentiality or specificity or uniqueness). One way that English realises a generic as opposed to an existential meaning of a sentence is by changing the aspect of the verbal predicate. In (1), the combination of a subject noun phrase with no article (a bare noun phrase) and a predicate in the simple tense results in a **generic meaning**: it is a general property of dogs that they bark. In (2), replacing the verb in the simple present tense with a progressive predicate means we naturally interpret the sentence as **existential**: there exists a specific group of dogs and they are currently barking.

(1) Dogs bark.

(2) Dogs are barking.

If you are a teacher of English as a foreign or second language (or a learner of English), you will likely have devoted a significant amount of time to considering the use of tenses as this is a complex area of English grammar. However, you might not have seen the difference between sentences (1) and (2) described in terms of generic and existential meaning. Some of the more typical characterisations of the difference rely on distinct, though similar, notions. For example, one might read in grammars or exercise books that the simple tense expresses a timeless truth while the progressive describes an ongoing event. One can detect here the affinities to generic versus existential meaning. If the typical characterisations to be found in grammar publications rely on broadly similar notions, what is the use of adding

1.3 Linguistics and Education

the generic/existential perspective? (Apart from getting to show off with some linguistic terminology).

The point here is that the generic/existential distinction can be seen as a facet of Virtual Grammar. It is a *potential* distinction which finds different forms of expression within an individual language, as well as explaining some comparative differences between different languages. By contrast, the more traditional approach of thinking in terms of a timeless or ongoing event focuses attention solely on the tense forms. Understanding of the more general grammatical concept provides deeper understanding of the full meaning of the verbal predicate. It can also be applied to a range of other grammatical forms beyond the realisation of tense and aspect on verbs. There is the opportunity, through a grammatical concepts approach, to provide a more holistic perspective by encouraging the making of links between different, seemingly only loosely connected points of grammar – and between different languages.

Let's look at how the generic/existential concept is manifested in different languages. An interesting example comes from Finnish (from Krifka et al., 1995, p. 118). Unlike English, Finnish has a rich system of case marking on nouns, and one way that this system is exploited is to realise the generic/existential concept. When a subject is marked with nominative case as in (3), the result is a generic reading. When marked with partitive case as in (4), one gets the existential meaning. For idiosyncratic reasons, the verb form also changes here so that partitive case takes singular agreement, but note that there is no aspectual change marked on the verb.

(3) Koir**at** haukkuvat.
    dogs.**NOM** bark.PL
    'Dogs bark.'

(4) Koir**ia** haukku.
    dogs.**PART** bark.SG
    'Dogs are barking.'

To an English speaker learning Finnish, the use of such case distinctions is likely to appear unwieldy and is no doubt hard to master (research shows that case marking systems are generally notoriously problematic in L2 learning). Nominative is the case category for subjects; it isn't a category specifically for genericity. This parallels the English example in which simple tense is a category for time distinction, not a category for genericity. But genericity is relevant in both these examples! An English-speaking learner of Finnish may well wonder: Why don't they just change the verb!? If our grammars were organised by grammatical concepts, this particular learning problem would be better addressed. But notice, if considered only in terms of genericity, this would cause difficulty explaining why nominative is used to mark subjects.

Leveraging knowledge of grammatical concepts does not magically make grammar learning easy, but it might provide a way to break down the opacity and complexity of the system by linking to aspects of meaning, especially when that meaning is already a familiar part of a language that is known by your learner, whether implicitly or explicitly. English speakers are perfectly capable of understanding and expressing the virtual conceptual generic/existential distinction; they are just accustomed to locating such distinctions in a different way, mainly in the verbal paradigm. By linking to this knowledge, we help to rethink notions of 'exotic' language features and foreignness. Languages do the same things conceptually; it is just that the tools used are in different corners of the morphosyntactic systems. Exoticism or strangeness is in the eye of the beholder: marking the generic/existential difference by changing tense and aspect would no doubt strike a Finnish speaker as a weird way of doing things.

A further example comes from French, which marks the generic/existential distinction in the choice of articles. A generic meaning requires the definite article as in (5), and an existential meaning the partitive article, as in (6).

(5) **Les** chiens   aboient
    the dog.PL   bark.PL
    'Dogs bark.'

(6) **Des** chiens   aboient.
    some dog.PL   bark.PL
    'Dogs are barking' / 'There are dogs barking.'

Note that French always has an article of some form accompanying nouns. The choice of article makes a difference, a potential issue for English-speakers learning French, for whom the presence or absence of an article contributes to encoding generic versus specific grammatical concepts, not the form of the article. In the other direction, for a French speaker learning English it poses a problem to know when to have or not have the article, and what meaning distinctions ensue. As already noted, considering these issues in light of grammatical concepts is not going to magically solve the learnability issues. However, it does provide an anchor point from which to consider the comparative

1.9 CASE IN POINT: PARTITIVITY

Partitivity is realised in different linguistic structures in different languages, including articles, particular morphemes, or case marking. Hungarian and Finnish are languages which have a dedicated partitive case. This appears on object noun phrases which are only partly or incompletely affected by the action of a verb. As in the Hungarian examples (i) and (ii) (Lyons, 1999, p. 218).

(i) Ette a süteményt
 Ate-3SG-OBJ the pastry-ACC
 'He/she ate the pastry.'
(ii) evett a süteményböl
 ate-3SG the pastry-PART
 'He/she ate some of the pastry.'

The English translation in (ii) uses a partitive construction 'some of the pastry', clearly illustrating the distinction. But this is just one way English realises the difference. There is a link between partially affected objects and aspectual differences such as incompleteness. In the Finnish examples in (iii) and (iv) (adapted from Kiparsky, 1998), we see the partitive case implicating an incomplete action (i.e. that the shot missed or didn't kill the bear), while accusative (iv) implicates a complete action.

(iii) Ammuin karhua
 shoot-PST-1SG bear-PART
 'I shot at the/a bear.'
(iv) Ammuin karhun
 shoot-PST-1SG bear- ACC
 'I shot the/a bear' 'I killed the/a bear' ' shot the/a bear dead.'

differences between languages, based on the underlying commonality of what it is that grammar can express. Even in this short survey based on genericity, we have made links between articles, uses of cases, and tense/aspect distinctions. The focus on grammatical concepts in the Cases in Point aims to highlight these links.

Of course, if you are a teacher of French, you do not need to know how Finnish partitive case works. Teachers will typically teach one foreign language, or perhaps two. Our aim is not to suggest that teachers need to know the grammatical details of languages they don't teach. However, consideration of how to think about and analyse grammar is indispensable. Comparing different languages in this way puts familiar grammatical properties into sharp relief and illustrates something about how language in general works. Because languages all express grammatical concepts in one way or another, appealing to these concepts allows for a way to connect into the language(s) that your learner knows. Even if you will never have to deliver a lesson involving partitivity or partitive case, knowledge of how generic/existential is implicated in a range of semantic processes may help you to recognise how it is manifested in the language you are teaching; it may allow you to understand (and then perhaps explain) some 'exception' to some rule which you or your students come across in class. Similarly, thinking about partialness of an event gives a view on verbs in English depending on the lack of a result, or an ongoing incomplete activity, as explored in the Case in Point 1.8.

As we progress through the Cases in Point, we will make some explicit connections between the different grammatical concepts and their realisations. Some concepts may be realised in different ways in different languages; a single morphosyntactic form may encode a range of grammatical concepts depending on interactions with other forms, etc. Some of the connections will remain implicit and we will encourage reflection on them in end-of-chapter questions and language puzzles. You may even make other completely new connections which have not occurred to us. In any case, if the Cases in Point encourage you to engage with familiar points of grammar or classroom learnability issues in new ways, or even just provide a fresh perspective, they will have achieved their aim. There's also the possibility that within your classroom there is a learner whose mother tongue implicates a particular grammatical form for the grammatical concept in question. Moreover, that learner may be struggling because of the *absence* of a distinct grammatical form for this feature in the language you are teaching. With this in mind, our view is that there is a valuable place for not just recognition, but also use of the mother tongue in the foreign language classroom. But this is not the view that has been commonly held by experts in teaching methodology in the recent past. We turn to language teaching as a field in the next section, starting with the question of whether or not there is a place for the mother tongue in the additional language classroom.

1.3.2 Brief Overview of (European) Language Teaching

The 'target language only' approach which developed within language teaching is starting to be challenged thanks, in part, to the work of Cook (2010) who focuses on the value of translation in teaching. Cook makes clear that the assumption that translation should not be used in

1.3 Linguistics and Education

language teaching is just that – an assumption. As formal linguists and researchers in second language acquisition, we agree that ignoring other languages is misguided.

An understanding of the history of language teaching clarifies how the target language only emphasis came to be. Our brief survey of the history of language teaching is very much oriented to developments in a European-language teaching context (Howatt & Widdowson, 2004, provide a comprehensive history). This is because this is our own orientation and because, arguably, the nature of English in the world generally means that language teaching from a European tradition has had a very strong influence on approaches to language teaching in general (for a comprehensive consideration of English-language teaching in the world, see Marr & English, 2019).

The Grammar Translation approach from the mid-1800s into the early 1900s was the accepted approach to teaching European languages. This approach relied on the translation of great works of literature, seeing this as a way of transmitting culture, but doing so by teaching the vocabulary and grammar encountered while translating. With a sample of literature as the object of study, teachers often found themselves defining words and explaining grammar rules through the medium of the students' mother tongue (for a description of Grammar Translation lesson in action, see Larsen-Freeman & Anderson, 2011). The approach to grammar within Grammar Translation reflected the way grammar was thought of by linguists at the time. As philologists, linguists at that time were particularly interested in charting the relationships between languages, guided by a structuralist methodology of systematically decomposing language according to its forms in order to identify patterns, or paradigms. You are no doubt familiar with declension tables still found in language teaching materials today, showing morphological patterns like: I eat, you eat, he/she/it eats, etc.

This 'traditional' approach to language teaching was challenged by what has come to be known as the Reform movement. We have already mentioned one significant achievement from within this movement, the creation of the International Phonetic Alphabet. In fact, one strong driver which motivated the creation of the IPA was recognition of the importance of spoken language, and the recognition that language teaching would benefit from systematic tools to teach pronunciation. For many, the efforts of these linguists in this era mark the beginning of Applied Linguistics as a field. The teaching method associated with the work of these linguists was the Natural Method, which also became known as the Direct Method. This approach, promoted in the early 1900s, insisted on use of the target language only, from the very first lesson and absolutely, regardless of the aims of the lesson. It promoted a natural immersion approach which relied on the active use of language instead of rules of grammar and long lists of definitions. This approach was very radical at the time, a strong reaction to Grammar Translation. But it still exists as the Berlitz Method, taught in private language schools bearing that name. While motivated learners who are willing to pay for a course seem to benefit from target language immersion, it is not an approach that saw success in the context of mainstream education.

What developed instead was more of an intermediate step away from the Grammar Translation approach. Though variants carried different names in different places, the mid-1900s saw the implementation of the Oral Approach in England, the Situational Approach in Australia, and the Audiolingual Approach in the USA. All three promoted an aural-oral component in language teaching. For the Oral/Situational approaches, this led to the organisation of teaching around real life contexts and themes with lessons with titles which you would recognise such as: Asking for Directions, or My Family. The Audiolingual Method prioritised listening and was strongly behaviourist in its reliance on habit formation, drills, and memorising dialogues, as perhaps appropriate in the eyes of the US government which funded its development for language training of military personnel. While the inclusion of more 'everyday' considerations was a positive step for language teaching, these approaches were still largely 'traditional' in that they maintained a structuralist view of grammar as rule-based, and they continued to be quite teacher-centred in orientation, with little consideration of learner autonomy or learner engagement.

It is against this backdrop that Communicative Language Teaching emerged. The basic premise of CLT builds on the aural/oral contributions from the Oral/Situational/Audiolingual approaches, and draws in elements of the Direct Method, viewing language as a vehicle for communication which develops through natural, real use. As an approach to how to teach, not a specific method for teaching, it can be described as having the following ten characteristics (Whong, 2013).

i. CLT prioritises fluency in language production over accuracy.
ii. The process of language development is important; not just the product/output.
iii. Emphasis should be on meaning over form.

1.3 Linguistics and Education

iv. Learners should be active users, not passive receivers of language.
v. Lessons should provide ample opportunity for interaction.
vi. Language materials should be authentic, or at least approximate authenticity.
vii. Teachers should be selective in correcting learners.
viii. A skills approach should integrate reading, writing, listening and speaking.
ix. Learner autonomy will lead to greater levels of success in language learning.
x. Teaching should be guided by humanistic principles, with recognition learner needs.

While there is very much to praise within Communicative Language Teaching as a general approach to language teaching, and every reason to recognise its strengths, one limitation, which can be seen as a legacy of developments in English language teaching, is a 'target language only' mentality that is often assumed within CLT. Another limitation is the extent to which there has been a move away from grammar. Just as Cook (2010) has called for a rethink of the potential for translation in language teaching, we argue that there is a need for more explicit consideration of grammar in language teaching – but in more contemporary terms. This is not to say that grammar has been completely ignored in communicative approaches to language education. Indeed, there are some extremely valuable contributions that have come from Functionalist approaches to grammar in particular. At the level of text and discourse, it is now commonplace in the language classroom to find explicit teaching of cohesive devices and discourse markers, with developments in understanding of genre providing useful contributions for teaching (e.g. Paltridge 2001; Swales & Feak, 1994). The use of cohesive devices and discourse markers are an overt way of signalling structure in text via the use of particular lexical items. Such suggestions are perhaps particularly useful for a language like English which has a rather rigid word order at the sentence level, and which typically indicates differences in emphasis with prosody, which is obviously not possible in writing (e.g. compare the different effects of *I'LL do the dishes, I WILL do the dishes, I'll DO THE DISHES*, etc.). Even in English, discourse and information interact with grammar in subtle ways, but across different languages there is a whole range of complexity in the way that grammatical properties interact with pragmatic or information structural properties (see Case in Point 1.10). Even where learners master the grammatical properties of a language, getting to grips with subtle features of information structure or pragmatics can prove elusive (see discussion in Chapter 4).

1.10 CASE IN POINT: INFORMATION STRUCTURE

One way to analyse how languages structure information is to divide them into subject-prominent types, such as English and Malagasy, and topic-prominent types, such as Hungarian and Mandarin (Li & Thompson, 1976). Languages do not necessarily fall discretely into just one type. English has subject-predicate structures, as in (i), and also more marked topic-comment structures, as in (ii). The relevant point is that a topic-prominent language will have structures similar to (ii) as the basic way to structure a sentence rather than as an optional extra.

(i) Harry has fed the dogs.
(ii) As for the dogs, Harry fed them.

In Hungarian, for example, word order is highly flexible, but the different permutations that are possible adhere to a topic-comment information structure so that a referent is foregrounded and then some predication or comment tells us something about the topic in each sentence, as illustrated in (iii)-(v) (from Kiss, 2002, p. 9).

(iii) Jánost elütötte egy autó
  John-ACC hit   a car
  'A car hit John.'
(iv) Jánosból hiányzik a becsület.
  from.John is.missing the honesty
  'Honesty is missing from John.'
(v) Jánosak összetörek az autóját.
  John-DAT they.broke the car-POSS-ACC
  'They broke John's car.'

In each of these sentences, John plays a different grammatical role, as indicated by the different case markings. In each case, however, he is the topic. In English, different strategies can be used to make sure that the topic and grammatical subject coincide, which is the preferred pattern: *John was hit by a car; John lacks honesty; John had his car broken.*

Especially as related to vocabulary and writing, contributions from corpus and cognitive linguistics have led to significant advancement for teaching. But contemporary formalist approaches to grammar have not seen significant impact. One main discussion which has implicated grammar comes out of research inspired by Long (1991) who called for a Focus on Form, as opposed to an exclusive Focus on Meaning as can occur in CLT, and in contrast to so-called Focus on

FormS, as inherent to 'traditional' grammar teaching methods. Our contention is that the reaction against traditional, structuralist understandings of grammar has led to too much of an across-the-board rejection of grammar in current approaches to language teaching. And that the current attempts in second language learning research to recognise grammar more often than not assume an outdated understanding of grammar. To be clear, we are not calling for a return to grammar rules as inherent to the approaches to teaching surveyed here. Instead, we note an absence of clear understanding of how formal linguists have come to understand grammar in the last few decades. Properties of language that are now clear and uncontroversial for formal linguists are simply absent from the repertoire of language teaching materials. Because research in language education and formal linguistics has not developed in collaboration with each other, there now exists something of a gap which would benefit from some attention. We hope this book goes some way to addressing this gap.

1.4 CONCLUSION: BRING BACK GRAMMAR

In the current, so called post-methods era, there is no single agreed-upon method for language teaching. Kumaravadivelu (2001) has noted that one reason for this is the pressure in teaching to look to theories of language learning. We have seen in this chapter that amongst academics with expertise in language, there are competing theories about how language works, with the question of whether Form or Function is the basis of language. There are also competing theories about how language develops, with variations on variations when contrasting child and adult language development. With such an array of theoretical frameworks, and competing understandings of research, it is not surprising if teachers, teacher trainers, textbook writers, curriculum designers and policy makers opt for a pick-and-mix approach. But one thing that is currently in short supply is a clear characterisation of contemporary understandings of grammar from the point of view of formal linguists. Of course, this viewpoint is premised on the assumption that there is something we can call grammar – an assumption that has itself been called into question by some language educators. But we stand firmly by the assumption that there is something called 'grammar'. While we will leave it to you to decide whether you find our concept of Virtual Grammar of any use, we hope you will agree that a solid understanding of grammar should be part of the expertise of language teachers. Before looking more closely at grammar, however, we turn to the notion of language, languages and Language.

1.5 EXERCISES AND QUESTIONS FOR DISCUSSION

1 Form vs Function

In this chapter we noted how grammar can be thought about in terms of Form or Function. Think about PAST TENSE in English.

i) Create an activity which could be used with learners of English to teach the PAST TENSE by focusing on Form. Include both grammatical forms (e.g. past tense *-ed* morpheme) and lexical forms (e.g. the word 'yesterday').

ii) Create an activity which could be used with learners of English to teach the PAST TENSE by focusing on Function.

iii) Consider how PAST TENSE is indicated in other languages that you know. What different types of forms are used for PAST TENSE in other languages? Are they limited to verbal morphemes and lexical forms like in English?

2 Deverbal nouns

i) Without stopping to think carefully, list ten verbs in English.

ii) Now consider each to see if it is possible to think of a nominal variant. Try creating example sentences with the nominal and verbal forms. Or you could find a freely available concordancing website to search a corpus to get real examples of your nominal and verbal forms. Based on your sets of examples, can you determine any regularities of use for deverbal nouns in English?

iii) Now consider the form of each nominal variant in your list. What generalisations can you give that describe now to make nominal forms of verbs in English?

iv) Is this an activity you could use with your language learners? How could you modify this to make it usable in a language teaching context?

3 Literal and Extended Word Meaning

i) List as many nouns in English as you can in 20 seconds. How many of them have additional extended meanings?

ii) Can you translate your original list into another language? How

1.5 Exercises and Questions for Discussion

many of them have extended meanings in the other language? Are the meanings the same or different? To what extent do they overlap?

iii) Find a short piece of text, for example a news feature from the Internet. Pick out examples of words that have meaning that extends the literal meaning. If you were teaching this text, would the focus on literal meaning add depth to an explanation of the extended meaning for all of the words you have identified?

4 Verb Classes and Locative Alternation

We saw that verbs can fall into classes depending on the grammatical patterns they allow. There is a set of verbs that can participate in an alternation in English called the locative alternation because there are two syntactic patterns which indicate movement of a substance to a place or container. An example of this alternation is: *Hannah sprayed paint onto the wall / Hannah sprayed the wall with paint.*

i) Here are some other verbs which include the same meaning of moving or applying a substance to a container or surface: *cover, load, pile, sprinkle, spill*. How many English verbs can you add to this list?

ii) Check how arguments are realised for the verbs listed, and others you have added. Do they allow the same locative alternation as *to paint*? Can you determine any commonalities in core meaning between them? How many meaning-based classes emerge? What generalisations can you make about the classes?

iii) Translate the verbs you have thought of into other languages that you know, or teach. Are there similar classes? Which differences are there compared to English? Which areas of overlap or similarity?

5 Verb Classes and Voice Alternations

We also saw in this chapter that certain verbs have alternations in their transitivity or voice patterns. Verbs of sound emission provide an example; some of these verbs allow causative alternations while others do not (see Levin & Rappaport Hovav, 2005, pp. 10–11).

Compare: *I clattered the teacups* (causative) with: *The teacups clattered* and **Peter rumbled the truck* (causative) with: *The truck rumbled.*

i) Construct similar sentences to check whether other related verbs follow the *clatter* pattern in allowing the causative alternation, or the *rumble* pattern: *babble, jingle, holler, rattle, buzz, whistle.*

ii) Can you think of a reason which explains the different behaviours of different verbs with respect to this transitivity alternation? (The term <u>causative</u> alternation provides a clue to the generalisation).
iii) Are there similar patterns in the other languages you know or teach? How could you use this sort of insight to develop ways to teach this vocabulary while taking account of the grammatical patterns?

6 Passive Forms

In this chapter, we compared different ways of forming a passive in different languages. Within the same language, there may also be a range of passive forms.

i) Think about the sentence *The door was closed*. This is clearly a passive form, but it is actually subtly ambiguous in English. Can you think of the two different meanings it may have?
ii) How does the additional context provided in sentences (a), (b) and (c) help to illustrate the different types of meaning?
   (a) The door was closed quietly by the student who arrived late for the exam.
   (b) The door remained closed for many years.
   (c) *The door remained closed for many years by the student.
iii) (a) is an example of a verbal passive, denoting an action, (b) is an example of an adjectival passive, describing a state. Translate these sentences into other languages you know or teach. Are there differences between verbal and adjectival passives in these languages? Is the difference marked overtly in the other languages you know? How might the patterns pose problems for learners?

2 Language and Languages

If anyone knows what language is, surely it is language teachers. Language teachers must be fluent users of the language(s) they teach; they must be experts in the properties of the language they teach; and they must have pedagogical expertise enabling them to effectively package and transmit their expertise to their students. Teachers are therefore expert linguists in the sense that they have themselves developed exceptional proficiency and specialist knowledge in their language(s). The academic variety of 'linguist', by contrast, is more interested in language as a phenomenon for study. As such, they do what all academics do, which is to continuously develop understanding within their discipline. This has resulted in a panoply of information and new insights within linguistics about language which is not always immediately accessible to language teachers, especially when developments are occurring in all the many subfields of linguistics. However, there are some core linguistic concepts which can be articulated. By conveying a linguist's view of language, we want to suggest a fresh way to think about that which is familiar, and as such, provide what we hope is a useful contribution to applied linguistics, following Larsen-Freeman who argues that 'a significant role of theory is to make the unconscious conscious. A theory helps us learn to look' (Larsen-Freeman, 2008, p. 292). Raising awareness of new and unfamiliar features can provide a lens through which to view more commonplace issues and reflect on further areas of knowledge, and how we use that in teaching. Case in Point 2.1 considers one way in which the familiar grammatical category of person marking finds expression in some languages of the world.

This is not to say that teachers need high levels of formal linguistic or theoretical understanding to be good teachers necessarily. People have always learned languages and it seems that for as long as civilizations have interacted, teachers, tutors or grammarians of one sort or another have produced materials to teach foreign languages (see

2.1 CASE IN POINT: ASSOCIATIVITY

Associativity is a type of person marking found in a large number of Austronesian and indigenous South American languages, as well as Vietnamese, Chechen, Gujarati, some dialects of Mandarin Chinese and Malay. In these languages, there are distinct first person plural personal pronouns to specify whether the person being addressed is included in the action. For example in Malay the two forms *kita* and *kami*, allow a speaker to be clear about whether the addressee is being included in the activity alongside the speaker, or not.

(i) **kita** meninggalkan sekarang
    we   leave   now
    'We, including you, are leaving now.'

(ii) **kami** meninggalkan sekarang
    we   leave   now
    'We, but not you, are leaving now.'

For a language with this linguistic property, the equivalent of the sentence 'We are invited' would automatically indicate whether you, the addressee, are also invited, or whether you have been excluded from the invitation. This distinction can also affect other linguistic elements in the grammatical system of a language. In the example from Ngiti (spoken in Democratic Republic of Congo), it can affect person marking on a verb as well as the choice of pronoun (see Cysouw, 2013).

(iii) ma   m-òdzɨ
      1SG.PRON 1-cry
      'I cry.'

(iv) **mà**   m-òdzɨ
     EXCL.PRON 1-cry
     'We (excluding you) cry.'

(v) **alɛ**   k-òdzɨ
    INCL.PRON INCL-cry
    'We (inclusive) cry.'

McArthur, 1988, for a general overview of history of reference materials; and Dickey, 2016, on Latin as a foreign language for the ancient Greeks). Successful language teaching does not necessarily require an abstract, 'scientific' understanding of what language is, but surely it is important for teachers of language to know as much as they can. And knowing as much as one can does not stop at the boundaries of the

2.1 What Is Language?

individual languages we teach; it is useful to know something about the way language works in general, in order to facilitate seeing familiar patterns and problems afresh.

When we use the word *language,* we are typically referring to a particular language or languages. As a teacher, you teach (a) particular language(s) rather than a general abstract notion of language. As a language user, you might be a Spanish speaker who has learned English as a second language, for example. Or a child of Turkish parents who grew up in Germany and can speak both languages fluently. In this chapter, as with the entire book, though we consider properties of specific languages, we are primarily considering **Language**, with a capital L, to reflect that we are not just exploring a single language, but instead, the nature of Language itself, as a phenomenon. As will become clearer, we are setting out a way of thinking about Language – and the intricacies of how Language works – which we refer to as Virtual Grammar. To be clear, this is not what we suggest should be taught to language learners directly or explicitly. Instead, it is designed to provide a cross-language basis for language teaching professionals to better approach the grammar of the particular language(s) that they teach. By looking at specific languages and the nature of linguistic diversity, we will see that Language is a distinctly human ability which, despite variation, abides by underlying principles. The nature of these underlying principles may prove helpful in questions of pedagogy, or at the least should prove interesting and provide a foundation on which to reflect on the teaching and learning of specific properties of language. We start with the fundamental question of what Language is.

2.1 WHAT IS LANGUAGE?

All sentient beings are able to interact and communicate. Many animal species exploit forms of, sometimes highly complex, display or vocalisation in order to communicate. But, however complex, these forms of communication are not linguistic. Let's think about the ways in which human communication and animal communication differ. We can consider the hissing sound represented by the string of letters *ssssss* in English. While articulation is different between humans and different animal species (i.e. the mechanics of lungs, throat, teeth and tongue will not be the same in different species), we do share with other animals the ability to produce a noise that we perceive as something we could represent with *sssssss*. When a cat produces a *ssssss* in your direction, you assume that you have done something to upset it and might want to get out of the way of a scratch-attack that is likely to follow. In this situation, there is 'meaning' to the extent that the cat has communicated a reaction to something in its environment via the production of this noise. A human may choose to make the same noise for the same effect, but the *linguistic* use of this noise is very different from the animal use (or the animalistic use if you are confronted by a hissing human). Usually when we produce 's', we do not do so simply as a noise or an instinctive reaction, but rather as a morpheme which combines in systematic ways with other parts of the language system. These combinations give rise to grammatical meaning. In English, there are different morphemes indicating plurality, possession and third person agreement. The addition of this same sound produces meaningfully different grammatical structures: 'book' + 's' gives rise to: *she bought some **books**; the **book's** author*; and *she **books** tickets*.

Notice in the previous sentence, we replaced the term 'noise' with the term 'sound'. In English, 's' is part of the sound system of the language; it isn't just a noise but rather a **phoneme**. As such, it is minimally different and distinguishable from other similar sounds in ways that make it meaningful for English speakers, so that even a small voicing difference results in major linguistic distinctions, allowing for both /s/ and /z/ in English. But despite these systematic morphemic and phonemic patterns and despite them giving rise to different meanings, there is nothing inherently meaningful in the soundstream of the individual sound itself. There is nothing specifically plural about the /s/ sound. Indeed, other languages form their plurals in radically different ways. Neither is there anything especially zitty about the /z/-/s/ distinction, a distinction which is exploited systematically by English to mark a range of lexical differences: sip/zip, sap/zap, sue/zoo, etc.

We can characterise these properties of Language as (i) **duality of structure** – meaningless sounds combine to make meaningful linguistic units; (ii) **discreteness** – minimal, gradient differences result in discrete linguistic distinctions; and (iii) **arbitrariness** – there is no consistent one-to-one mapping between linguistic element and meaning. These are three of the 'design features' of human language which distinguish it from the communication systems of animals. Charles Hockett, a prominent figure in the shaping of modern linguistics, identified a total of thirteen such design features (Hockett, 1960). While some of these features are shared between animal communication and human languages, only human language has all thirteen.

2.1 What Is Language?

So, language is something qualitatively different from other forms of communication in the animal kingdom. However, while general design features define Language with a capital L as something uniquely human, there is clearly a range of variation within Language, as exemplified by the whole range of grammatical complexities we see across different languages. Every individual language includes its own very subtle grammatical phenomena, but the sheer range of potential sophistication when we start to look at different languages is striking. Indeed, this is what often proves so daunting and problematic, but often also interesting and intriguing, for learners of foreign languages. Sticking with the example of phonetics for the moment, if you are a mother-tongue English speaker, it seems natural that 'l' and 'r' are distinct, unconfusable sounds. If you set out to buy a lamp, you are unlikely to be confounded by phonetic issues and come home in possession of a ramp. In Japanese, however, the choice of 'r' versus 'l' makes no meaning differences and is thus irrelevant in the sound system of Japanese. Speakers of Japanese have a hard time disentangling in English what for them is essentially the same sound (see Brown, 2000). One's dominant linguistic system can make one seemingly deaf to phonetic distinctions in new languages that we are not accustomed to making in our entrenched language system(s). What's important to bear in mind is that we can physically make and perceive different sounds, but whether or not a particular difference will be linguistically meaningful can differ from one language to another. This point can be clearly seen when considering tone languages including Chinese, and other Asian languages, Vietnamese, Thai, etc. as well as a number of Bantu languages spoken in Sub-Saharan Africa, and some Native American languages (Case in Point 2.2).

The sounds of language provide a relatively clear example of issues with respect to language learning, which we can readily hear in the form of foreign accents. When applied to grammar, the principles remain the same. Though the human vocal tract can physically produce a vast range of sounds, only a certain number of discrete sounds is produced within the sound system of a specific language; equally, the human facility for language makes a certain range of grammatical concepts available for linguistic use. However, these concepts can be realised in different ways in different languages, as we saw in the example of the inclusive/exclusive variant of the grammatical concept of **person** in Case in Point 2.1 on Associativity. Even more familiar meaning-based concepts can illustrate distinctions which give rise to intricate variation when encoded in the grammar of particular

2.2 CASE IN POINT: TONES

Some languages rely on differences in tone to create meaningfully distinct sounds. And meaningfully distinct sounds lead to meaningfully distinct words. Mandarin Chinese, for example, has four tones. A word will have a completely different meaning if it is spoken with a level tone (i), a rising tone (ii), a falling-rising tone (iii) or a falling tone (iv).

(i)   mā   'mother'

(ii) má   'hemp'

(iii) mǎ   'horse'

(iv) mà   'scold'

Other varieties of Chinese make even more tone distinctions. Cantonese makes six meaningful distinctions:

High level	si	'poem'
Low level	si	'matter'
Mid level	si	'try'
High rising	si	'history'
Low rising	si	'market'
Falling	si	'time'

(Yip & Matthews, 2017, p. 13)

languages. **Number** marking is something that is cognitively obvious: one can easily identify how many entities one might want to refer to. But different languages impose different restrictions on the morphosyntactic expression of number (see Case in Point 2.3). 'Often the situation in languages like English is taken as normal, whereas it represents only one of the possibilities. ... for some languages the expression of number is in a sense optional, while in others it is a category which speakers cannot avoid' (Corbett, 2000, p. 9).

The range of linguistic phenomena that exists across languages is perhaps not surprising given the wide range of thoughts, feelings and intentions that are a natural part of being human. But at the same time, because we are all human, and, in principle, capable of the same range of human expression, it might be surprising that there is such apparent divergence. Careful study of languages reveals that alongside interesting differences, there is also a great deal of constancy. A groundbreaking example of linguistic research showing similarity across languages is work by Joseph Greenberg who set out forty-five **language universals**, based on a sample of thirty languages. In

2.3 CASE IN POINT: NUMBER

English distinguishes between singular and plural forms of nouns. Speakers are required to mark whether one or more entity is referred to in communication (but see also **Mass/Count/Collective Distinctions**).

(i) I bought a book.
(ii) I bought books.

Number, cross-linguistically, can require more refined distinctions. The singular–plural distinction can additionally include **dual** number, which requires a specific grammatical marking when referring to two entities. A language may also have **paucal** number which marks a number of entities somewhere between two and many, with the exact dividing line between 'two' and 'many' depending on context and conventions in different languages (see Corbett, 2000, ch. 2). The grammatical marking will apply to different categories depending on the morphological properties of the language in question and may require agreement on other elements together with changes on nouns and pronouns.

To illustrate, Upper Sorbian, a Slavonic language spoken in Germany, distinguishes between singular, dual and plural (Corbett, 2000, p. 20).

(iii) singular   dual   plural
     hr**ó**d 'castle'   hr**odaj** 'two castles'   hr**ody** 'castles'
     ja 'I'   mój 'we two'   my 'we'

Bayso, a Cushitic language spoken in Ethiopia, has dedicated forms for paucal (Corbett, 2000, p. 11).

(iv) singular   paucal   plural
     lubán-**titi** 'a lion'   luban-**jaa** 'a few lions'   luban-**jool** 'lions'

As indicated by the English translations, the same notions can be expressed perfectly well in English by using expressions that quantify. The underlying concept of number is at work in all languages, but distinctions are marked morphosyntactically in the grammatical system in some languages.

Universal 42, for example, Greenberg notes that all languages have a pronoun system that involves at least three persons and two numbers (Greenberg, 1963, p. 96). In other words, there is no language which does not have distinct grammatical forms for first vs second vs third person pronouns, and a distinction between singular and plural in the pronoun system. This is not to say that all pronoun systems make a singular/plural distinction on all three person forms. It is likely that, as an English speaker, you will have sometimes found it necessary to clarify whether *you* means only the person you are speaking to, or a number of people. (And in some dialects, plural forms such as *yous*, and *y'all* are used for this purpose, reflecting a possible encoding of plurality in English.) It is also very common in languages from Italian to Japanese to Arabic for there to be no need to include a pronoun as the subject or object in a sentence at all if the context makes the referent clear. However, the point is that all languages have a system which allows for clear distinction of the person (or thing) being referred to without having to name the particular person or thing. And in your language classroom, your learners will have an in-built system for this distinction which has seen realisation in terms of the language(s) that they already speak.

This may strike you as unremarkable, but it is a remarkable fact. Of the infinite array of meanings and functions that humans can express and understand, a few find grammatical expression in all languages (e.g. person, number). And while some meanings find specific morphological expression in some languages but not others (e.g. associativity, dual and paucal, etc.; see Cases in Point), all languages are able to express these core meanings grammatically. The shared possibilities are what we refer to as a **Virtual Grammar**. Given the sheer range of linguistic variation that is possible, it is striking when certain grammatical concepts or features are universally expressed in all languages; this tells us something about the underlying nature of Language. One fundamental defining feature of all languages is that of hierarchical **structure dependence**. Because structure dependence is universal, it can be seen to be at work in a wide variety of grammatical phenomena. A specific Case in Point is the formation of questions. As shown in Case in Point 2.4, structure dependence is a kind of abstract syntactic scaffolding which places constraints on which words and phrases participate in grammatical patterns based on where they occur in the structural hierarchy of the sentence in question. Knowing that all languages depend on an abstract syntactic scaffolding may provide some comfort for teachers. Even when your learners are producing structures which seem unconstrained, you can rest assured they are subject to structure dependence and other rules – though potentially not the rules you have taught. As we will discuss more fully in Chapter 3, they are not unconstrained wild grammars.

2.1 What Is Language?

> ### 2.4 CASE IN POINT: STRUCTURE DEPENDENCE AND QUESTION FORMATION
>
> Forming a yes/no question in a language like English might seem to be captured in a rule like: 'move the copula or auxiliary to the start of the sentence'. This rough and ready rule will work for many simple instances, as in (i).
>
> (i) The baby **is** happy. → **Is** the baby happy?
>
> But it needs a **structure dependent** refinement to hold true as a rule. The hierarchical syntactic structure of sentences means that the verbs occupy specific *syntactic* positions, not just a linear order in the clause. Consider a minimally more complex situation where two auxiliaries are involved. Following a rule which just moves the first auxiliary encountered in the sentence to form a question would lead to a word jumble, as in (ii).
>
> (ii) The baby who **is** playing with building blocks **is** happy.
> → ***Is** the baby who playing with building blocks **is** happy?
>
> In this case, the structure of the sentence seems to be complicated by the presence of the relative clause; structure dependence dictates that it is the auxiliary of the sentential subject which must move, regardless of whether it happens that the auxiliary is the first, second or third auxiliary that occurs in the sentence.

When Greenberg drew up his list of Universals, he was deliberate in his choice of thirty languages in order to include those that represent the human population across the world in geographic terms. While initial study of 'other' or foreign languages often leads to pleasant surprise at the diversity and creativity of languages (even if we don't always manage to master this creativity), the degree of regularity and the existence of 'universals' also forces the vexing question of why Language is as consistent as it is. The answer is to do with our earlier point that language is uniquely human; as such it is a distinguishing trait of the species *Homo sapiens*. In this sense, Language is biological. And in this biological sense, it can be said that language 'grows' just as a child grows from infancy. This growth is constrained in certain ways, for example by structure dependence, which provides a blueprint for linguistic growth in the same way that biological growth is constrained: as a child grows, his limbs will develop and get stronger, but the child will not develop a second pair of legs. This is ruled out by the genetic blueprint for a human body. But there is of course still variation in physical growth, with some children becoming taller or fatter or fitter adults than others. Similarly, working within constraints of the overall linguistic blueprint for what a language can be, there is linguistic diversity, with some languages making distinctions that others do not. They are all expressions of Language nevertheless.

Some aspects of grammar are more directly connected to meaning than others. One feature of Language that illustrates this in interesting ways is **gender**. The connection between gender and pronouns in English is so obvious that it seems odd to name it. If you are an English speaker who has learned another European language you will have quickly realised that gender goes far beyond biological sex. (See Case in Point 2.5). Gender assignment for entities not involving biological sex shows a range of complexities, which typically prove to be frustratingly difficult for second language learners to master. This is perhaps due to the apparent randomness of gender assignment with intricacies involved in conceptual, semantic and grammatical factors which determine gender. In fact, language imposes order on nominal elements in a variety of ways, with gender just one mechanism by which nouns are sorted into categories. In other words, noun classification is a natural property of Language, which sees realisation through different grammatical mechanisms, including classifiers (e.g. Chinese) and declension classes (e.g. Russian). The point is that Language is a complex system for expressing meaning, with some connections much more transparent or direct than others. As seen in our discussion of noun classification, some connections to meaning depend on higher levels of abstraction than others.

Two crucial points emerge from this discussion. Firstly, marking of nouns with classifiers, or number distinctions involving dual or trial or paucal might appear to be complex from the perspective of a speaker of a language which lacks classifiers and gender, and only marks singular or plural. But marking of more distinctions is not inherently more complex or difficult in any meaningful way. A child exposed to dual, paucal and plural marking will acquire these distinctions just as readily a child exposed to just singular versus plural does. Secondly, even if there is significant variation, it is still quite tightly constrained. Languages never grammatically express exactly seven, or approximately forty-five. One can imagine that it might be useful in specific communicative contexts if they did, but there is in fact an upper limit of how many distinctions can be made in expressions of grammatical number (see Corbett, 2000, ch. 2). Similarly, other

2.1 What Is Language?

2.5 CASE IN POINT: GENDER AND NOUN CLASSIFICATION

For speakers or learners of Indo-European languages, gender is a familiar, if often frustrating, aspect of grammar. It comes in the form of the requirement that nouns categorised as masculine, feminine or neuter trigger agreement on determiners (e.g. articles, demonstratives), adjectives and other parts of speech.

In these languages, there is often a relatively clear connection to biological sex, such that male animate or human referents typically are assigned masculine gender, female referents carry feminine gender as in (i) and (ii) in German. However, even if biological sex is a semantic core of gender assignment, the link is often tenuous beyond this core. As illustrated in (iii–v), German assigns the semantically similar objects of *spoon, knife, fork* to distinct grammatical genders.

(i) **der** Mann
 the.**MASC** 'man'
(ii) **die** Frau
 the.**FEM** 'woman'
(iii) **der** Löffel
 the.**MASC** 'spoon'
(iv) **die** Gabel
 the.**FEM** 'fork'
(v) **das** Messer
 the.**NEUT** 'knife'

This type of feminine/masculine/neuter system is just one instance of systems by which languages classify nouns. In a sense, gender just refers to 'class' and is not (necessarily) connected to biological sex. In fact, there are a number of languages that make use of classifier systems, including Chinese and the range of variations of Chinese. We illustrate, however, with Jacaltec, a modern-day Mayan language, starting with classifiers for reference to people, which are based on an interaction of gender, age and kinship relations, as in (vi), (from Craig, 1987).

(vi) cunam male (diety)
 cumi' female (diety)
 ya' male/female (older generation)
 unin male/female (infant)
 ho' male (same age, kin)
 xo' female (same age, kin)
 naj male (same age, non-kin)
 ix female (same age, non-kin)

Objects in the physical world take one of twelve classifiers based mainly on their properties, but with some exceptions, as in any gender/classifier system. This is illustrated in (vii).

(vii) atz'am + nouns for salt
       ch'en + nouns for stone, rock, glass, metal and objects made of these
       ha'   + nouns for water
       ixim   + nouns for corn, wheat and products made from corn, wheat
       k'ap   + nouns for cloth
       k'a'   + nouns for fire
       metx   + nouns for dog
       no'   + nouns for animals other than dog, and animal products
       te'   + nouns for plants except corn and products from plant material, except rope, thread and cloth
       tx'al + nouns for thread and woven materials
       tx'añ + nouns for fiber, rope and objects made from rope
       tx'otx' + nouns for ground, dirt, objects made of dirt or clay

The substance of which a product is made is therefore the basic source of noun classification in Jacaltec. Consider these examples of nouns with their associated classifiers.

(viii) **ha'** ha'   classifier+water (not recommended for drinking)
(ix)   **no'** lech classifier+milk
(x)   **te'** cape classifier+coffee

If you or I were creating a classifier system, we might create a single classifier for liquids. But in Jacaltec, we've just seen that it is the material that defines classes; so coffee takes a plant classifier, and milk takes an animal classifier.

universal properties of the language faculty impose constraints on the possible forms that language can take.

These constraints are so deeply ingrained in our biology that they are simply taken for granted without impinging on our awareness, as with other innate facets of being human. You are aware that you breathe, for example, and there are times when you make conscious efforts to control your breathing. But for the vast majority of the time you breathe without thinking about it, and you most likely take for granted that you breathe at all. Similarly, the ability to make full use of the very complex hierarchical structural system that underlies

2.1 What Is Language?

language is something that we tend to take for granted. It is often only when confronted by the unexpected properties of a foreign language that our implicit control of complex, yet also mundane, features of language are thrown into sharp relief. While for English speakers it is unremarkable that a pronoun will immediately identify whether the person you are referring to is male or female, for Korean speakers, this is not an assumed part of grammar and could be surprising for a monolingual Korean speaker who encounters English for the first time – just as it is likely surprising to you, but not Malay speakers, that it is possible in some languages to indicate whether you as a listener are being included by the choice of first person plural pronoun.

A final aspect of Language as a natural phenomenon that we will mention here is the degree to which it is an interconnected system. The majority of Greenberg's universals are implicational; they set out linguistic features in a dependent relationship with other features. Universal 36, for example, captures the observation that every language that includes gender as a grammatical category, always has number as a grammatical category as well (Greenberg, 1963, p. 95). Within number, we have seen that every language that has dual also has plural. The specific choices made by languages as to the grammatical properties they instantiate are therefore clearly not random but instead interconnected as part of a wider system (see Case in Point 2.6).

Overall, when considering the nature of Language, our answer to the question, 'what is **Language**' is: a rich system of communication, sharing specifically linguistic design features, which is an innate biological characteristic of the species *Homo sapiens*. Though a shared property, as with any biological mechanism, the underlying unity permits a rich variety of forms to surface. The interesting feature of Language when considering languages cross-linguistically, is the interplay of unity and diversity. While the range of linguistic diversity grows from the same shared root of Language, this diversity is fundamentally constrained. As we develop our understanding of this unity and diversity in terms of the idea of Virtual Grammar, we will see that *all* forms of language are constrained in shared ways. Language learners cannot escape these constraints, even if the language we produce as learners of another language might diverge from the variety that proficient speakers speak. Even at early stages, learner language is not wild, with unconstrained variation. Discussion of language learning will be left for Chapter 4 so that we can turn to the matter of diversity amongst languages in the next section.

2.6 CASE IN POINT: NUMBER, GENERIC AND SPECIFIC MEANING

Case in Point 2.3 on Number showed that languages make different levels of plurality distinction by expressing dual and paucal number in addition to singular and plural. The Cushitic language Bayso is one such language, with paucal and plural marking (examples from Corbett, 2000, p. 11).

(i) luban-**jaa**   foofe.
    lion-PAUCAL   watch.1SG
    'I watched a few lions'

(ii) luban-**jool**   foofe.
    lion-PL   watch.1SG
    'I watched a lot of lions.'

However, in addition to a singular form, Bayso also has a 'general' number which does not entail a commitment on the part of the speaker to reference to either one or more than one entity. The singular form refers to one entity, in particular for a specific referent, i.e. a specific lion in (iii). General number does not specify the number of referents involved, *lúban* in (iv) may mean *a lion* or *lions* (examples from Corbett, 2000, p. 11).

(iii) lubán-**titi**   foofe.
    lion-SG   watch.1SG
    'I watched a lion.'

(iv) lúban   foofe.
    lion.GENERAL   watch.1SG
    literally: 'I watched lion' (one or more than one).

As with other grammatical concepts, the marking of this sort of general/specific distinction can be found cross-linguistically. It is just that the distinctions might be encoded in different corners of the grammatical system. In English, the general versus specific meaning arises in the interaction of (in)definite articles and plural marking on nouns whose referents are conceptualised as being inherently countable individual entities or a mass substance.

2.2 LINGUISTIC DIVERSITY AND DIVERSITY IN LINGUISTICS

The question of how many languages there are in the world is both controversial and complex, not least because of the vexed issue of determining the boundaries between one language and another (see next section). The generally accepted estimate for the number of

2.2 Linguistic Diversity and Diversity in Linguistics

languages that are actively still in use is between 6,000 and 7,000 (Ethnologue: Simons & Fennig, 2018). In our discussion of Language, we have seen that there are numerous ways in which aspects of language are classified. We could use this as a way of grouping languages. For example, we could distinguish between languages with associativity marking versus non-associativity marking, or tone versus non-tone languages. We have also seen glimpses of more systemic relationships in the form of implicational universals. In this section we will explore ways in which we can classify and study languages, whether by typological features or genetic relationships. The theme of unity and diversity continues. We will see that languages which are genetically closely related may be typologically different and vice-versa (although there is obviously a tendency for related languages to be typologically similar). And we will connect this back to how different approaches to linguistics account for the different properties within a single language, and the differences between languages.

You are probably familiar with classifications of language by language family. Like human families, a language is said to be in the same language family when it descends from another shared language, or **proto-language**; this is expressed as genetic relationships between languages. Again as with humans, whether or not one language is said to be genetically related to another depends on how far back you want to go. It is generally accepted that English is related to German, Dutch and Swedish, for example, because these all descend from a Proto-Germanic language. But in order to claim that English is genetically related to French or Spanish, one would need to go back to the common Proto-Indo-European language which is the 'parent' (or grandparent) to both Proto-Germanic and Proto-Romance languages. You can think of this as English and German being siblings while Romance languages are their cousins.

While these genetic relationships can be clearly represented in the form of language family trees, things are rarely so clear-cut in practice. Via **language contact**, unrelated or distantly related languages which have existed in close geographic proximity for extended periods can influence each other so that they come to share certain lexical and grammatical features. These are referred to as **areal features**, which are shared by unrelated languages in a particular geographical area. A well-researched example is the Balkan Language Area (see Friedman, 2007), in which the Slavic and Romance languages share certain features with neighbouring Greek, Albanian and Turkish but not with other Romance and Slavic languages which are genetically related, but geographically more distant. Of course, careful linguistic and philological scholarship is required to establish such patterns of relatedness as opposed to accidental similarities which can be found between very distant languages. For example, the word for a domesticated canine happens to be *dog* in both the English and Mbaram Australian languages (see Campbell & Mixco, 2007, p. 29, on false cognates), but this does not betray any connection between these languages.

The English/French/German relationship mentioned can illustrate different types of relatedness. Even though English is genetically more closely related to German, the Romance languages have had a strong influence on modern-day English for historical reasons. This is especially true at the lexical level, as can be clearly seen in the two types of verbs that exist in English. 'Native' (i.e. Germanic) English verbs often have associated particles, as is common in the sister Germanic verb systems with so-called **satellite-framed** verbal systems (see also Case in Point 2.7). However, for many of these verbs in English, there is also a Latinate variety which follows the Romance family so-called **verb-framed** pattern of expressing meaning in a single lexical item (see Case in Point 2.7 on expressing motion). Some examples are given in the Table below.

Consideration of language by type in terms of particular linguistic phenomena shows us that languages that are genetically related but with quite a lot of distance may still share similar properties. The distantly related Romance and Semitic languages, for example share the property of both being verb-framed, while the more closely related Germanic and Romance languages differ with respect to this property.

While it makes sense that genetically related languages will be typologically similar, we also find typological similarities between languages without close genetic connections; for example, indigenous American and Australian languages tend to be typologically similar

TABLE 2.1 *English verb variants*

Germanic	Latinate
go in	enter
get together	congregate
talk over	discuss
put out	extinguish
take off	remove
get over	recover
put together	connect

2.7 CASE IN POINT: VERBS AND MOTION EVENTS

A range of different elements may be encoded within verb phrases to capture the nature of an event involving, for example, motion: the cause of the motion, the location of the motion, etc. If we consider the encoding of semantic aspects of an event, we see that languages divide into different types according to how they realise certain features grammatically. We explore this here in terms of path of motion and manner of motion (see Talmy, 1991).

Verb-framed languages (including Romance and Semitic languages) encode an element of meaning in the verb itself. For example, the path of motion is inherent to the meaning of the verb, with different verbs specifying different paths. If another meaning is needed, like the manner of motion, it is expressed by an adverbial expressions. This is illustrated in Spanish.

(i) La chica salió de la casa.
     the girl exit.3PAST of the house
     'The girl went out of the house.'

(ii) La chica **salió** de la casa **corriendo**.
     the girl exit.3PAST of the house running
     'The girl ran out of the house.'

This contrasts with languages which use a **satellite-framed** mechanism: they don't include the path as part of the meaning of the verb itself, but use extra particles or adverbials to express the path of motion instead. Germanic, Finno-Ugric and Chinese languages are considered to be satellite-framed in this way. Examples from Hungarian serve to illustrate:

(iii) Kiment   a házból.
      out.leave   the house
      'he/she left the house.'

(iv) Kifutott   a házból.
      out.run   the house
      'he/she ran out of the house.'

What you will have noticed if you thought about the Hungarian examples carefully is that while Hungarian is satellite-framed with respect to path, it looks like it is verb-framed if considered in terms of manner of motion; the verb in (iv) includes the manner of the leaving, namely, running. We discuss the challenges of typology below.

with respect to their use of morphology, even though they share no genetic relationship (see Case in Point 2.8). Linguistic **typology** has a long history, with typologists devoted to descriptive analysis of languages based on careful collection of attested linguistic forms. We have, in fact, already begun to see how some of the world's languages differ typologically. We have seen this in terms of semantics, for example motion events (see also Talmy, 1985), syntax (as in Greenberg's work), and phonology (e.g. Case in Point 2.2 on Tones and see Maddieson, 1984).

The classical approach to typology took morphology as its basis because the ways in which languages exploit the basic building blocks at the level of the word can be very different. Just as the same building materials can be put to use to form very different architectural structures, the same sort of linguistic material can be put together in ways which give rise to what might look like wildly different linguistic structures. Early typology work divided the world's languages into isolating, inflectional and agglutinative languages based on the shape that languages take. In so-called **isolating languages** there are few, if any, grammatical words or affixes; instead the language is made up of predominantly contentful lexical items. The Chinese language family is often given as an example of an isolating language because it has relatively few purely grammatical words or morphemes.

By contrast, **agglutinative languages** are characterised by rich morphological affixation, with whole sentences being expressed through one single, complex word. Languages as distinct as Navajo, Turkish and Mongolian are all said to be agglutinative languages, as are Bininj Gunwok and Cayuga, as shown in the Case in Point 2.8. More recent work on morphologically rich languages has introduced the term **polysynthesis** to refer to languages that rely on complexes of affixes to create full sentences or utterances.

In the third category, **inflectional languages** have a different shape in that there are mostly free-standing lexical items, like in isolating languages. But there is also the tendency for lexical items to readily change form through grammatical suffixation. With Latin being the classical inflecting language, its genetic descendants, French, Italian, Spanish, etc., would all fall into this category. In reality, this approach was never entirely convincing because it isn't possible to shoehorn any one language entirely into one of these types. Instead languages make use of all of these morphological possibilities, some doing so to more extreme levels than others. English,

2.8 CASE IN POINT: SENTENCE–WORDS

Some languages with rich agglutinative morphology are said to form sentence-words. That is, the various functions and meanings that are encoded in individual words in isolating-type languages are realised as bound morphemes in agglutinative or polysynthetic languages. This is typical of Indigenous American and Australian languages as well as others. Examples in (i) and (ii) illustrate from Bininj Gunwok (Australian) and Cayuga (American), respectively (from Evans & Sasse, 2002).

(i) Nga-ban-mame-yawoih-**dulk**-djobge-ng.
1SG.SUBJ-3PL.OBJ- BEN-again-**tree**-cut-PP
'I cut another tree for them.'

(ii) Ę-s-kakhe-**hona't**-á-yęthw-ahs.
FUT- REP-1SG.SUBJ/3PL.OBJ-**potato**-SJ-plant-BEN:PUNC
'I will plant potatoes for them again.'

The unfamiliar morpheme glosses in these examples are:

BEN = Benefactive; PP = Past Perfective; REP = Reciprocal;
SJ = stem joiner; PUNC = Punctual

Elements that English encodes either as individual words or by grammatical construction appear are affixes on the verb above, including subject and object pronouns, tense, aspect (punctuality), as well as predicate-argument relationships (benefactive).

Because lexical items ('tree' and 'potatoes' above) are incorporated into these 'sentence words', these direct objects are seen by linguists as having become part of the verb, a process known as **noun incorporation**.

---

for example, makes relatively little use of affixation as compared to both agglutinating and inflectional languages. In this way, English could be said to be more typologically similar to Chinese. But obviously, Chinese and English are not closely related as languages. In other words, from the set of options available within morphology, Virtual Grammar gives rise to actual languages, some of which exploit some word formation tendencies over others.

Language typology is useful because it allows us to know which features of language are common and which are unusual, or **marked**. Thanks to language typologists we know, for example, that the use of relative pronouns like *who* or *which* in relative clauses is very common in European languages but very infrequent across the rest of the world's languages (Comrie, 1989). We also know that the pronunciation of 'th' in English is very infrequent cross-linguistically. That English has both a voiced and unvoiced version of 'th' means that most learners of English as an additional language will find the correct pronunciation of words with the voiced variant like *this*, *father* and *bathe*, as well as its unvoiced counterpart, *thing*, *author* and *teeth*, very challenging indeed.

Typological study of large samples of specific languages, looking for general tendencies, allows linguists to identify features of language that are frequent or infrequent. However, the sheer existence of a language, to say nothing of its dominance or effect on other languages, is dependent on non-linguistic realities like the political power its speakers hold, nothing to do with the inherent properties of the language itself. This reality means that we ought not to put too much stock in how common any specific linguistic feature is given that its existence is just one more happenstance of history. While the inherent nature of language has nothing to do with how often any specific feature of language might occur across languages, by studying linguistic properties across a range of languages we can gain better understanding of more abstract unifying principles, or universals such as structure dependence or agreement, for example. It is the recognition of universals that supports a view of language as biological. The study of universals in terms of linguistic properties as revealed through typological studies has defined formal approaches to linguistics. As we saw in Chapter 1, there is diversity in linguistic explanation; the diversity in the world's languages is yet one more reason why the diversity in approaches to linguistics exists.

One facet of linguistic diversity which can play out in different ways in language teaching, is consideration of language as a cognitive linguistic system on the one hand, and language as integral to social systems on the other. While both are valid and valuable from a scientific perspective, they should not be viewed in isolation when considered from a pedagogical perspective. A curriculum oriented around grammar, for example, will benefit from understanding of the cognitive linguistic system that underlies it, while a curriculum which prioritises interaction and communication will require good understanding of social systems and cultural norms. In practice, teaching involves aspects of the abstract grammatical system and the social and cultural import of language. As a teacher, it is well worth having the widest repertoire possible when considering how to teach language. This is true when considering the interplay between genetic and typological relatedness for different features of languages being learned and/or taught. The language you are teaching might be very similar to the language your learners already know, whether in terms of genetic closeness or in terms of typology. This may lead to a perception of 'foreignness' amongst your learners which might create unhelpful barriers to learning. A view of unity underlying diversity – even at the level of grammar – may help you to combat this.

We will return to consideration of similarity and 'foreignness' in the later chapters as we move to questions of language learning. We'll close this section on diversity with the reminder that all languages are expressions of a uniquely human ability and all normally developing children come to develop (at least one) fully formed language system. However, while knowing a language includes being able to speak it, abiding by very complex linguistic constraints to produce language with subtle and sophisticated nuances, there are aspects of language which don't come through sheer exposure to language, but instead which need to be learned. This is true both for aspects of the first language one encounters and for a language learned later in life. The ability to read and write is one example, as we will discuss in the next section.

2.3 LANGUAGES WITHIN LANGUAGES

We have explored Language with a capital L, highlighting abstract principles and universals. In this section we will explore the variation that exists within a language, asking what is *a* language. What we find is that there are variants within a language which are complex and different enough that they could be thought of as languages within languages.

2.3.1 Varieties and Dialects

Posing the question 'what is a language?' inevitably confronts us with fuzzy issues of definition and value judgements, which terminology is often ill equipped to clarify. Dimensions of a language, such as *variety*, *dialect*, *patois* and other terms are not always easy to define in technical linguistic terms, quite apart from the added complications of connotations associated with their non-technical uses. A regular line in introductory linguistics courses is that *a language is a dialect with an army and a navy*.[1] This characterisation points to the historical and political dimensions of defining (national) languages. To some extent, this way of thinking relates to the genetic relationships between languages discussed in the previous section. While some closely related linguistic varieties are subsumed as dialects of a particular language, genetically distinct varieties cannot be categorised in this way. As an illustration, the Celtic language Breton, spoken in Brittany, an administrative region within France, has the status of a 'regional language'. It is much more closely related to Welsh and other Celtic languages than it is to French. For this reason, it cannot be called a 'dialect of French'. This contrasts with Alemannic language varieties spoken in south-western Germany and Switzerland, which are closely related to German. Their regional proximity and linguistic similarities allow them to be categorised as 'varieties' or 'dialects' of German. Note, however, that these German 'varieties' can be as unintelligible to a German speaker from, say, Berlin as the related language Dutch is. Though Dutch is considered a distinct language from German, the languages are in fact extremely closely related to one another. It is only by accidents of history that when considering German, we talk of an Alemannic dialect on the one hand, but Dutch as a separate language, on the other. Had things played out differently, we could just as well today be talking of the Netherlandish dialect of German, or a Berliner dialect of Dutch. (See www.dialectsyntax.org for a range of research on dialectal variation in Europe).

We will follow the practice of understanding a **dialect** to refer to variants of a language which have distinct forms in terms of lexical items and morphosyntactic patterns, as well as pronunciation. This range of differences distinguishes dialects from the term **accent**, which is generally restricted to differences in pronunciation only. When thinking about dialects, it is useful to think in terms of a **dialect continuum**, which helps to contextualise the status of national standard languages. We can illustrate by returning to the Dutch-German example. Let's consider a traveller setting out eastwards from Amsterdam in the seventeenth century before the advent of strict international borders and national education systems. This imaginary Amsterdam traveller would speak the dialect of the city, and after a journey of ten kilometres would come to a village where the local speech is more or less the same as the Amsterdam variety. The next leg of the journey to a village a further fifty kilometres away

---

[1] There is some debate about the source of this saying. It is often attributed to the linguist Max Weinreich (see Notes, *LiS*, 1997).

2.3 Languages within Languages

would confront the traveller with local speech that is more different from the Amsterdam variety but still shares the majority of lexical, phonological and grammatical features so that our traveller can easily understand and be understood. After the next leg of the journey, a further fifty kilometres eastwards, our traveller would arrive at a village where mutual comprehension becomes more difficult but with enough shared features to allow communication, and to trigger at least mutual recognition of a shared linguistic heritage. A further fifty kilometres and perhaps the traveller would face significant communication problems with the locals. And so on. This illustrates the continuum. On a journey from Amsterdam to Berlin, there would be no clear *linguistic* dividing line where Dutch ends and German begins. The various dialects along the way would differ incrementally such that mutual comprehension between neighbouring speech communities is not a problem, but at either end of the continuum, we find mutually incomprehensible varieties such that the Amsterdamer does not understand the Berliner, and vice-versa. It is only the creation of an arbitrary international border with different standard 'national languages' on either side of it that breaks this continuum into distinct languages. If divorced from political and historical context, consideration of the linguistic properties of varieties of German and Dutch could support a view in which they are seen as dialects of the same language (Pereltsvaig, 2012, p. 6).

If it is possible to consider Dutch and German as dialects of the same language, one logically wonders what language they are dialects of. This confronts us with the tricky notion that a standard language is necessarily an abstraction, or indeed an ideology (Armstrong & Mackenzie, 2013, p. 5; Milroy & Milroy, 1999). The forces behind standardisation are social and educational and involve questions of hierarchical power relations within nation-states and questions of linguistic prestige and supposed purity. Detailed consideration of these issues would take us far beyond our discussions here (we return to these issues with respect to prescriptive grammar in Chapter 3). The relevant point is that there is nothing linguistically special about national standard varieties. There is no linguistic basis on which to claim that Canadian English is any better or worse than American or Irish English, for example. Each of these standard varieties illustrates the same range of grammatical features and complexity as any other, and indeed as any of the many 'dialectal' varieties within each of these national varieties. And they are each also in a continuous state of change, removing the spurious notion that the variety with the oldest history is somehow a more 'true' variety. But obviously, it is the codified national language that is taught as a foreign language to learners outside the speech community, and it is the codified national language that is the basis of literacy education for pupils within the speech community. These facts create certain issues for language teaching given the tension between providing instruction in a codified standard language and the messy reality that language is an abstraction. This reality speaks to another aspect of our concept of Virtual Grammar, as we will return to later.

An interesting situation arises when differences between many recognisably different national varieties are seen to have a common standard, as is the case with Arabic. Modern Standard Arabic (MSA) is used in writing and the media, and it is the form of Arabic taught in schools in Arabic-speaking countries; it is also the form taught to learners of Arabic as a foreign language. In reality, however, a large number of varieties of Arabic, which diverge from MSA to differing degrees, are spoken from North Africa to the Levant and the Gulf of Arabia (Holes, 1995), giving us for example, Libyan Arabic, Syrian Arabic and Saudi Arabic, and others. Each of these varieties is distinct from each other and from MSA. This situation has given rise to the phenomenon of **diglossia**. In diglossic speech communities, speakers have command of two recognisably distinct forms of a language, changing from one to the other according to circumstance, context or mode (see Case in Point 2.9). However, because the 'high' language version (MSA in the case of Arabic) tends to be explicitly taught as part of common literacy rather than acquired naturally, it has even been suggested that MSA is more like a second language for Arabic speakers (Khamis-Dakwar et al., 2012, p. 71). In particular, switching between varieties of Arabic seems to evoke similar cognitive responses as code-switching in bilinguals (Khamis-Dakwar & Froud, 2007). Where MSA differs from a local variety, children show more evidence of variability in the standard and have less determinate judgements of the grammaticality of constructions in MSA – for example on the form of dual versus plural marking (Khamis-Dakwar et al., 2012). This obviously poses intricate challenges for education in these contexts.

Whether one standard spans across national boundaries or multiple standards exist in different nations, there is a degree to which any language can be said to be an abstraction. From New Zealand to South Africa to Ireland, English itself is an abstraction. And, of course, we know that within any national standard, there are dialects. In Britain, the varieties often carry names and associations with geographic regions, like Geordie, Cockney or Brummie. In the USA, there are varieties associated with ethnicity, such as Black Vernacular English.

2.3 Languages within Languages

> ### 2.9 CASE IN POINT: PLURAL AND DUAL IN A DIGLOSSIC LANGUAGE
>
> Arabic is one of the languages which differentiate between singular, dual and plural number marking. However, in the linguistic variety that exists in Arabic, this number feature is also realised in variable ways. As is common for spoken varieties of any language (as compared to standard literary varieties), there is often simplification or neutralisation of complex grammatical forms.
>
> In Standard and Classical Arabic, verbs and adjectives have to have dual marking that agrees with nouns in the dual form, and plural agreement with plural nouns, as in (i) – (iii).
>
> (i) ʔalbana:**tu** daxal-**na**
> The.girl-**PL** entered-3.FEM.**PL**
> 'The girls entered.'
>
> (ii) ʔal**bint-a:ni** daxal-**ata**
> The.girl-**DUAL** entered-3.FEM.**DUAL** (Holes, 1995, pp. 120–1)
> 'Two girls entered.'
>
> (iii) ʔaloa lada:n yadhaka:n
> the-boy- DUAL PRES-smile-3MASC.DUAL (Khamis-Dakwar et al., 2012)
> 'The two boys are smiling.'
>
> Regional varieties do not maintain this agreement pattern. Instead, dual occurs only on nouns, as illustrated in Cairene Arabic (iv-v) and Palestinian Colloquial Arabic (vi).
>
> (iv) il**bana:t** daxal-u
> the.girl.**PL** entered-3COMPL
> 'The girls entered.'
>
> (v) il**binte:n** daxal-u
> the.girl-**DUAL** entered-3COMPL
> 'Two girls entered.'
>
> (vi) ʔil**ualade:n** bIdhaku
> the.boy-**DUAL** PRES-smile-3MP
> 'The two children are smiling.'

All of this leaves much food for thought about the status of languages and what is defined as a language at all for language teaching (see papers in Makoni & Pennycook, 2007). We return to these issues in Chapter 5.

Despite these issues concerning the status of languages and varieties, when we are thinking of teaching or learning a language we are typically talking about a discrete *other*, in other words, an additional or foreign, language. Globally, there is general acceptance that including language as a subject in school is a normal option within a school's curriculum. But, of course, the schooling of young children in education systems across the world also includes significant amounts of time devoted to the language they already know in order to ensure that children learn to read and write. This intersects with notions of standardisation as the written form is typically the accepted national standard language, and may differ more or less radically from the spoken form children acquire prior to schooling. Part of becoming literate is learning the set of conventions associated specifically with the written form of the language. This includes everything from the alphabet to spelling to conventions of punctuation. As literate adults, it is easy to think of all of this as knowledge of one's language. But in fact, these aspects of language can be seen as **artefacts of language** in the sense that they have been developed by society, a point underlined by the existence of spoken languages which don't have a written variant. Typically, these artefacts form the bulk of what is taught in school precisely because these are socially constructed conventions and not part of the biological, inherent understanding of language we have been considering thus far in this book.

2.3.2 Language Register

While dialectal variation develops as a natural part of language evolution, **register** differences are understood to be more functional and employed with distinct communicative goals in mind. The difference in register between speech and writing is referred to as a difference of **mode**, or medium, and it holds irrespective of dialect differences. Mode or medium is one of three aspects of register in language (see Biber & Conrad, 2009, for extensive discussion of issues of register with respect to English). The mode of writing sees differences to speech which can range from lexical choice to grammatical structure. You will know this from your own experience when you attempt to capture some feature of spoken language to include in a text message and realise that there is no 'correct' spelling for it. The opposite occurs when you look for ways in speech to use conventions developed for writing, such as the finger-gestured 'air quotes' often used in speech to convey a sense of speculation.

As with the other types of variation we have encountered, register variation is also constrained by linguistic principles. Variation is not linguistically or grammatically random, even if some forms might be considered to be 'lower' register, or simplified compared to 'correct' or written forms. An indicator of a spoken or colloquial register in

2.10 CASE IN POINT: SUBJECTLESS SENTENCES

One way in which languages vary is whether or not they overtly express the subject/object arguments of verbs when the arguments are pronouns. Languages such as Chinese may freely omit any argument (i–ii), provided the discourse context makes the intended referent clear.

(i)   _ kanjian ta le
    _ saw   him PERF
    'He saw him.'

(ii) Ta kanjian _ le
    He saw   _ PERF
    'He saw him.'

Languages like Spanish can omit all subject pronouns.

(iii) _ lo vi
    _ him saw.
    'I saw him.'

Languages like English cannot omit arguments.

(iv) *_ saw him

And some languages, like Finnish, can only omit arguments of certain persons (first vs third) or in certain tenses.

(v) _ näin hänet
    _ saw   him
    'I saw him.'

(vi) Hän näki hänet
    He saw him

(vii) *_ näki hänet

However, as pointed out, certain registers of English do in fact allow subject pronouns to be dropped.

(viii) Wish you were here!
(ix) Cried yesterday morning: as if it were an hour for keening: why is crying so pleasurable? (*The Journals of Sylvia Plath*, discussed in Haegeman & Ihsane, 2001)
(x) Will be late! (cf. I will be late).

Even though such examples represent a less formal or more colloquial register, this doesn't mean they are grammatically unconstrained (Haegeman, 2017). For example, even if the register

> and context is appropriate, subjects cannot be left out of subordinate clauses (xi), nor from questions (xii) (Haegeman & Gueron, 1999, p. 617).
>
> (xi) *I must work, as __ told Sally G.
> (xii) *Am __ jealous?

English would be the use of a reduced or 'telegraphic' speech style which does not require expression of certain grammatical elements (see Case in Point 2.10). An utterance such as *there in 5* is a perfectly natural realisation of the grammatical sentence *I will arrive there in 5 minutes*, if the mode is a phone call or text message between friends. However, even such reduced registers are constrained by quite sophisticated grammatical properties which are to be found operating across different languages or language varieties.

A second area of register difference is by **domain**, or field. You will be familiar with differences in language use in academic contexts compared to journalism, which differs again from language used in social media, and so on. As with the difference between speech and writing, these differences range from word choice to grammar. Language for advertising, for example, will employ a rich range of adjectives to entice the listener or reader in a way that is normally deemed inappropriate in language used for an academic essay, a rail station announcement, or a memorial service. But variation extends beyond general function to differences within a single domain as well. There is a rich body of literature within genre analysis showing that within the domain of academic language, for example, there are clear differences to be found from one academic discipline to another (Hyland, 2004).

The third way in which a language shows register variation is by **tenor**, or formality. This cuts across mode and domain as it is possible to be formal and informal in both speech and writing and in different domains of use (although some domains will more naturally require certain levels of formality than others). We have devoted quite a bit of discussion to sociolinguistic ideas of variation so far in this section, and while much of this variation is linguistically expressed in functional and communicative ways, many languages also grammatically encode certain aspects of these features. While tenor may be expressed by choice of words and communicative strategies, some languages encode aspects of politeness or formality, for example, in the grammatical system itself (see Case in Point 2.11).

2.11 CASE IN POINT: POLITENESS

A number of languages have specific pronoun forms which are formal, or polite variants of the regular form, as did English in the past, with what used to be the informal variant *thou* now included in the more broadly extended *you* form. Some languages go much further than this. In Korean (and Japanese), there is an extensive system of honorifics. It implicates both the nominal and verbal systems, and is employed in writing and in speech. Every sentence and utterance which includes reference to someone for whom deference is expected will employ a separate verb ending, or honorific marker, *si*.

(i) a. apeci-ka   o-**si**-nta
    Father-SUBJ   come-**HON**-PRES.PROG
    'Father is coming.'
  b. tongsayng-i   o-nta
    sibling-SUBJ   come-PRES.PROG
    'Brother/Sister is coming.'   (Lee and Ramsey, 2000, pp. 239–40)

But this is the tip of the iceberg in Korean. Traditionally, there are in fact six 'speech levels', with every verb in Korean required to reflect one of the six levels, though the 'middle' levels, blunt and familiar, are no longer routinely used (Sohn, 1999, p. 413). The verb endings for each of the levels (in declarative sentences) are as follows:

Plain level	-ta
Intimate level	-a/-e
(Familiar level	-ne-y)
(Blunt level	-(s)ol-(s)wu)
Polite level	-(a/e)yo
Deferential level	-(su)pnita

In addition, at the lexical level, there are sets of words for which there is a separate form altogether, including:

	Honorific form	Plain form	Meaning
Verbs:	capswusta	mekta	'to eat'
	tolakasita	cwukta	'to die'
	kyeysita	issta	'to stay'
Noun:	tayk	cip	'house'
	yensai	nai	'age'
	cinci	pap	'meal'

All languages are, of course, able to express politeness, with linguistic conventions and routines often an important part of a school curriculum as well as fundamental to what is considered good parenting. The extent to which any register difference features when studying a new language is certainly central within a language for specific purposes context. A language course designed for students planning to study abroad will need to focus on formal features of written language in a way that a language course designed for learners wanting to visit a country as a tourist, for example, need not concern itself. There will also be considerations which are particular to the language in question. Teachers of Arabic as a foreign language, for example, have traditionally taught MSA, leaving students of Arabic who spend time in an Arabic-speaking country struggling to communicate in the 'everyday' Arabic they hear around them. In this example, the issue goes beyond formal or informal register to the question of variety of language.

2.3.3 Pidgins and Creoles

A final aspect of languages within languages that we will consider is that of pidgins and creoles. **Pidgins** derive from different language communities in such intimate contact, and under enough pressure to communicate, that hybrid forms emerge. This hybrid form typically includes core lexical items from both languages. It may be light on, or even devoid, of grammatical morphemes as the pressure to communicate privileges the use of meaningful content words, with heavy reliance on the immediate context to convey meaning. Nevertheless, the realisation of pidginised forms may indicate the importance of underlying grammatical concepts. In Case in Point 2.12, words from English have been repurposed to fit the conceptual requirements of the substrate Central Eastern Oceanic in the formation of Melanesian Pidgin. Like Central Eastern Oceanic, Melanesian Pidgin realises associativity and different plural forms.

A **creole** refers to subsequent forms of the hybrid language, which typically emerge from subsequent generations who sometimes speak only the hybrid version of the language. When the hybrid forms provide the input for mother tongue development, the developing generation imposes upon it grammatical features that do not exist in the pidgin form. A pidgin is thus said to have become a creole when it is the mother tongue for a generation of speakers. This pattern of creolisation is known to have happened in several places in the 'new world' from the 1500s, when Europeans settled on already populated lands or forcibly dislocated and brought together different speech

2.12 CASE IN POINT: NUMBER AND ASSOCIATIVITY IN A CREOLE LANGUAGE

The Melanesian creole language, Bislama, is one of the many languages that express associativity grammatically (see Case in Point 2.1), as well as differentiating between different forms of number. Bislama is a creole derived from a substrate Central Oceanic language and English, the so-called lexifier language for Bislama. English forms have been pressed into service as markers of inclusive/exclusive distinctions as well as markers of dual and trial number. In the paradigm outlined here, tu and tri (from 'two' and 'three') are added to pronouns to mark dual and trial number. The element *-fala* is a plural marker derived from 'fellow' (Siegel, 2008, after Keesing, 1988, p. 96).

	Singular	Dual	Trial	Plural
1st person inclusive		yumi**tu**(fala)	yumi**trifala**	yumi
1st person exclusive	mi	mi**tufala**	mi**trifala**	mifala
2nd person	yu	yu**tufala**	yu**trifala**	yufala
3rd person	hem/em	**tufala**	**trifala**	olgeta

This closely follows the paradigm in Central Eastern Oceanic, as illustrated by Tangoa (Siegel, 2008, after Camden, 1979, p. 88). The forms *rua* and *tolu* correspond also to 'two' and 'three' as independent words, illustrating the sort of equivalence that has been established between the languages, a useful mechanism employed in the pidgin as well.

	Singular	Dual	Trial	Plural
1st person inclusive		enra**rua**	enra**tolu**	enra
1st person exclusive	enau	kamam**rua**	kamam**tolu**	kamam
2nd person	egko	kamim**rua**	kamim**tolu**	kamim
3rd person	enia	enra**rua**	enra**tolu**	enra/enira

communities (see Aboh, 2015, ch. 2). A more recent example is that of Tok Pisin, 'talk pidgin', in Papua New Guinea which developed last century. Tok Pisin has been seen as distinct from English since the mid-1900s, and became an official language in 1981.

What is interesting from a linguistic and language acquisition point of view is how grammaticalisation emerges with new generations of speakers. Leaving aside many particulars, we can assume that when simplified pidgin languages are filtered through children's innate grammar-making capacities, a fuller and more complex creole language emerges. This real-life opportunity for new language creation has received a good amount of attention from researchers as it offers a way to study how language develops. (See Kegl, 1994, for one famous example, and Singler & Kouwenberg, 2008, for more on pidgins and creoles in general.)

There are interesting issues that one might explore with respect to the extent to which pidginisation/creolisation and second language acquisition resemble each other and share similar features (see papers in Lefebvre et al., 2006, for example). For the moment, it suffices to say that the emergence of a hybrid linguistic system due to contact between speech communities bears interesting analogies to the hybrid system that emerges when different languages come into contact in the mind of an individual learner.

2.4 CONCLUSION: MOVING FORWARD

In this chapter we set out to explore the nature of language and languages. The main theme that has emerged is unity in diversity. Language can be seen as a natural biological phenomenon which is specific to the human species and distinct from other forms of communication. This unifying human cognitive capacity diverges into a range of particular instantiations in the form of families of languages, and these further diversify into particular individual languages. But the divergence between languages is tightly constrained and not random. We see genetic and typological relationships, which can help to reveal the underlying nature of language as a biological and cognitive phenomenon. Within each particular language, we see diversity in the form of dialectal variation which constitutes a continuum of varieties of languages. And within each variety, we have a range of functional variation according to domain and mode of use. We finally arrive at the level of the individual speaker who controls a number of varieties of language(s) which can be exploited in a range of different social and communicative contexts as appropriate.

As we shall see in Chapter 4, the underlying cognitive and biological unity of language simplifies the task of acquiring a language for young children by providing a blueprint for what the grammar of a language can possibly be. So, one can think of this as providing a head start to language learning. When we come to learn an additional language, in some ways, the problem is that we have too much of a head start. We will have already established the properties of (at least) one language, and these specific linguistic properties are entrenched thanks to years of continuous activation of the individual underlying properties that give rise to the totality of the language system in question. For this reason, getting to grips with new and seemingly strange grammatical properties can prove difficult. Baker (2002, p. 6) says that '[m]uch of the difficulty in coming to grips with an unfamiliar language is that there are many layers of difference. Each layer might be understandable enough in its own terms, but the differences magnify each other until the total effect is overwhelming.' But we take the view that the ability to abstract away from a language to Language can facilitate language learning. As we turn to grammar more specifically in the next chapter, we hold onto the point made by Baker (2002) that even apparently wildly different languages share a common core. We agree, and have developed the notion of Virtual Grammar to try to capture this for the context of language learning, as we will discuss in the next chapter.

2.5 EXERCISES AND QUESTIONS FOR DISCUSSION

1. Linguistic Complexity and Difficult Languages

It is a maxim of Linguistics that no language is superior to any other. Because all languages are equal as a communicative vehicle for human thoughts and feelings, it might also be assumed that no language is inherently more complicated or difficult than any other language.

i) Even if you agree with this, as a language learner or a language teacher you have also likely experienced that the grammars of some languages seem harder to come to grips with. Which languages have you learned/taught that seem more grammatically 'difficult' than others? How would you characterise what it is about those languages that seems to make them more grammatically difficult?

ii) A typical answer to this question is that languages with elaborate morphological paradigms are 'difficult' while languages without such paradigms might be considered to have 'no grammar' or 'simple grammar' (see Case in Point 2.8 on sentence-words). Consider your opinion on this and how morphological elaboration might interact with other areas of grammar to result in patterns that appear 'difficult' to learners. Why do you think morphologically complex languages tend to be considered difficult? (see discussion of acquisition in Chapter 4).

iii) What have you learned about aspects of grammar from this chapter that illustrate 'hidden complexity' that is not immediately obvious from the surface forms of languages?

2. Language Diversity and Language Learning

Languages spoken by small homogenous groups tend to be more elaborate in their grammatical patterns than languages with large and dispersed speech communities. It has been claimed by John McWhorter that the less elaborate grammars of widely spoken lingua francas are a result of simplifications to these languages because they have been learned imperfectly by adult speakers at various points during their history. The simplified grammatical patterns from imperfect mastery by adult learners are then incorporated into the standard language. McWhorter (2007, p. 15) says, 'The human grammar is a fecund weed, like grass. Languages like English, Persian and Mandarin Chinese are mowed lawns, indicative of interruption in natural proliferation.'

i) Given what you know about learner language, what sort of simplifications do you expect in English, Mandarin and Persian? (Or in any language learned as an L2).

ii) If McWhorter is right and English, Mandarin and Persian are linguistically simplified, does it affect your view of these languages? What does this tell you about language status in terms of linguistic complexity and socio-political power?

3. Language Families and Language Learning

i) Reflect on the genetic or typological relatedness of the language you teach and the language(s) that your learners typically know.

ii) To what extent does the dissimilarity between your learners' languages and the languages being taught pose learnability issues? To what extent does similarity facilitate learning for your learners?

iii) Consider a point of grammar in the language you teach which seems unusual or exotic compared to the grammar of the language(s) your learners typically know. Can you think of a connection to a grammatical concept or form in the learners' languages which makes the exotic or 'unusual' point of grammar seem more familiar or relatable? How could you use L1–L2 connections like this in your teaching?

2.5 Exercises and Questions for Discussion

4. Dialect and Standard

i) Consider the variety of the language that you speak as a primary language. Which grammatical feature(s) do you use in your dialect that are not considered typical in the standard variety? If you speak the standard variety, what are some of the features that distinguish it from other varieties?

ii) Even if the dialectal features might be considered non-standard in your speech community, they will still be subject to sophisticated grammatical rules. For the dialect patterns you have thought of, can you formulate grammatical rules or regularities for them? How do the rules compare to the standard variety? Are they more or less complex?

iii) How are these features viewed in education, and in popular culture? To what extent are they stigmatised? To what extent are they used as indicators of identity?

5. Politeness

i) In this chapter, we pointed out how politeness may be manifested grammatically in Korean. For European languages, there is often a choice of familiar versus polite pronoun (*tu-vous* in French, *du-Sie* in German, etc.). In what other ways are levels of familiarity or politeness encoded in the languages you speak or teach? Consider: forms of address; grammatical patterns; choice of lexical items in interaction.

ii) How are communicative phenomena like politeness addressed in the teaching materials you are familiar with? To what extent are communicative or register phenomena included within information on grammar and grammar practice activities?

iii) How do you create contexts which favour or require the use of different levels of politeness or register variation in the classroom context? To what extent do you include these contextual features in the teaching and use of grammar practice?

6. Number, Mass and Genericity

i) The example of 'general number' in this chapter illustrated that some languages do not force nouns to be marked for number. A literal translation of general number would give a bare noun in English, as in 'lion' in (a). This is ungrammatical, but a similar pattern, like (b) is possible, though with a different interpretation. How is the referent of 'lion' being conceptualised differently in (a) versus (b)? How do concepts like count, mass and genericity help you understand and explain these differences?

    a) *I saw lion.
    b) I don't like lion.
    c) I don't like lions.

ii) The meaning or referent of a noun will change how it patterns with respect to concepts like mass, count, etc. How are concepts of mass/count, definiteness/specificity at play in (d–f)? (compared, for example, to (a) – (c)).

    d) I don't like wine.
    e) I don't like the wine.
    f) I don't like German wines.

iii) How are concepts like number, genericity and definiteness/specificity expressed in the language(s) you teach compared to the language(s) that your learners know? Are they realised in the same or different types of constructions (e.g. articles)? How do the concepts interact in these languages? Which difficulties might arise for learners as a result?

7. Person, Number and Associativity

i) English plural reflexives can sometimes appear in singular forms (such as *ourself* or *themself*). Consider your reaction to the sentences in (a) – (d). Some speakers would use all of these, although one of the forms would be considered non-standard. Some English speakers might consider it completely ungrammatical. Which one? (see Collins & Postal, 2012, for studies of acceptability).

    a) Have you washed yourselves?
    b) Have you washed yourself?
    c) Have we washed ourselves?
    d) Have we washed ourself?

ii) For those English speakers who accept all of these sentences as grammatically possible, there are distinctions in meaning connected to agreement and associativity. Using the concepts of person, number and associativity, how might you analyse the differences in meanings expressed by these sentences? Can you think of a communicative situation where they would be used? Pay particular attention to the sentence that might have struck you as ungrammatical – for those speakers who use it, what is the rationale for its use?

2.5 Exercises and Questions for Discussion

iii) Consider how non-standard variants in the languages you teach or know might be motivated by expression of grammatical concepts for particular communicative purposes. Can you think of a grammatical usage which is non-standard or dialectal but which can be analysed fruitfully in terms of grammatical concepts?

8. Structure Dependence

i) We saw that some elements of a sentence can be analysed as having 'moved' in the syntactic structure. How can these sentences (a) – (c) be said to illustrate this (from Radford & Felser, 2011)? Pay attention to the prepositions highlighted (and see also Chapter 3).

   a) He sent it straight back **from** where it came **from**.
   b) Tiger Woods, **about** whom this Masters seems to be all **about**, is due to tee off shortly.
   c) **To** which of these groups do you consider that you belong **to**?

ii) You will have noticed that these structures seem to show that the prepositions are pronounced in both their original and moved positions. Can you think of other phenomena in colloquial language production that illustrate the structure-dependence of language? How can one differentiate between production phenomena like repetition and false starts and grammatical phenomena, illustrated in (a) – (c)?

3 Grammar and Grammars

In the previous chapter, we discussed the nature of Language and languages. Because this is a book on grammar, the way we are approaching language means that there are times when we have used the words 'language' and 'grammar' as near synonyms. Given that they are not the same thing, this chapter will explore grammar more closely, further developing the notion of Virtual Grammar. As such, we continue to be linguistic in orientation, but guided by usefulness for questions of teaching and learning. A starting point for the notion of Virtual Grammar is as an abstract innate property which constrains the range of potential structural forms that are expressed in the world's languages. We saw in the last chapter that one important way of categorising languages into different types is precisely along the lines of grammatical similarity or difference. Indeed, just as language and grammar can be used interchangeably in many respects, for some academics, linguistics and grammar refer to essentially the same thing as well. It is worth a reminder that the academic study of language includes both formal and functional approaches to grammar. For some, the close identification of language with grammar as presented here may bear too close a connection. This is a product of our orientation as linguists who are interested in grammar. At the same time, given our commitment to language education, we try to temper this discussion of grammar by looking to educational and pedagogical issues to guide us. Grammar provides an interesting perspective on educational questions because questions of grammatical accuracy are often considered crucial, both in language education of the shared speech community, and in the teaching and learning of additional languages. Based on our understanding of what language is, the discussion of grammar(s) to follow will seek to put some of these educational assumptions with respect to grammar in a different light.

Grammar suffers from an image problem. Some immediate word associations (at least in English) are likely to be 'mistake', 'pedant' or 'school'. These all relate in some way to the notion of accuracy and the idea that there is correct usage of grammatical properties to which speakers must conform. The impression in education is perhaps too often one of a set of arbitrary paradigms, rules and exceptions which need to be inculcated to learners, either to make them correct users of a proper L1 grammar, or to make them accurate users of an L2 grammar. Indeed, language learners often seem to have internalised such thinking about grammar when they give opinions that it is 'necessary but boring' (see Jean & Simard, 2011). In addition to the general image problem, grammar does not have a single locus in the curriculum. The teaching of grammatical properties may be distributed across curricula in national language literacy, literacy support (in second/additional languages), foreign language subjects, classical languages and academic skills such as reading and writing as applied to a range of other subjects.

Before we pursue questions of acquisition, learning and teaching further, we need to unpack the concept of grammar some more to come to a better understanding of what we mean by 'grammar'.

3.1 WHAT IS GRAMMAR?

In some ways, this might appear easier to answer than the question *what is language*. One response to the question what is grammar, which avoids any abstract complications, would be simply to point to a physical object such as a tome on a bookshelf and say that it is a grammar. It might be a grammar of English or Tamil or Japanese, etc. In one colloquial sense, of course, this is a perfectly true statement. Publications such as these contain a summary of the grammatical rules of a language that we might turn to in order to seek clarification on points of usage. The existence of grammars in the form of books or websites or databases provides one answer to the question what is grammar. However, their very existence as an answer might conceal other equally valid understandings of what grammar is. We know that grammar is also something abstract and cognitive. It is, however, more difficult, conceptually and pedagogically, to define this sense of grammar, and to put it to use; a challenge that our formulation of Virtual Grammar seeks to address.

The book on the shelf that we reach for to settle an argument about some point of usage can be labelled a **reference grammar**. This is only one of a number of conceptualisations of grammar that are often discussed in the applied linguistics literature. Discussions of grammar also include the terms pedagogical grammar, prescriptive grammar, descriptive grammar, school grammar and linguistic grammar, to name a few.

The connections between the ideas underlying these various labels are intricate, and the elements on the list are not discrete. For example, a reference grammar may set out to be **descriptive** (describing how the language is used), or it might be **prescriptive** (prescribing how the language ought to be used). One complication is that the very fact that a grammatical rule appears somewhere in black and white automatically lends it some authority in regulating usage. Thus, a descriptive grammar might acquire prescriptive overtones. If the description is at odds with your usage, you might feel like your usage needs to be changed in line with the description, as will be considered in the context of so-called Grammatical Viruses later in this chapter.

All of the above characterisations of types of grammar rely on the use to which grammar is put, or the audience that it is aimed at. This masks any independent reality of grammar. It seems to imply that grammar is not an entity in itself, but rather only takes on some concrete form in the way that it is exploited. It is of course vital for educators to understand these various conceptions of grammar in order to use them appropriately. Claiming that grammar has an independent reality beyond the uses to which it is put is not intended to negate or replace other conceptualisations. The intention is instead to provide a different perspective that is not standardly dealt with in language teaching or teacher-training. We hope that such a perspective might prove a useful complement to existing ideas, and provide a way of reflecting on the learning and teaching of grammar.

We start by considering grammar as a phenomenon that can be thought about in two related ways. Firstly, there is the mental grammar possessed by individual speakers which allows each of us to produce and understand utterances. At the level of the individual, this will include a degree of variability because all individuals have had a different linguistic experience. But there will be enough overlap between individuals that we can identify speech communities which can be said to share the same grammar. Secondly, at a higher level of abstraction, there is the general mental capacity for grammar. This general mental capacity is fixed across the human species and is the faculty which allows us to acquire any particular grammar. However, as we have begun to show in this book, this generality is constrained. Even though the grammars of different languages might on the surface appear to be very divergent, they are all variations on a unified underlying theme.

Even if grammar in these two senses is something real, its reality is cognitive and tacit and, as such, only partially open to conscious influence or reflection. When speaking our most entrenched language(s), whether our birth language or a 'foreign' language in

3.1 What Is Grammar?

which we have attained high proficiency, it is not typically the case that we would (or could) reflect on the cognitive processes that are millisecond by millisecond producing the right words, sounds or other structures to put our thoughts into grammatical form, or integrate what we hear into a syntactic structure. What's more, the grammatical element of language processing is heavily influenced by factors such as plausibility and frequency (see Case in Point 3.1), which would in any case make the range of possible interpretations less obvious. This is even true in a language laboratory setting in which sentences have been constructed to be ambiguous.

The highly abstract properties of grammar which facilitate and constrain the acquisition of any specific language can only be indirectly characterised, making use of a research methodology that compares and contrasts the properties of different languages in order to establish the similarities which betray the underlying unity of the abstract human grammar capacity. Indeed, we are trying to develop your ability to do linguistic analysis in the way we have presented language data to exemplify the points we are making in this book. Ultimately, we aim to convince you that an understanding of grammar in this abstract sense can be pedagogically useful. The danger associated with this is if it leads to the conclusion that the teaching of foreign languages should be equated with the teaching of linguistics. This is not the aim, and one reason why we are using the term Virtual Grammar. Surely it would be absurd to suggest that a Beginners Spanish class would include a test on a 'virtual' grammar. Instead, we use the term Virtual Grammar as an approach for thinking about the abstract reality of grammar that is studied in linguistics, but in a way that is pedagogically useful for the teaching of any languages. Before considering this approach further, we will discuss more familiar notions of grammar in a little more detail.

3.1.1 Prescriptive Grammar and Descriptive Grammar

A good jumping off point for a discussion of grammar is the well-known **prescriptive** versus **descriptive** dichotomy already alluded to. This is a distinction in approach between the academic linguistic commitment to description of grammatical patterns as they are used in speech communities, and a traditional attempt to limit grammatical patterns to some purist ideal defined often in historical or supposedly logical terms (see Armstrong & MacKenzie, 2013, and the discussion which follows here). Hudson (2008, p. 59) states that 'prescription tries to change language by proscribing forms that are in fact used and prescribing alternatives, whereas description accepts all forms that are used'.

3.1 CASE IN POINT: STRUCTURE DEPENDENCE AND ATTACHMENT AMBIGUITY

Saying that hierarchical structure regulates grammar may sound like syntax imposes rigid limitations on language. But in fact, there is ambiguity in meaning that can be attributed to options in hierarchical structure. Syntactic ambiguity arises when words or phrases can be analysed as occupying different positions in hierarchical syntactic structures. The sentence in (i) is an example of prepositional phrase attachment ambiguity as the phrase *with binoculars* may be interpreted in relation to two different positions in the syntactic structure:

(i) I saw the police officer with binoculars.
Verb Phrase Attachment = I used the binoculars in order to view the officer.
Noun Phrase Attachment = The officer that I was looking at was using binoculars.

So-called relative clause attachment, has been of major interest to psycholinguists as it can reveal interesting properties about how we parse different languages. When a relative clause follows a complex noun phrase, it may be read as attached to, and thus modifying, either the first noun in the complex phrase, or the second. Consider example (ii) (from Dussias & Sagarra, 2007). Who was on the balcony?

(ii) An armed robber shot the sister of the actor who was on the balcony.

If you said *the actor*, you have a preference for 'low attachment'. You have parsed the relative clause as attached to the second noun, and thus lower in the syntactic structure. This is the typical preference of English speakers. While the same sentence in Spanish, as in (iii), is also ambiguous, Spanish speakers will typically say that la hermana (=the sister) was on the balcony.

(iii) Un ladrón armado le disparó a la hermana del actor que estaba en el balcón.
a robber armed CL shot to the sister of.the actor who was on the balcony

Afrikaans, Dutch, French, German and Greek share this 'high attachment' preference with Spanish, while Arabic, Brazilian Portuguese, Norwegian, Romanian and Swedish pattern with English in having a low attachment preference (Dussias & Sagarra, 2007, p. 102).

3.1 What Is Grammar?

The prescriptive notion of grammar is often intimately linked to the idea of education and standardisation or codification that was discussed in Chapter 2. Once a particular regional variety, or a variety linked to a particular social class, is established as the national idiom and codified as the system to be taught and used, especially in writing, any grammatical deviation from this codified form may be considered bad or wrong grammar (see, for example, Armstrong and Mackenzie, 2013, on French and Spanish; Langer, 2001, on German). This is not to say that such notions can then be dismissed as irrelevant. Quite the contrary, it is important to know about and be able to navigate the ways in which your language use might affect how other people make judgements about your social background or level of education. However, it should be emphasised, once again, that these questions of correct grammar are fundamentally social rather than linguistic or grammatical. The language faculty permits grammatical variation, and the fact that some variants are stigmatised but others are not is a historical-social judgement. Nevertheless, a knowledge of language should also equip speakers to be able to resist truly spurious prescriptive rules, or at least to put them into some perspective. This alone is a valuable contribution for language education to make.

An example of a spurious rule is the injunction against split infinitives in English. According to such a rule, *to boldly go* is grammatically wrong and should be rendered as *boldly to go*. If anything, the non-split version of the phrase seems more awkward and less natural English than the supposedly ungrammatical version. The source of this particular rule is not very clear, but it seems that it derives from apparently rational or aesthetic judgements. It is possible that nineteenth century admirers of Latin as a purer and more logical language tried to apply its rules to English (Cutts, 2009, p. 111). As Latin infinitives are formed with a morphological ending attached to the verb rather than an independent morpheme, Latin infinitives are unsplittable, so, according to this logic, English infinitives should also not be split. Even a basic understanding of languages exposes the grammatical absurdity of such thinking. We saw in Chapter 2 that different languages take different approaches to how to combine their morphological building blocks. Even if morphological elegance is the measure of language, why should we take Latin as the language to which English should conform? Why not Cayuga instead? Latin was of course the point of comparison due to the social and cultural status it traditionally enjoyed as the language of classical learning in Europe. But it is absurd to assume that Latin does morphology better than English; it simply instantiates one of the options available within Language.

Often, comparisons between languages can be truly informative as to the nature of abstract rules and the arbitrary connection to prescription/description. Case in Point 3.2 below illustrates that splitting linguistic phrases, or **constituents**, is an interesting cross-linguistic phenomenon. Attempts to shoehorn one language into the grammatical forms of another will result in unnatural rules divorced from any true grammatical properties of the language. When grammars interact in terms of contact, they naturally influence each other in certain ways, as we saw in our discussion of creolisation in the last chapter. However, imposing the standards of one grammar on another language for reasons of aesthetics or purism results in unnatural and difficult usages.

Other forms of prescriptive grammar are really not related to grammar as such, but rather to spelling and punctuation. As mentioned in the last chapter, spelling and punctuation are artefacts of language. As such, they are not fundamentally grammatical in the linguistic sense. Most of the world's languages spoken today have never had a written form. Unfortunately, many such languages are at risk of becoming extinct and in the absence of a written record, they will be completely lost to history (see www.eldp.net). But the exclusively spoken language of even a very small speech community has a grammar as rich as any other language, even if it has never been written down. In fact, small language communities tend to have greater grammatical complexity than languages with large numbers of widely dispersed speakers (see discussion questions in Chapter 2).

We can conclude that any issues with respect to spelling and punctuation are issues of literacy, in effect connected to one's ability to manipulate the technology of writing, rather than a grammatical problem, even though they can often reflect grammatical properties. English apostrophe usage is a familiar target of 'grammatical' opprobrium. The 'greengrocer's apostrophe' in plurals such as *fresh banana's* or *tomato's from Italy* will rightly be deemed wrong by any English teacher. But what does 'wrong' mean here? Marking possessive *-s* with an apostrophe is an arbitrary orthographic device in English which must be learned as one learns the conventions of writing. Anyone who has not completely mastered this and produces the deviant *tomato's from Italy* has a command of English grammar, they just haven't mastered this rule of writing which is used to demark a particular grammatical difference. There are real grammatical properties involving phonological changes which underlie the addition of 's' to root words in English. For example, adding 's' to a final vowel results in *tomatoes* having a voiced plural ending sounding like /z/, while addition to a voiceless consonant, as in *tomato plants*, results in

3.2 CASE IN POINT: DISPLACEMENT AND DISCONTINUITY

Displacement is a term used to capture a structure with an interpretation which reflects an association which seems displaced in the structure. Linguists often conceptualise such situations as the word or phrase having 'moved' syntactically; this captures the sense of it having originated somewhere else in the syntactic structure to where it occurs in speech/writing. In (i), the word *who* refers to the object of the verb *meet*, and so is said to be displaced from object position, represented by ___. (Note that a prescriptivist might claim that this is wrong, as the object form of *who* should be *whom*. If you are an English-speaker, you can reflect on your own usage of this. Typically in conversation one would use *who*. *Whom* might occur in more careful monitored speech, or in formal writing.)

(i) Who did you meet ___ ?

English also allows a question form in which there is no such displacement. A so-called **echo question** is usually related directly to a declarative: *He met my friend.* Echo-question: *He met who!?*

Displacement is universal but its implementation differs between different languages: what can be displaced, how far and under what circumstances. Moreover, displacement can create syntactic **discontinuities**, or split phrases, in some languages which are impossible in others. In Croatian, noun phrases can be split in ways that are ungrammatical in English, as illustrated (ii-iii) (data from Fanselow & Cavar, 2002).

(ii) a. Ivan se   popeo   **na veliko drvo.**
        Ivan SELF climbed **on big tree**
    b. **Na veliko** se Ivan **drvo** popeo.
        On big   SELF Ivan **tree** climbed
    Both mean: "Ivan climbed the/a big tree."

(iii) a. Ivan   je kupio   **crveni auto.**
         Ivan   has bought   **red car**
     b. **Crveni** je Ivan   **auto**   kupio.
        Red   has Ivan   **car**   bought
     Both mean: "Ivan bought the/a red car."

While this type of displacement phenomenon is more widespread in some languages than others, it is still constrained by syntactic properties. Only some types of split phrases and discontinuities are possible in Croatian. Compare (ii) with (iv) and (v).

(iv)	*Drvo	se	Ivan	popeo	**na veliko**.
	Tree	SELF	Ivan	climbed	**on big**
(v)	*Ivan	se	**drvo**	popeo	**na veliko**.
	Ivan	SELF	**tree**	climbed	**on big**

a voiceless /s/ sound. Fluent speakers of English have control of this subtle, and real, phonological rule, though most have never thought about or been told about it – and regardless of how they might punctuate these words.

So far we have seen that targets of grammatical prescription can be broken down in two ways. Natural grammatical rules may acquire social overtones for non-linguistic reasons, and secondly, grammatical prescription may not actually target grammar in the linguistic sense at all. You might now wonder: is anything truly ungrammatical? If familiar prescriptive notions of ungrammatical usage often turn out to be either unfounded, or not really connected to grammar, does this result in a grammatical free-for-all when it comes to teaching? The answer is no. Hudson (2008, p. 59) observes that description entails defining the limits of, and border between, particular codes. He notes that the noun phrase *those books* is, purely descriptively, a component of the English code, but not French. Similarly, the phrase *them books* is descriptively a component of various English varieties, but not a component of the written Standard English code. But it contrasts with truly ungrammatical noun phrases such as *this books*, where the number agreement relation has been violated. As has been discussed, number and agreement are abstract grammatical properties. The violation of number agreement, as a consistent property in English noun phrases which include a demonstrative, is the reason why *this books* is 'disallowed' by the properties of English.

From this point of view, a function of teaching in an English-speaking context, including English as a second or foreign language context, would involve contextualising descriptive differences in order to delimit what might be considered a usage or register issue and what might be a true grammatical error. In practice, the dividing line between prescriptive error and true grammatical error is not necessarily clear-cut. In thinking about such cases more carefully, one can start to appreciate the complexity of the abstract grammar. As illustrated in Case in Point 3.3 below, the oft-cited stricture that you should not end a sentence with a preposition does not stand up to a linguistic analysis. English speakers come to master the subtle syntactic and semantic

3.3 CASE IN POINT: DISPLACEMENT, DISCONTINUITY AND PREPOSITION STRANDING

In English, when certain prepositional phrases are displaced, they either take their associated prepositions with them, or the prepositions stay in their original position. These options are referred to as preposition pied-piping and preposition stranding respectively. Descriptively, these are simply two variants of displacement properties, with the pied-piped variant sounding somewhat more formal. Prescriptively, however, the stranded variant is sometimes condemned as 'bad'. (i) illustrates a stranded preposition, (ii) a pied-piped preposition.

(i) **Which** glass did you drink **from**?
(ii) **From which** glass did you drink?

One might hear from a prescriptive grammarian that 'you cannot end a sentence with a preposition'. This prescriptive blanket ban underestimates the true, sophisticated grammatical properties that English speakers implicitly know. For example, certain particle verbs, as shown in (iii), allow sentence-final or non-sentence-final prepositions. Interestingly, however, when the same particle verb is included in relative clause variations with displacement, not only is a sentence-final preposition possible, it is required! In this case, obeying the prescriptive ban on stranding prepositions would lead to gobbledegook (vi).

(iii) She **threw out** the rubbish. / She **threw** the rubbish **out**.
(iv) That is the rubbish which she **threw out**. / *That is the rubbish **out which** she **threw**.

Notice that we just used the term *particle*. There are some verb + preposition phrases which don't allow the two options. As seen in (v), the sentence-final version isn't possible. And what's interesting, when used in the relative clause variation, in contrast with the gobbledegook above, English allows the pied-piping version (vi).

(v) She **ran up** the staircase. / *She **ran** the staircase **up**.
(vi) That is the staircase which she **ran up**. / That is the staircase **up** which she **ran**.

Even more intriguing, when used in a more metaphorical or idiomatic context, *to run up* exhibits yet another pattern. These particles don't like to be stranded from their verb in any of the options.

> (vii) She **ran up** a huge bill. / *?She **ran** a huge bill **up**.
> (viii) Look at the huge bill which she **ran up**! / *Look at the huge bill **up** which she **ran**!
>
> English speakers implicitly know all these complex and intricate rules without being told. We see that what is proposed as a prescriptive rule is linguistically ill-informed, and much less interesting than the real grammar.

distinctions without anyone explaining these patterns. Any simple injunction not to end a sentence with a preposition becomes patently ridiculous in light of the real grammatical patterns, and reveals this to be an oversimple rule, which can never hope to capture the true complexity of the patterns which grammar permits.

By looking at issues such as preposition stranding though an analytical linguistic lens, we begin to see past the familiar concepts of descriptive, prescriptive and reference grammar to the underlying principles of grammar. In many ways, the pedagogical rules provided for foreign language instruction are similar to the prescriptive rule discussed with respect to preposition stranding. Not that we are suggesting that pedagogical grammar rules are ill-informed! But formulating these rules presents a difficult conundrum for materials developers and teachers: there is inevitably a tension between packaging information about grammatical properties in a way that is clear, digestible and useful for language learners, and accurately capturing the range of intricacies that are inescapably associated with the abstract grammatical concepts underlying even apparently simple properties. If learners assume that the pedagogical rules represent clear and discrete grammatical facts rather than summarised rules of thumb, then the rules risk becoming overly simplified prescriptions that do not cover the range of abstract properties at work in acquisition (and this tends to have effects on grammatical development, as we will see in Chapter 5).

In this abstract sense, **grammar** is the full set of linguistic constraints that can be found in Language; and **a grammar** is a specific subset of actually encoded phonological, morphological and semantic features which make up a particular language. For example, we saw in the Cases in Point that grammar in the abstract sense allows a range of syntactic operations which rearrange the order of words in clauses. Different languages exhibit specific variations on these operations. Concepts like Displacement, or as we saw in Chapter 2, Number, Gender and others are all universal categories, with languages

3.1 What Is Grammar?

choosing whether and how to mark them. Some languages make number distinctions that others do not: Arabic marks dual number agreement as well as plural and singular, English does not. Italian and English each make a binary singular/plural distinction, but the realisation differs: Italian marks this on definite articles and adjectives as well as their associated nouns, English does not: *il libro scolastico / i libri scolastici* vs. *the scholarly book / the scholarly books*.

When we say that speakers of a language have a grammar that allows them to produce and comprehend grammatical utterances, we mean that they have knowledge of these requirements. But, at least in the context of a fully entrenched grammar, this grammatical knowledge is inherently hidden. While it guides communication, it does not avail itself to introspection as it does so. It is the nature of grammar that a speaker is able to create an infinite number of linguistic outputs that display subtle properties and distinctions, even if the speaker has no conscious awareness of these properties.

This abstract conceptualisation of grammar, distinct from specific descriptions or prescriptions of grammatical features does not replace or deny other possible uses of the term grammar. A set of cognitive constraints which can generate an infinity of potential utterances obviously must stand in some relationship, however tangential, to the set of rules presented in a descriptive or reference grammar. In the previous chapter, we compared language to breathing. Breathing is a complex physiological activity which we rarely consciously think about, unless there is some physical problem which draws our attention to it. Grammar is a hugely complex cognitive activity which we rarely think about or comment on when we use it, unless we are unsettled by an awareness of (often spurious) prescriptive rules, or confronted with a linguistic ambiguity. Indeed linguistic ambiguity is often the basis of jokes and the bread and butter for many comedians. In short, our every utterance contains feats of mental grammatical complexity which are subject neither to description nor prescription, precisely because they happen implicitly and are taken for granted. In our use of less familiar or 'foreign' language grammar, this is not typically the case, especially if we are not proficient users of the language. In the context of language teaching, description and prescription of foreign language grammar often go hand in hand in the form of pedagogical grammar.

3.1.2 Pedagogical Grammar

When considering pedagogical grammar, we are confronted with the same dichotomy between the specific and the abstract that we have discussed. The image of a book on a shelf again provides a straightforward characterisation of a pedagogical grammar. Searching the Internet with the phrase *a pedagogical grammar of ...* will return a wide range of books and electronic resources for different languages. It would be logical to assume that what unites the results of such a search would be the pedagogical nature of the grammars. That is, they present the grammatical rules and constraints of a particular language in such a way as to facilitate learning the grammar of that language for communication.

At this point, we encounter the by-now-familiar problems of definition and distinction. One can argue that *any* publication calling itself a grammar is in some sense pedagogical or didactic. As an example, take the monumental and well-respected *Cambridge Grammar of the English Language* (Huddleston & Pullum, 2002). This is billed as a 'new and comprehensive *descriptive* grammar of English'[1] (our emphasis). Incidentally, it might also be called a linguistic grammar given that it is based on linguistic principles, or it might be characterised as a reference grammar given that it is an authoritative and exhaustive work to which one can refer to adjudicate on points of usage. It would probably not standardly be assumed to be a pedagogical grammar in its conception. But it is likely that teachers and learners of English have used it as some form of pedagogical resource, either to learn something or to teach something about the English language.

Thus, the pedagogicalness (to coin a phrase) of a pedagogical grammar is in some ways in the eye of the beholder. It is not immediately obvious what it is about so-called pedagogical grammars that makes them specifically pedagogical. It will of necessity be descriptive in that it describes the grammatical patterns of the language in question. It may acquire elements of prescription to the extent that people who refer to such a grammar may interpret the descriptive generalisations to be strict and invariant rules to follow. One distinguishing feature of a pedagogical grammar is the inclusion of elements specifically related to teaching and learning, such as practice activities or tips for how to present grammatical features in a language classroom (Cowan, 2008, and Parrott, 2010, are representative examples for English). In our quest for a definition, we will dispense with the specific, moving away from *a pedagogical grammar,* to talk instead about pedagogical grammar in conceptual terms. From this perspective, pedagogical grammar may be defined as 'a research domain that is concerned with how grammar can most effectively be taught in

---

[1] www.cambridge.org/gb/academic/subjects/languages-linguistics/grammar-and-syntax/cambridge-grammar-english-language

3.1 What Is Grammar?

the second language classroom' (Keck & Kim, 2014, p. 1). Pedagogical grammar can be seen as a general framework or approach, the application of which may result in *a* pedagogical grammar of a particular language. But it is also a way of thinking about the pedagogic aspects of grammar, rather than just fixed sets of rules or properties to be taught in L2 contexts.

As a framework, then, pedagogical grammar is intimately tied to more general trends in language teaching policies and practices (See Keck & Kim, 2014, ch. 2, for a historical overview). Keck and Kim (2014, p. 3) characterise the research domain as the interface between work on grammar description, L2 grammar acquisition and L2 grammar instruction. Description of the grammatical system may be considered 'an essential starting point for proper pedagogy' (Larsen-Freeman, 2011, p. 521). As linguistics is the go-to discipline for providing descriptions of grammar, it necessarily has some role in pedagogical grammar. However, recall that the formal–functional divide, among other conceptual and methodological controversies within linguistics, may lead to descriptions which focus on different aspects of grammar, resulting in different pedagogical treatments. As discussed by Larsen-Freeman (2011, p. 520), a formal linguistic analysis may formulate generalisations that are too abstract for effective direct use in teaching, while a functional, usage-based approach may formulate a large number of micro-generalisations connected to the use of particular words and phrases that are too narrow.

Whether derived from formal or functional linguistic work, pedagogical rules are based essentially on descriptions of the observable, surface phenomena of a language. It is an open question whether and how any pedagogical presentation of particular pieces of language data become knowledge of the target language in the sense of the underlying mental grammar of language learners. Our contention here is that teachers who have an understanding of something of the nature of the abstract properties of grammar, in the sense of Virtual Grammar or Grammatical Concepts, will be better positioned to critique existing pedagogical materials and grammar exercises, and make informed choices about when to use which approaches to address particular points of grammar for the learning and communicative goals in their classroom teaching.

The grammar of English articles provides an interesting illustration (see Case in Point 3.4). Pedagogical grammars attempt to capture rules for article usage, but these tend to be riddled with exceptions. This is not because of some inherent weakness in pedagogical grammars. The distribution of articles is extremely complicated; we have already seen that it is regulated by an

3.4 CASE IN POINT: DEFINITENESS AND SPECIFICITY

A first association with definiteness for learners of English is likely to be articles. (In)definiteness is clearly encoded by the choice of the definite vs indefinite article in English. We saw in Chapter 1 that the semantic property of specificity is also encoded in English articles. While NPs can have (un)specific meaning in English, there is no difference in the choice of article form that distinguishes specific vs unspecific contexts. It is definiteness which regulates the choice. The examples from Chapter 1 are repeated here.

(i) He didn't see **a car** parked at the door
   until two men got out of it and asked for directions. = *specific*
   so he knew the visitors hadn't arrived yet. = *unspecific*

(ii) I didn't meet **the professor** during my visit to the philosophy department yesterday morning
   but I managed to get hold of him in the afternoon. = *specific*
   so I began to wonder whether that chair had been filled yet. = *unspecific*

Samoan, like English, also has two different articles. But what's interesting is that the two forms implicate (un)specificity, not definiteness, with the form *le* for specific referents and *se* for unspecific referents. Notice the form of the Samoan articles in relation to the English translation.

(v) Sa   i ai   **le**   ulugāli'i 'o Papa **le** tane a 'o
    PAST   exist   ART   couple PRES Papa ART husband but PRES
    Eleele **le**   fafine.
    Eleele ART   woman
    'There was a couple, Papa, the husband, and Eleele, the wife.'

(vi) 'Au-mai   **se** niu.
     take DIR ART coconut.
     'Bring me a coconut.'

intricate mix of grammatical, semantic and discourse/contextual features. As is the case with practically any grammatical feature, there is therefore a tension between the messy linguistic reality, and the pedagogical drive to present facts in clear and comprehensible ways for learning. Our answer is to provide teachers with an explanation of the abstract grammatical concepts that are understood by linguists to be relevant for article use. We also see value in

3.1 What Is Grammar?

teachers having light training in linguistic analysis which equips them to gather and sort examples into linguistic data sets, in order to work out what may be going on. With an understanding of properties that don't standardly appear in descriptive and pedagogical grammars but which will underlie the knowledge and performance of learners, teachers will have an extra weapon in their armoury which may prove useful for presentation, discussion and correction of points of grammar as necessary.

Learners of English whose existing language(s) does not have articles at all often have problems acquiring the use of articles and the meanings associated with the choice of article, or the presence versus absence of articles. However, it is not simply the case that these learners randomly distribute or omit articles. For some learners, the choice of *a* versus *the* may be guided only by specificity without consideration of definiteness as their mental grammar attempts to construct a rationale for this new type of word within the bounds of what the language faculty permits. This is not what English does, but it is a perfectly logical option which works in Samoan. Learners who optionally rely on specificity in regulating article distribution will overuse *the* in specific, non-definite contexts and overuse *a* in non-specific, definite contexts (see Ionin et al., 2004).

In addition to this sort of grammatical difficulty, the status of nouns as mass or countable co-determines article usage, and the interpretation of articles in English (see Case in Point 3.5). These, along with further properties of discourse context, render article usage in English (and other languages) difficult for learners, especially if the language(s) they know does not have articles at all. Addressing this learning issue with effective pedagogical material is also difficult: distilling this whole range of intricate grammatical features into a pedagogically useful package poses a formidable task for materials developers and teachers. For example, ESL/EFL materials will typically distinguish between countable/uncountable nouns, but it might be questioned on linguistic grounds whether these are discrete categories (Pelletier, 2012). At higher levels of proficiency, it might be beneficial to use different criteria to explore the use of different types of noun phrase in context. Even at lower levels of proficiency, it is likely that learners will encounter usages which 'break' the count/non-count rule. As discussed, we see the issue of a tension between a more deliverable rule of thumb and a more complex linguistic pattern.

Let's relate this back to the idea that pedagogical grammar is really a research domain at the intersection of grammar description, grammar acquisition and grammar instruction. There are a number of relevant issues for this notion of pedagogical grammar that emerge

3.5 CASE IN POINT: NUMBER, COUNTABILITY AND GENERICITY

In Chapter 1, we saw how the concept of number varies across languages. One further way in which this is manifest is the concept of countability, or a mass/count distinction. In a language like English, uncountable nouns do not accept plural marking and cannot be used with counting articles.

(i) Books are on the shelf. / *Furnitures are in the room.
(ii) A book is on the shelf. / *A furniture is in the room.

Uncountable nouns may represent abstract concepts or masses (iii). However, abstract concepts may also be countable (iv), and in general there are exceptions in all directions so that many nouns may appear in countable and uncountable configurations (v) (see Pelletier, 2012).

(iii) Knowledge is valuable. / *A knowledge is valuable / *Knowledges are valuable.
(iv) *Idea is valuable. / An idea is valuable. / Ideas are valuable.
(v) Beer is good. / A beer is good. / These beers are good.

Mass nouns tend to have a generic meaning when used without articles (as in (iii)). For countable nouns, we can add generic meaning as a further intersection with definite and specific forms/meanings. In (vi)–(viii), we are talking about the generic concept of 'dogishness', rather than any specific or contextually relevant individual.

(vi)   A dog makes a good pet.
(vii) The dog makes a good pet.
(viii) Dogs make good pets.

But even these apparently similar meanings are subject to subtly different constraints. For example, if generic meaning is encoded by the type of predicate, which has to refer to a kind or type, the indefinite generic is not possible in English (Krifka et al., 1995).

(ix) *A dodo / the dodo is extinct. / Dodos are extinct.

from the discussion. Firstly, any point of grammar is potentially highly complex and intersects with other grammatical phenomena in intricate ways. As an illustration, Case in Point 3.5 has only really scratched the surface of concepts such as generic meaning or mass/count distinctions, and only for English. Entire books have been devoted to discussion of the intricacies of such ideas in different languages (e.g. Carlson & Pelletier, 1995; Massam, 2012). Thus, any

3.1 What Is Grammar?

simple pedagogical grammar rules of thumb can never hope to cover the full range potential issues that might be at play in grammar acquisition. As a consequence, it is more useful to think of pedagogical grammar as a research domain to be explored rather than a discrete set of set rules. Secondly, given the potential complexity of this research domain, we suggest that it is more useful to foster a way of thinking about grammar as opposed to fostering knowledge of particular points of grammar. Finally, one way of developing this way of thinking is to approach it from a Virtual Grammar perspective, drawing on abstract or universal semantic and morphosyntactic properties which provide an underlying unity to different features of grammar. In this way, it is possible to connect different areas of knowledge across a range of languages, which risk being seen as randomly and mysteriously divergent when viewed simply from the perspective of surface (dis)similarity.

Seeing pedagogical grammar as a way of thinking rather than a set of rules has the extra advantage of building connections to work in language acquisition research. A range of work in second language acquisition has pointed to the difficulties in the acquisition of points of grammar, which can be analysed productively using abstract grammatical concepts (see, for example, Ionin et al., 2004; Ionin et al., 2011; Snape, 2008, among others on specificity, definiteness and genericity; see discussion of interlanguage grammar in Section 3.1.3). Building on these acquisition findings, work on L2 grammar instruction has begun to explore the application of these concepts to the classroom (e.g. Lopez & Sabir, 2019; Snape & Yusa, 2013). So we seem to have a clear case of pedagogical grammar in action as a field of research.

It is the endeavour of this book to pursue this version of pedagogical grammar. Most features of grammar will resist straightforward distillation into pedagogical rules. Of course, this is not to say that existing pedagogical grammars are in any way defective or unsatisfactory. In many contexts, a quick summary rule can be an effective sketch of some point, or a useful answer to a grammatical question. At the same time, however, we have to recognise that the imperative to condense highly abstract and complex patterns into quick summary rules will inevitably mean that important features of the complexity will be reduced or ignored along the way. It is in some of these occluded areas of grammar that difficult acquisition problems reside, and for this reason, we contend that it is useful to supplement traditional pedagogical grammars with some knowledge of the abstract, virtual properties associated with grammar. Even if the ideas are not immediately applicable in tomorrow's lesson, by raising awareness, teachers can develop a catalogue of grammatical properties that are susceptible to this different view on grammar and so provide potentially useful ways to reflect on one's practice. At the very least, this approach should shed new light on the nature of knotty acquisition and teaching problems. Adopting this sort of analytical framework may therefore be more informative with respect to learners' underlying grammars. It is to this that we now turn.

3.1.3 Interlanguage Grammar

Chapter 1 briefly introduced the concept of **interlanguage** (IL) as a description of a learner's current stage of development. As a description of a learner's grammatical system, it characterises the mental properties which underlie learner performance at any given point in L2 development. As Selinker (1972) intended in his original proposal, an interlanguage grammar is a natural grammar and so is a particular instantiation of the abstract human capacity for grammar, just as Polish or Swahili are particular instantiations of the human grammar capacity. It is therefore amenable to the same sorts of analytical principles. Interlanguage grammar differs from the grammars of established speech communities inasmuch as it is more variable and is not itself associated with a particular well-defined speech community. As the name suggests, you can consider it a variety of language which is somewhere 'between' the existing dominant language(s) that the learner already speaks and the properties of the language being learned. The important point is that it is not a wild mix of grammatical properties, but is constrained by the general human capacity for grammar in the same way as other linguistic varieties. It follows its own internal rules, which are amenable to analysis and explication as with any other natural language grammatical system.

Key elements of IL are its systematicity, variability and dynamism. It is systematic as, at any particular point in development, there is a set of abstract, mental grammatical rules which define a learner's grammar. Analysis can reveal the systemic nature of these rules. But at the same time, the system allows variability in grammatical properties which seems to show evidence of apparently contradictory rules: again the fluctuation between specificity and definiteness as determinants of article choice illustrates the principle. Being simultaneously systematic and variable is not, however, a contradiction. We saw in our discussion of varieties and registers that variability is a property of grammatical competence. Variability is in principle permitted by an individual's mental grammar, it is just the nature of the variability in IL which differs from the grammar found in established speech communities. Finally, IL is also

3.1 What Is Grammar?

dynamic in that its grammatical rules are prone to change and, as one would expect given greater variability, they are likely to be less stable. Nevertheless, the understanding is that at any given time, the interlanguage grammar has some degree of internal consistency. It moves stepwise 'from stable plateau to stable plateau' (Selinker, 1992, p. 226). We can think of this as stages of development as the grammar changes.

A formal linguistic approach to interlanguage grammar sees an IL as definable in terms of the same sorts of formal properties that we know constrain the properties of any language. A pertinent illustration is the constraining influence of **unaccusativity** on patterns of L2 grammatical development (see Case in Point 3.6). An oft-cited error in L2 English is illustrated by sentences in (1) and (2) discussed in Zobl (1989, p. 204); many others have also studied the phenomenon: Balcom (1997), Oshita (2000; 2001), Yip (1995), among others. This type of error indicates overgeneralisation of English grammatical properties as passive morphology has been used to construct verb phrases in active contexts.

(1) The most memorable experience of my life was happened 15 years ago.

(2) Most people are fallen in love and marry with somebody.

Overgeneralisation is a typical phenomenon in language development, and is typical in IL as well. It captures the tendency to extend a rule to contexts or examples which go beyond the actual limits of the rule. The important point about these errors as exemplified here is that the overgeneralisation is not a random addition of morphology to just any verb. These errors occur exclusively with a class of verbs referred to as unaccusative by formal grammarians. It can therefore be assumed that this virtual formal distinction between types of verbs is represented in the IL grammar. There is a rationale underlying this grammatical system; it is grammatically logical to treat the syntactic subject of unaccusative verbs and passive predicates in a similar fashion. Learners who produce passive-unaccusative structures have a grammar which is seeking to overtly mark this abstract commonality between passive and unaccusative structures. The interesting point is that the learners in the research cited don't know about this explicitly. Few teachers and very few materials for teaching include anything about unaccusativity. We suspect that your knowing about this would help you to address this kind of error if it was happening with your learners. Our point here is that the IL of these learners reveals the underlying systemic nature of the error. What at first sight might seem like random overgeneralisation of passive verb forms becomes on closer inspection a logical and sophisticated implementation of abstract grammatical properties to the English system.

We see that the same type of constraint applies in interlanguage grammar as well as any other language. It is just that its occurrence differs from what the English system happens to instantiate. This insight may in turn be leveraged for research on instructional effectiveness (see Hirakawa, 2013). And thus, we see the framework for pedagogical grammar in action again.

This perspective on IL grammar assumes that the same grammatical concepts underlie any natural language. Particular features will have different consequences in different languages, but these may be related to certain underlying universals, which allows us to account for IL as a general phenomenon, and as an instantiation of the abstract properties of grammar which all humans have as part of their language faculty.

In terms of instructional effectiveness, there is no guarantee that the use in instruction of concepts which derive from the underlying grammatical properties would be any better or more effective than any traditional grammatical description or pedagogy. Questions of which methods and approaches are used in teaching are usually answered by educational policies which differ according to socio-cultural norms for education, and which are liable to change over time (see Chapter 5). The point is not that the view we are developing here should replace any existing practices or be assumed to be better, however 'better' might be measured. The point is that it provides a potential enrichment of existing approaches to pedagogical grammar and opens up different avenues that teachers might explore in their approaches to questions of what to teach in order to promote the learning of grammar.

3.6 CASE IN POINT: UNACCUSATIVITY

In Chapter 1, we saw that languages grammatically align the arguments of verbs in different configurations. Further instances of this turn up on closer analysis of intransitive verbs. Sentences (i) and (ii) look similar, but they turn out to be semantically and grammatically different.

(i) The manager arrived.
(ii) The manager chatted.

We refer to verbs like *arrive* as **unaccusative** and *chat* as **unergative**. One defining feature is that the subject of an unaccusative is not interpreted as an active agent or initiator of the action of the verb:

arrival is something that happened to the manager, not something s/he actively did, in contrast with the controlled initiated action of chatting. Unaccusativity, and subdivisions thereof, can help us analyse a number of properties of different languages. It is relevant across languages, and has different types of grammatical consequences depending on the properties of the language in question. For example, in English, unaccusativity plays a role in word order variation: unaccusatives allow the impersonal *there*-construction, while unergatives do not.

(iii) There arrived a new manager.
(iv) *There chatted a new manager.

Unaccusativity is also relevant for auxiliary choice in languages like Italian, which have either *to be* or *to have* as auxiliary verbs: unaccusatives are more likely to take *be*, and unergatives *have* (see Sorace, 2000).

(v) I ospiti **sono** arrivati.
    the guests **are** arrived
    'The guests arrived.'
(vi) I colleghi **hanno** chiaccherato tutto il pomeriggio.
    the colleagues **have** chatted whole the afternoon
    'My colleagues chatted the whole afternoon.'

As with any concept, an even finer level of detail can reveal deeper regularities. For example, Sorace (2000, p. 863) proposes a subdivision into different verb classes with strict auxiliary selection at the ends of the continuum, but variable behaviour in the middle:

CHANGE OF LOCATION   SELECTS *BE* (LEAST VARIATION)
CHANGE OF STATE
CONTINUATION OF A PRE-EXISTING STATE
EXISTENCE OF STATE
UNCONTROLLED PROCESS
CONTROLLED MOTIONAL PROCESS
CONTROLLED NONMOTIONAL PROCESS   SELECTS *HAVE* (LEAST
                                        VARIATION)

While (v) and (vi) illustrate consistent auxiliary choice, a class in the middle will have variable behaviour, as illustrated for existence of a state in (vii) (from Sorace, 2000, p. 869).

(vii) Il cibo è / ha scarseggiato tra i terremotati.
    the food is / has run short among the earthquake victims
    'Food ran short among the earthquake victims.'

3.2 THE USE AND ABUSE OF GRAMMAR

The discussion thus far has assumed that grammar is something that is pedagogically worthwhile. However, we noted at the start that grammar also has an image problem. Grammar has been used and abused in the wider culture as well as in education. This impinges upon the perceived value of grammar. It is both loved and loathed. Often loved by grammar mavens who regulate usage (with often spurious prescriptive rules), and typically loathed by those on the receiving end. This reality, together with the inherent complexity of conceptualisations of grammar, complicate the task of providing grammar instruction, whether in national language literacy or in foreign language contexts. Two images are insightful. Pullum (2018, p. 177) suggests that published grammars and usage guides for speakers of English as a first language often cater to 'perverts' who 'lust for someone to force them into unnatural posh-sounding constructions, as if they want to be harshly disciplined for fantasised grammatical transgressions'. Hardly an uplifting vision for delivery of grammatical knowledge. Similarly, in foreign language learning, Larsen-Freeman (2003, p. 7) notes that 'when students are asked to shift from a communicative activity to, say a grammar exercise, there is often an audible response of displeasure'.

The source of this image problem likely derives at least to some extent from traditional prescriptively informed presentation of grammatical topics, and connotations in both national and foreign language learning contexts which continue to inform people's perceptions after schooling. This might explain some of the loathe side of the attitudes to grammar, but it does little to explain the enduring interest and apparent love side of the equation. The continued publication and regular appearances on bestseller lists of grammar and usage-related books aimed at the general public attest to the enduring interest and popularity of the topic (e.g. Truss, 2003, on English, Sick, 2004, on German, among many others). It should surely be possible to leverage this inherent interest in grammar for grammar instruction in language education.

In the same way that even the most proficient speakers seek out grammar guidance and correction, research on foreign language learners' attitudes finds that grammar instruction is often perceived to be beneficial. But it is also considered especially tedious (see Jean & Simard, 2011; Loewen et al., 2009). Teachers face difficult choices in the face of this love–hate relationship. Indeed, teachers themselves might share the

3.2 The Use and Abuse of Grammar

same ambivalence of seeing grammar as simultaneously 'boring but necessary'. There is no shortage of teaching methods or ideas that have been proposed to improve or facilitate the teaching of grammar (consider the outline of differing approaches to teaching described in Chapter 1, and see discussion in Chapter 5). For now, in keeping with the theme of this chapter, we will discuss how grammar can be reconceived in potentially useful ways for pedagogic purposes.

Recalling the distinction between grammar on the one hand, and orthography and punctuation on the other, potential problems arise if there is conflation of 'grammar and punctuation' or 'grammar and writing'. Spelling and punctuation do not come naturally to anyone: they must be taught. An internet search, however, will testify to the range of pedagogical and reference works available which seek to address 'bad grammar', when in fact the problem is one of conforming to the rules that have been imposed on language and are part of the technology of writing. Now, we would not wish to imply that this is necessarily a bad thing, nor that such works are necessarily unhelpful. Quite the contrary, we *need* help with punctuation in the same way that we follow instructions to get to grips with any technological devices. Stating that a particular type of apostrophe placement is wrong is surely uncontroversial: in English writing, apostrophes do not mark plurals and using an apostrophe in such a way is incorrect. However, stating that a particular grammatical structure is wrong is a much thornier issue, at least with respect to national language usage. And interesting issues extend from this to other/foreign language learning too.

3.2.1 Grammatical Viruses

One potentially enlightening way of understanding the intricacies involved in grammatical accuracy and issues of instruction is grammatical viruses. These occupy a grey area between prescription and description in language use, and, as we will see in Chapter 5, one can think of effects of pedagogical rules in language learning in terms of grammatical viruses. The slightly pernicious term, virus, is used because certain grammatical phenomena are analysed as parasitic on natural morphosyntactic properties. These parasitised features are then co-opted to produce forms which are treated as correct and prestigious. However, once such a virus is established, it spawns its own rules of usage and any description of the grammar of a language then has to address the nature of these rules, and instruction is tasked with equipping learners to be able to use socially important rules. Noam Chomsky has an interesting take on these questions:

> I think sensible prescriptivism ought to be part of any education. I would certainly think that students ought to know the standard literary language with all its conventions, its absurdities, its artificial conventions, and so on because that's a real cultural system, and an important cultural system ... It's not better, or more sensible. Much of it is a violation of natural law. In fact, a good deal of what's taught is taught because it's wrong. (Chomsky, interviewed in Olson and Faigley, 1991, p. 30)

One might question whether this view is really helpful in clarifying questions of accuracy and naturalness in grammar. Viruses may not be pleasant, but they are part of the natural world; the same can be said to apply to grammatical viruses. Indeed, Armstrong and MacKenzie (2013, p. 67) propose that grammatical viruses 'can be regarded as a natural and perhaps inevitable by-product of the emergence of a standard language ideology'. It might be expected that any standardised national language is infected, and this has been documented for a number of cases (see Lasnik & Sobin, 2000, Sobin, 1994; 1997, on English; Armstrong & MacKenzie, 2013, p. 78ff, on Spanish and French; Mackenzie, 2013, on French; Sundquist, 2011, on Norwegian).

How can we spot viral a construction? These structures are lexically specific, sensitive to directionality, and subject both to over- and undergeneralisation. These properties are illustrated on the basis of pronoun case in Case in Point 3.7.

Take a moment to consider your reactions to sentences (iii) – (vii) in Case in Point 3.7. Do you consider them all to be equally acceptable? In which contexts would you expect to hear or use the different forms? What, if anything, have you been taught about these properties? It has been argued that the *linguistically* natural forms are those in (iii) and (v). By linguistically natural, we mean that if there were no prescriptive rules and no educational intervention, these would be the forms that would be learned by English-speaking children because these are the forms that people actually say, and therefore exist as part of the ambient input that drives language acquisition amongst very young children.

Sobin (1997) says that the issues illustrated in the Case in Point 3.7 stem from the viral ... *and I* rule. This rule is lexically specific as it applies only to the pronoun *I*. This is unexpected for natural syntactic rules which apply to whole categories. A language which has case on noun phrases, marks case on all noun phrases, not only on some depending on the words used in the phrase. This explains why (vii) stands out; the 'rule' to use subject forms does not seem to extend to other pronouns as the presence of *she* rather than *I* makes this sentence sound much less acceptable.

3.7 CASE IN POINT: CASE MARKING AND PRONOUNS

Case is a pervasive linguistic property across the world's languages. English instantiates one of the simpler systems of case, as it is only clearly marked on pronouns. Nominative pronouns are also called subject pronouns because they appear in subject position, e.g. *I, she* in English, whereas accusative, or object pronouns, appear in object position, e.g. *me, her* in English.

(i) **I** met **her** in the shop.
(ii) *****Me** met **she** in the shop.

This simple pattern is much trickier, however, when the subject and object phrases are coordinated noun phrases (i.e. combined with *and*). Consider the distributional patterns illustrated in (iii–vi).

(iii) Jo and me went to the shop.
(iv) Jo and I went to the shop.
(v)   Jane came to the shop with Jo and me.
(vi) Jane came to the shop with Jo and I.
(vii) ?Jane came to the shop with Jo and she.
(viii) ?I and Jane went to the shop.

English contrasts with a language like German, which more clearly and consistently marks case not just on pronouns (xi, xii), but on noun phrases as well, as illustrated in (ix) – (x). Notice that the object noun phrase occurs after the verb in (ix), but German allows it to occur before the verb as well (x). The order of occurrence of pronouns in coordination does not affect case marking in any way (xii).

(ix) Johann traf   **den** Arzt.
     Joe   met   **the.ACC** doctor
     'Joe met the doctor.'

(x) **Den**   Arzt   traf   Johann.
     The.ACC doctor met   Joe
     'Joe met the doctor.'

(xi) Johann traf **mich** und **ihn**.
     Joe   met **me.ACC** and **him.ACC**

(xii) Johann traf **ihn** und **mich**.
      Joe   met **him.ACC** and **me.ACC**

The same logic applies to directionality. The grammatical form of a word should not be affected by its local context and linear order of occurrence relative to other words it is coordinated with. For a language like German, which clearly and consistently marks case on nouns and pronouns, the order of occurrence of pronouns with coordinating conjunctions does not affect the morphosyntax. Accusative forms occur in (ix) and (x) to indicate the same subject and object roles, even if the order of occurrence changes. Similarly, the case marking on pronouns in (xi) and (xii) consistently marks the object role regardless of order within the coordination. In English, by contrast, (viii) seems to be worse than (iv), which is unexpected of a naturally applicable rule of grammar.

Finally, such forms tend to be subject both to overgeneralisation and undergeneralisation in unexpected ways.[2] It seems that the viral *and I* rule began as an injunction against 'object' pronouns in subject position, as in (iii). However, this prescriptive rule has been overextended to cases where it makes less logical or linguistic sense, for example to coordinated phrases in object position where there is no motivation for a subject pronoun. This usage is reflected in the often-discussed phrase *between you and I* (compare to *between I and you*). Once a viral rule is established, its limited applicability and tendency towards unpredictable over/undergeneralisation means that it can give rise to a cycle of prescriptive purism. A naturally occurring coordinated subject form as in (iii), repeated here as (3), is condemned as incorrect according to prescriptive ideas about how language *should* function. That is, *me* is an object form, *Joe and me* functions as a subject, therefore using the *me* form must be incorrect (despite the fact that monolingual speakers of English will say this).

(3) Joe and me went to the beach.

Once natural usage of this form is condemned and corrected by prescriptively aware parents, teachers, etc., speakers may develop a general aversion to phrases of the form *X and me*. They then tend towards **hypercorrection** and produce phrases such as *between you and I* as a hypercorrect form of the perfectly acceptable *between you and me*. The hypercorrect form can then itself become the target of purists' opprobrium. Cochrane (2003) goes so far as to use this phrase as emblematic of what is 'wrong' with English in a work entitled *Between You and I: A Little Book of Bad English*. Bernstein (1965, p. 322) is also withering in his condemnation:

---

[2] Obviously, over the course of historical development, the scope of rules can change naturally, but the point with respect to the viruses is that over/underextension occurs together with the other properties of lexical specificity and directional sensitivity to suggest that over/underextension is not a natural development but rather indicative of speakers' lack of implicit control of the rule, unlike properties which are part of tacit competence.

3.2 The Use and Abuse of Grammar

Uncomprehending souls who have heard strictures about 'It is me' tend to think of 'me' as a naughty word, particularly when it is associated with 'you,' which they mistake for a nominative case. Thinking they are leaning over backward to be correct, they somersault onto their faces and come up with BETWEEN YOU AND I.

Returning to questions of teaching and prestige usage and grammatical viruses, we have seen that Chomsky proposes that such structures are taught to speakers who have acquired their language from birth precisely because they are add-ons to the naturally developed grammar and so require instruction in order to regulate use. No teacher would dream of explaining the properties of wh-questions, or the formation of the imperative form to monolingual speakers. These, and the rest of the abstract grammatical system, develop naturally and need no extra educational support. The viral, prestigious properties can (and should) be addressed in education because, as Sobin (1994, p. 57) points out, grammatical viruses are 'linguistically superfluous but socially significant'. Learning to navigate social life in our communities is an important element in general education.

However, the issues become more intricate still when we consider the impact of similar questions in foreign language learning. Harley (1993, p. 251) proposes that principles of analytic grammar teaching in foreign language instruction entail, among other things, paying attention to features which may create confusion or negative attitudes among first language speakers. Such features are of course variable, but variability presents practical difficulties for teachers of foreign languages. A feature which is socially variable in the ambient speech community may be presented as a core part of the grammar when repackaged as pedagogical grammar for foreign language learners. As a result, it may be expected that foreign language learners master patterns of 'accuracy' which do not hold for those for whom the foreign language is their primary language.

In the foreign language classroom, it might not always be clear what distinguishes a pedagogical rule from a descriptive rule from a prescriptive rule or a viral rule, resulting in issues for delivering grammar instruction. For example, consider how one might teach the grammar of coordinated pronouns in English as a foreign language, or participle agreement in French as a foreign language (Case in Point 3.8) in light of the issues discussed in the Cases in Point in this section. There is a pedagogical rationale for providing grammatical rules which are simplified enough to be digestible for pupils and applicable to the sort of communicative contexts that occur in the classroom. However, there is a risk that such simplified pedagogical rules could become viral and

3.8 CASE IN POINT: AGREEMENT AND PARTICIPLES

Languages with gender and number require agreement between different types of constituents, such as adjectives and nouns so that the forms match in terms of number and gender, much like how one must add a plural to the noun if one says in English: *I read three books*. Romance languages require a very specific type of agreement: between a participle and a preceding direct object phrase. Notice how the participial forms of the verb in (i) and (ii) have a feminine ending to agree with the preceding feminine object *la section* and *la promesse* (from MacKenzie 2013, p. 19).

(i) **Cette** section de l'autoroute, ils l'ont **refaite** il y a six mois.
that.FEM section of the motorway, they CL.have **rebuilt**.FEM there are six months
'That section of motorway, they rebuilt it six months ago.'

(ii) **Quelle** promesse a-t-il **faite**?
which.FEM promise has he **made**.FEM
'What has he promised?'

While linguists have attempted to understand this in theoretical terms, it may be that this is a viral rule rather than a real grammatical rule. It seems to be subject to over- and underextension, as is typical of grammatical viruses. While (iii) is said to be ungrammatical because the noun *la femme* is the object of *épouser* in a subordinate clause, rather than *dire* in the main clause, such agreement structures are found in French, presumably as an overextension of the viral rule, as in the number agreement on the participle in (iv).

(iii) *****Quelle femme** ai-je **dite** qu'il veut épouser?
which.FEM woman have-I **said**.FEM that it wants marry
'Which woman did I say he wants to marry?'

(iv) **Ces systèmes périphériques**... sont **dits** être des modules.
these systems peripheral.PL.. are **said**.PL be the modules
'These peripheral systems are said to be modules.'

only partially account for the language input data. Ultimately, this may result in a partial or viral grammatical system with rules which cannot generate the full range of target language structures that a teacher might have in mind when providing the rule in the first place. We would not want you to be worried about this, but instead suggest that having a fuller understanding of what may be going on with your learners will help you to make decisions about what to focus on and what to overlook.

Academic linguists, especially of the formal variety, have little compunction in talking about natural and unnatural rules. This is where the idea of grammatical viruses came from. When applied to questions of teaching and learning (about) grammar, for monolingual, proficient and additional language learners, issues of naturalness interact in convoluted ways with questions of prestige and standardisation to complicate pedagogical questions related to grammar. One way of working around these issues is to consider how to think about grammar rather than just seeking to deliver a set of discrete grammatical rules.

3.3 VIRTUAL GRAMMAR AND LANGUAGE EDUCATION

Virtual Grammar is how we formulate a way to think about abstract grammatical concepts for educational purposes. The three elements we draw upon to motivate the idea are: linguistics, language acquisition and education. The linguistic logic can be traced back to founding ideas in linguistics (and anthropology). In discussing linguistic differences between cultural communities, Boas (1938, p. 133) says 'while for us definiteness, number, and time are obligatory aspects, we find in another language location near the speaker or somewhere else, source of information – whether seen, heard or inferred – as obligatory aspects'. We see these sorts of features of language as categories of Virtual Grammar. That is, there is a *potential* suite of grammatical distinctions available to all humans by virtue of having the capability to develop language. Some of these distinctions will find grammaticalised expression in some languages but not others. Because the potentially meaningful distinctions are universal, we can all understand and express them. However, the ways in which they are grammatically expressed differ radically from language to language. For example, evidentiality is perfectly expressible in English through a range of circumlocutions when you have a specific reason for including this information (*I have reason to believe that* ... ; *It is evident that* ...). Evidentiality may also be consistently marked in a language's grammatical system, as is the case in Japanese, Korean and Tariana. In those languages, it is included even at times when you may not feel the need to specify the nature of the evidence underlying the thought. It would therefore be understandable if grammatical differences like this were an area of difficulty for language learners.

The acquisition research we draw on to motivate Virtual Grammar is explicated in more detail in Chapter 4. For the moment, it suffices to point out that once we have established entrenched particular instantiations of grammar in our primary language(s), developing the new properties required by an additional or foreign language may pose problems. This is not to say that it is impossible. As mentioned, we can in principle comprehend any of the virtual grammatical properties that language makes available. However, the grammatical complexities of our existing linguistic system and how this compares to the grammar of the language being learned make the process of learning additional languages difficult. For example, if the language you are learning makes an aspectual distinction which your primary language does not, it is likely that you will encounter difficulties in consistently marking or interpreting the new distinction in ways that the target language system requires (see Case in Point 3.9).

The educational facet of the Virtual Grammar idea owes a debt to the work of Henry Widdowson (see Widdowson, 2002; 2003, and in particular 2016) who invokes the notion of 'virtual language'. His proposal for language education is that it would be beneficial for all learners to explore the nature of language prior to learning actual specific languages. The rationale is that a learner who is primed by understanding something of the nature of language and the communicative possibilities of grammatical patterns will have an easier time understanding 'new' or 'unusual' linguistic patterns in a specific target language. The intuition is that this would enable a learner to exploit their knowledge in an informed and strategic fashion, in order to learn better.

Such thinking could address broader educational goals that are associated with language learning and teaching. These include the promotion of multi- or plurilingual proficiency and the promotion of intercultural rapport. Widdowson and Seidlhofer (2008) argue that the way that language teaching is currently organised actually works against these stated educational goals. This is because practice tends to concentrate on a single target language, and in a way that dissociates the target from the learner's 'native' language knowledge (or knowledge from any other previously acquired languages). In doing so, the essential foreignness of the language is emphasised as opposed to being seen as sharing the same virtual grammatical foundations as any variety. One way of addressing this is by exploring the virtual communicative and cultural potential of Language by investigating how communicative and cultural features are expressed by different codes. This includes both codes with labels that distinguish them as languages (English vs Spanish, for example), and codes which are distinguished by dialect or by register.

Taking this line of thinking to a logical conclusion, Widdowson even suggests that rather than teaching particular foreign languages at school level, the subject that should be offered is the study of language, with the

3.9 CASE IN POINT: ASPECT – HABITUALITY AND INCOMPLETENESS

Different aspectual meanings can be packaged into individual tense/aspect morphemes. Like English, French has a past tense morpheme that also indicates meaning beyond the past. The French *'imparfait'* (imperfect) paradigm can denote either past ongoing/incomplete actions, or past repeated habitual actions.

1SG	v+*ais*	1PL	v+*ions*
2SG	v+*ais*	2PL	v+*iez*
3SG	v+*ait*	3PL	v+*aient*

Without context, a sentence can be ambiguous in terms of its aspectual interpretation, as indicated by the potential English translations (see McManus & Marsden, 2017).

(i) Il **jouait** au foot.
he **play.IMP** to.the foot
'He played football regularly / he used to play football.'
'He was playing football.'

Similarly, the past tense used alone is ambiguous as it can indicate either a completed action or a habitual repeated action. This can be disambiguated by adding a clarifying clause which forces one of the potential interpretations.

(ii) a. Il **jouait** au foot quand j'ai appelé
he **play.IMP** to.the foot when i.have called
'He was playing football when I called.'
b. Il **jouait** au foot quand nous étions petits
he **play.IMP** to.the foot when we were small
'He played football when we were young.'

This feature of past tense is true for English as well.

(iii) a. He **played** football once last year.   (completed past action meaning)
b. He **played** football every Saturday.   (habitual past action meaning)

While the same distinctions are at play in each language, the way they are grammatically packaged differs. The tense morphemes *-ait* / *-ed* can both be used to express a habitual meaning, but they differ for a secondary meaning, with French *-ait* encoding an incomplete past action and English *-ed* a complete past action (McManus & Marsden, 2017).

national language and any other language drawn upon to illustrate relevant grammatical facts. 'The purpose of [this type of] course would be to get students to invest in a more general awareness of the nature of language and culture by specific and comparative reference to other languages and to their own' (Widdowson & Seidlhofer, 2008, p. 211). This is a rather grand vision which would involve rethinking the organisation of language education on a policy and curricular level. While questions of policy change take us far beyond our discussion, we note that conclusions from a range of approaches to language education point in a similar direction: e.g. Awakening to Languages (Candelier, 2008), bilingualisation (Butzkamm & Caldwell, 2009), Knowledge about Language (Mitchell et al., 1994), Language Awareness (Hawkins, 1984) and translanguaging (Garcia & Wei, 2014).

While the details differ between these various ideas, the point on which there is agreement is that the teaching of individual languages isolated from each other is not necessarily the most appropriate approach to language education. The single-language approach results in a lack of cross-fertilisation of linguistic knowledge from the national language to the foreign language, or from foreign languages to linguistic and literacy skills in the national language. Current practice within communicative language teaching compounds this issue. While a communicative approach justifiably emphasises communicative abilities in the target language as a counterweight to a traditional focus on grammar-translation, instruction exclusively using the target language with active avoidance of explicit comparisons between languages means that existing linguistic knowledge is not leveraged for new learning. It is surely pedagogically questionable to ignore the rich sources of knowledge that are available from learners' existing languages. Modern forms of education rely on scaffolding, building upon and exploiting the range of skills and knowledge that a learner brings to bear when engaging with new knowledge and abilities. Assuming that new foreign languages are separate subjects which start from scratch without explicit reference to existing linguistic know-how is not only pedagogically debatable, but, as we will see in Chapter 4, the process of additional language development implicates existing sources of grammatical knowledge whether this is used in the classroom or not.

The essential pedagogic notion for teachers is that grammar is not just the bits and pieces of grammatical machinery outlined in morphological paradigms or lists of rules and exceptions. Virtual Grammar encompasses the range of potential properties and features of meaning and usage which may find particular grammatical expression in any language. Particular properties may be more or less relevant in any particular learning context. Consider the notion of unaccusativity that we discussed above. Unaccusativity is a virtual, grammatical concept, which regulates the occurrence of a range of morphosyntactic and lexical constructions in different languages. As such, it will be at play in the acquisition processes of our learners, whether we as teachers know about the concept or not, and whether we choose to work with the concept in some way or not. So, should teachers actually teach unaccusativity to their learners? No, or at least not necessarily. But your knowledge of unaccusativity might shed light on any number of teaching and learning issues: passive formation in an English classroom, auxiliary selection in a French classroom, etc. With this knowledge a teacher could make more informed decisions about what and how to address specific points in teaching, or how to correct occurrences of ungrammatical performance which may implicate unaccusativity.

Fellow linguists might recognise in our notion of Virtual Grammar a certain reliance on Universal Grammar, or UG, which is the bedrock of formal generative approaches to language. Our use of the term, Virtual Grammar, is an attempt to introduce a notion which does not immediately elicit pre-conceived views with respect to theories of language. We also think a new term is needed because Virtual Grammar, while sharing some affinities with UG, goes beyond the concept of UG as it is not limited exclusively to the mechanics of grammar. In addition, it is oriented explicitly towards that which is pedagogically useful in the teaching of language.

We see Virtual Grammar as a way of emphasising the shared properties of grammar in order to leverage and extend existing knowledge with the aim of facilitating analytical skills for future language learning. Teachers with an understanding of this sort of approach will be better able to sensitise learners to the abstract grammatical tools that language makes available. This is suggested as a way to address general educational aims of awareness raising, as well as priming learners for the learning of specific languages by raising awareness of how different languages may in principle work.

Our contention is that teachers with higher levels of expertise in the grammatical concepts of Virtual Grammar will have additional options for strategically exploiting that knowledge in grammar instruction. There is empirical evidence showing that such an approach can be effective. McManus and Marsden (2017) have shown that English-speaking learners of French improved their knowledge and processing of the use of the *imparfait* in French when grammatical information about the use of this versus other aspectual distinctions in the verbal system of

French was provided. More crucially, however, in addition to information about French aspectual distinctions, a second group of learners received instruction about tense and aspect distinctions in their first language, English, with explicit comparison to French. These learners performed even better on their sensitivity to tense/aspect mismatches in French compared to those who only got the French teaching.

Expanding this thinking, we can suggest that knowing about tense and aspect, and understanding how these properties function in general can facilitate teaching and learning. In other words, the use of the virtual grammar of tense and aspect provides a potential approach to a challenging area of grammar. We suggest that with a Virtual Grammar mindset, a teacher would be able to alter their approach in a wide range of language learning situations. Widdowson (2016, p. 33) suggests that one can conceptualise any particular linguistic code as 'a set of general encoding principles which are independent of their partial selective use and which represents an inexhaustible potential for meaning making'. Thus, tense and aspect (or indeed any of the grammatical concepts we've outlined) provides a wide variety of potential for meaning making which is realised differentially in the selections that any particular language makes. And understanding this grammatical meaning potential is applicable across different codes.

Our focus on grammatical properties might raise the spectre of a traditional grammar-translation teaching method. But if properly understood, it will not because we are not advocating the teaching of a newer more updated set of grammatical rules. Instead, we suggest a move away from a rigid rule-based mentality to a more dynamic understanding of the range of ways linguistic properties can be realised grammatically, both across languages and within a language. A teacher with a view of grammar as a mechanism for instantiating grammatical concepts which are shared by virtue of being human, will emphasise the shared nature of languages, instead of teaching something 'foreign'. From this 'virtual' starting point, the wonderful array of ways that languages express specific grammatical concepts provides a fascinating window into the human mind. As learners discover new ways of conveying meaning in the new language, they will encounter new specific properties of grammar. Exploration is likely to lead to some regularities which appear to conform to patterns which could be called rules. You may decide the context or level of the class means that limiting the learning to a rule is appropriate. However, true exploration even at low levels of proficiency is likely to reveal examples which do not fit the rules found in grammar books and teaching materials. Light-touch linguistic analysis will allow learners and teachers to unpick the language, tracing it back to its grammatical concepts. This way of focusing on the meaning being expressed allows for the recognition that there are different grammatical mechanisms available to the learner. In time, the more proficient learner will be able to use a wider range of grammatical features, and with more ease and comfort. In sum, by conceiving of grammar as the virtual properties which are realised differentially in different languages, we can begin to develop grammatical concepts that can be exploited in order to promote learning of individual foreign languages, as well as highlighting what is shared between all languages.

3.4 CONCLUSION: MAKING THE MOST OF GRAMMAR

Grammar and grammars mean different things to different people. A language teacher and an academic linguist will have different views on the nature of grammar. The grammar presented in a schoolbook is different from the grammar presented in a reference work. The multifaceted understanding of grammar can be advantageous as it permits a full range of focus for analysis, academic understanding, teaching and learning. However, this also masks the fact that grammar has an underlying unity as part of the human cognitive facility, which underlies all languages. Brumfit (2001, p. 17) has pointed out that '[l]anguage is the cheapest scientific data available to schools, and pupils, in my experience invariably enjoy thinking about it, as a socially significant system and as an abstract system alike, if the teacher is committed, knowledgeable, and enthusiastic.'

Our elaboration of the idea of Virtual Grammar addresses this proposal and aligns with existing recommendations based on the importance of language awareness in foreign language learning, and within language education more generally (Hawkins, 1984). We assert that better knowledge of the full capacity of language in terms of Virtual Grammar, will enable teachers to develop the grammatical awareness of their learners, and to do so based on sound foundations. Comparisons of specific instantiations of grammar in languages of the world also enrich our understanding of the elements of meaning and the communicative features that can be encoded in grammar. Learners with some understanding of broad grammatical concepts will be better primed for linguistic input which instantiates new and different ways to encode meaning. And with newly acquired grammatical properties they will be able to explore the communicative and pragmatic import that the different grammatical choices hold. In addition, the Virtual Grammar notion provides a way in which existing, tacit knowledge of one's existing language(s) can be leveraged so that learners actively use their linguistic knowledge, linking it to those elements being learned in the new target language. In this way, grammatical properties which may otherwise appear alien are rendered more familiar as they will be seen as variations of the same grammatical themes and concepts which constitute all languages.

3.5 EXERCISES AND QUESTIONS FOR DISCUSSION

1. Pedagogical Grammar

i) Consult your favourite grammar for the language(s) you teach or have studied. What makes it a good grammar for you? Clarity? Coverage? etc.

ii) Are there any rules or usages you have identified in reference or pedagogical grammars which strike you as not quite right compared to your knowledge of how the constructions in question function? If so, how have you adapted or extended the information presented in such grammars to make it fit what you know intuitively about the language?

iii) To what extent are reference or pedagogical grammars useful for teaching? Can you think of ways to use them that address some of the issues raised in this chapter? Try adapting or extending information from reference or pedagogical grammars to make it appropriate for use with your learners. Which details would you adapt or change? What information do you need to be able to extend or supplement grammatical information?

2. Pedagogy and Grammatical Explanation

i) Consider this statement by Diane Larsen-Freeman in which she talks about what should be taught with respect to grammar:

> My idea is to teach reasons so that students understand that language is the way it is. Also, I think reasons tend to be broader-based than rules, and if you understand the reason why speakers make the choices they do, you have some access to the way that people think in that language, the culture of speakers of that language. (Pérez-Llantada & Larsen-Freeman, 2007, p. 160)

3.5 Exercises and Questions for Discussion

What kind of 'reasons' for why language is the way it is have been discussed in this book so far?

ii) Think about ways that 'reasons' can be conceptualised in terms of grammatical explanation (see also discussion of form, function, etc. in Chapter 1). How useful do you think it is to teach reasons for grammatical patterns? In your teaching, when would you use explanations of patterns as opposed to concentrating just on paradigms and rules?

iii) Choose a grammatical pattern which is often taught as a simple rule or paradigm. Can you think of a deeper generalisation that gives a reason for the pattern? Alternatively, can you find in available grammars underlying reasons for the patterns? How useful would this information be in your teaching?

3. Grammatical Ambiguity

i) The sentence in (a) is ambiguous. Consider what you think the two possible meanings are. One meaning is more obvious and occurs more frequently than the other. (see also Chapter 4 and Case in Point 4.9 on quantifiers).

   a) Someone read every book.

ii) Consider how you could exploit ambiguity in communicative contexts to illustrate points of grammar. Newspaper headlines often provide amusing examples: 'Students Cook and Serve Grandparents'. Collect some headlines and consider whether any of them are ambiguous, and what the ambiguity might illustrate about grammatical properties of the language in question.

iii) Create examples of ambiguous sentences. How could you use these examples, or ambiguity in general, in teaching?

4. Grammatical Viruses

i) We saw some examples of viral grammatical constructions with coordination in this chapter. Similar issues apply to other constructions in English involving case and pronouns. Which of these sentences do you think is the result of a viral grammatical rule, and which is the natural rule that English speakers will tend to say in colloquial speech?

   a) It was I who answered the phone.
   b) It was me who answered the phone.

ii) We can test for viral rules by exploring whether they are restricted to certain contexts. Sentence (c) shows a context which requires a first person pronoun after a form of the verb *to be*, just as in (a) and (b). However, in this case, there is no choice between *I* and *me*. Only one would be accepted as grammatically possible by English speakers. Which do you think it is?

c) That is ____ wearing the funny hat in the photo.

iii) What is your view on prescriptive vs descriptive grammar in relation to language teaching? If teaching English, how would you respond to these choices of pronoun use? Does it depend on the type of class? The particular student? The context in which these choices arise? Something else altogether?

iv) What is your view on grammatical correction in general? Accepting that grammatical accuracy plays a role in language teaching, what is your view on the extent to which it should be emphasised? Are you comfortable with making a distinction between prescriptive and descriptive norms in your approach to accuracy? Do your views change if applied to writing as opposed to speaking?

5. Virtual Grammar and Grammatical Concepts

As one illustration of virtual grammar, we saw in this chapter that in English, specificity plays a role in the distribution of (in)definite articles. Even though English does not have an article or morpheme for specificity, this virtual concept is relevant to English grammar.

i) Choose a difficult point of grammar that you deal with in the language(s) you teach and find explanations or rules for it in pedagogical or reference materials.

ii) Do these materials make reference to any underlying concepts in their explanations of the grammar point you have chosen? Can you identify any underlying concepts which help to make sense of the grammatical pattern(s) you have identified? In trying to identify underlying grammatical concepts, try to think of how the language works beyond looking at specific grammatical forms. (In the same way that specificity helps explain the distribution of English definite versus indefinite articles and their associated meanings.)

4 Language Learning and Acquisition

In the absence of physical or cognitive impairments, we all come to master the core grammatical properties of the language(s) we are exposed to from birth. When compared to the learning of additional, foreign languages later in life, this fact presents something of a paradox. As infants with still-developing cognitive capacities, we manage to build and start to use a complex, abstract grammatical system within three or four years of exposure to the **ambient language** we hear around us. As adults, the outcome of language learning is less certain, with many of us finding we have limits where further development seems impossible. And worse, so-called **fossilisation** often occurs at a level of development sometimes far removed from that of people who have acquired the language from birth. This can happen despite conscious effort and dogged determination to learn, and despite intensive instruction about the properties of the language, which themselves are carefully curated by materials developers, specifically in order to promote learning.

This observation raises a number of interesting and potentially tricky questions. Do second language acquisition and first language acquisition rely on fundamentally different cognitive processes? Are the resultant grammatical systems fundamentally different? Is there a window of opportunity for natural language learning in infancy beyond which language learning is compromised, or even impossible? Does the existence of a fully developed, entrenched grammar hinder acquisition of the grammar of a subsequent language? In addition to these linguistic and cognitive questions, there are also, of course, social and motivational variables which distinguish 'mother tongue' from 'foreign' language acquisition settings.

These issues are crucial for teachers interested in successfully guiding the language development of their learners. While scholars are not short of potential answers, for many of the same reasons that there is a lack of agreed consensus in the field of linguistics, there is little which qualifies as uncontroversial agreement in adult language development research, even in terms of the right questions to ask! Against this background, it would be foolhardy for us to try to provide definitive resolution to the questions listed. This is not our aim. Instead, our focus here, as with the rest of the book, takes the view of the formal linguist, focusing on cognitive research in second language acquisition. One main motivation for doing this is our view that the voice of formal linguists is often missing in language education, as a result of the disconnect between linguistics and education as academic fields.

In our discussion, we make comparisons to child language development – with a view to illustrating that there are areas of overlap and similarity between the two – instead of assuming difference, as has become the more usual practice in foreign language education. In this chapter, we will follow the convention within the field of formal second language acquisition (SLA) to refer to the existing grammar of the language(s) acquired from birth as the L1, or first language, even if there is more than one. The additional language(s) being researched will be referred to as the L2, regardless of whether it is the second, fifth or twelfth language. For this reason you will find that we talk about L1s and L2s in the plural. In other words, our approach in this chapter abstracts away from interesting questions of multilingualism, saving that for the next chapter. We will also avoid the contentious 'native language' issue in this chapter. As will become clear, the way we focus on grammar at the cognitive level means that the 'language' a learner is developing is itself an idealisation, whether being acquired from birth or as an adult. In other words, in this chapter, 'language' really refers to the abstract grammatical features of a language. As should be clear from earlier chapters, there is wide variation within what is supposedly the grammar of any single language, and we are well aware that grammar alone does not capture the full entity of a language. But we take this more narrow focus because we think there are useful contributions to be made.

In a nutshell, this chapter explores the SLA research to show how, in cognitive terms, L1 and L2 acquisition are the same and different. We hope to pull out points that find general agreement among researchers who focus on grammatical development from the point of view of form-oriented linguistics. In doing so, we extend the view of Virtual Grammar developed in this book to the arena of language development. We hope that this might help you to think differently about features of grammar so that you can take a more informed and targeted approach in your teaching. Note, however, that because the ultimate aims in the language classroom should be more holistic than single grammar points, we are not suggesting that the research explored in this chapter provides direct application for teaching a specific lesson. Instead we aim to show how a critical understanding of the linguistic issues provides a foundation which allows you to reflect on pedagogical content and practice from a linguistic point of view. In doing so, we hope to enhance your own expertise in the area of linguistic development.

4.1 ADDITIONAL LANGUAGE LEARNING: FUNDAMENTALLY DIFFERENT?

One question in L2 research is the extent to which second language learners follow the same developmental path as children acquiring their first language. Early, and highly influential, studies of the acquisition of English morphemes suggested that there is a 'natural order' of acquisition of morphemes in L1 and L2 English (see Dulay & Burt, 1974; Dulay et al., 1982). This led some early researchers to boldly claim that language learning is essentially the same process in childhood and in adulthood, following an internal timetable which one cannot substantially alter by teaching. The claim that L2 learning recapitulates the L1 sequence has, however, since been called into question, due in part to a range of empirical issues with the original studies (see Goldschneider & DeKeyser, 2001), to say nothing of the overgeneralisation of morpheme development to 'language' or even 'grammar'. The logical opposite pole to the 'essentially the same' idea is that L1 and L2 acquisition are fundamentally different. This position has also been espoused, with proponents claiming that L1 and L2 acquisition result in distinct types of knowledge (Bley-Vroman, 1990; 2009), or by assuming that linguistic knowledge is put to use in language processing in fundamentally different ways (Clahsen & Felser, 2006).

On balance, there are problems with both the fundamentally different and fundamentally identical extremes. It may be that the strong claims made based on the early morpheme studies encouraged a reaction towards the other extreme. Our reading of the literature is that more educationally oriented research has left this question for linguists and seems to assume a 'basically different' position in its orientation. We see value in returning to the 'difference' perspective as a starting point from which to consider the range of research that now exists. To be clear, we don't want to repeat the past by denying the differences that exist. There are manifest differences between L1 and L2 development, and between the end results of each process. This becomes abundantly clear within minutes if you listen to most people speaking their 'home' language(s) as compared to a 'foreign' language whether or not they are still trying to learn it. This kind of observation is the basis of the **Fundamental Difference Hypothesis** outlined by Bley-Vroman (1990; 2009). The starting point of the FDH is the assumption that humans are equipped with an innate, **domain-specific** cognitive system which deals exclusively with language. This explains how children can develop an abstract formal system at a stage of development where their general cognitive abilities cannot handle other abstract symbolic systems. However, according to this hypothesis, the language-specific system does not operate indefinitely, due to maturation effects around puberty. Language learning after this **critical period** is assumed to resort to non-linguistic, general learning mechanisms. In other words, adults apply their well-developed general problem-solving and skill-acquisition abilities to language learning. The catch of course is that general problem-solving is not well-suited to dealing with the abstract formal grammatical system which underlies language. Bley-Vroman (1990) lists ten factors which you will likely agree distinguish L2 learning from L1 development:

i. Lack of success
ii. General failure
iii. Variation in success, course and strategy
iv. Variation in goals
v. Correlation of age and proficiency
vi. Fossilisation
vii. Indeterminate intuitions
viii. Importance of instruction
ix. Negative evidence
x. Role of affective factors

These bear the hallmarks of skill development, unlike the natural development which allows humans to see, hear, feel emotions and, arguably, develop language as infants. Skill development applies to activities like driving, reading or learning to play a musical instrument. Even if you have never taken music lessons, you will know that there is variation in outcomes and most people will not become expert musicians (i and ii); different people will attain different levels of competence in their musical ability depending on their goals (iii and iv); those who start younger are more likely to reach higher levels (v); some people will not progress beyond a particular level of ability regardless of practice and motivation (vi); most will not have perfect pitch regardless of how good their teachers are (vii and viii); most need

4.1 Additional Language Learning: Fundamentally Different? 121

explanation and explicit correction of mistakes, known formally as **negative evidence** (ix); and there is a role for our attitude towards music and the instrument we are playing (x).

Of course, Bley-Vroman illustrated each of these ten fundamental differences in terms of L2 language development, not music. The list may seem depressing, but the language teacher need not despair, even in response to the pessimistic claim that '[l]anguage is not merely difficult to learn with only general cognitive strategies, it is virtually impossible' (Bley-Vroman, 1990, p. 7). The very reason we teach subjects within school curricula is precisely because they do not develop naturally on their own. And even to the extent to which they do, we value **meta-knowledge**, giving us understanding *about* things. Humans have a natural intuition for physics, for example. We know implicitly that objects remain motionless unless a force acts on them; we expect objects to fall if not supported. Yet we still teach physics at school because we believe that it is important to understand how these laws of nature work. Without sophisticated explicit training, most humans do not naturally develop an affinity for physics beyond being able to judge the velocity and trajectory of moving objects in order to avoid being crushed by a rolling boulder or run over by a bus when crossing the street. Similarly, humans develop sophisticated linguistic knowledge at a very young age, without explicit awareness of the properties of language.

In Chapter 1, we introduced the concept of the poverty of the stimulus, whereby the stimulus, or input made available to any child is 'poor' in relation to the rich grammar they develop. How does this notion work with respect to L2 learning? Like the L1 context, the L2 context includes language input. Additionally, however, it also includes the learner's previous linguistic experience, and typically some kind of instruction about L2 properties. A naïve assumption, then, is that there is no poverty in the stimulus because anything 'missing' from the 'naturally occurring' input can be provided through instruction. However, as we have shown in earlier chapters, there are a number of linguistic properties that are very subtle. Many of these are not explicitly known by fluent speakers of a language, including language teachers if they have not been exposed to high levels of linguistic training. And, because many of these properties remain confined to discussion in academic SLA research, they are typically not included in pedagogical grammars or language teaching materials. For L2 researchers, however, this provides an opportunity. There is, in fact, a body of research that has aimed to explore precisely those phenomena in second language acquisition which cannot be derived directly from the input and are not addressed in teaching because they are not widely known. The third factor in this research angle is ensuring that the properties being investigated do not exist in the same way in the learner's L1. In other words, if points of grammar (a) don't exist in L1 grammar, (b) are not clear in the input, and (c) are not explicitly taught, but they are found to be successfully acquired by the L2 learner, then it would seem as though there is still some role for internal cognitive mechanisms in L2 development (Schwartz & Sprouse, 2013). As such, the fundamental difference position would be too strong.

Good grammatical candidates for testing this are subtle properties of interpretation which are not transparent in the input. Linguists have explored such properties and shown that L2 learners can develop the same sort of interpretive patterns as L1 speakers of the languages, despite the apparent learnability difficulties. To exemplify, there is a study that tests the ability of English-speakers to acquire distinctions in the acceptability and interpretation of complex noun phrases (NPs) in French. A noun denoting the result of an action in French can mark the agent of that action either with the preposition *de* (= *of*) or *par* (= *by*) while a noun denoting a process can only mark the agent with *par* (see Case in Point 4.1, refer also to information in Case in Point 1.5).

The distinction between process and result nominals is not overtly marked in French (or English) in the sense that is there is no piece of morphology on nouns that overtly signals to learners 'I'm a process noun' versus 'I'm a result noun'. The property is not taught in French classes and is not included in French foreign language textbooks or pedagogical grammars. It is useful to research English learners of French because English provides no help.[1] Dekydtspotter et al. (1997) tested English-speaking learners of French by providing them with contexts which required either the result or process interpretation of the NP and studying learners' acceptance of the different prepositional complements in French. Despite all the odds stacked against them, this research found that by higher proficiency levels in French, L1 English-speaking learners can reliably make the appropriate grammatical distinction, a distinction which requires the interpretation of French nouns as denoting either a process or a result. It seems, therefore, that at least in some areas, successful L2 grammatical development can take place even in the absence of instruction or clear evidence from the target language input.

---

[1] Even though English can mark possessives with post-nominal *of*-phrases, the occurrence of multiple *of*-NP combinations is ungrammatical (e.g. *the version of the 9th of Karajan*) and therefore of no use for application within French grammar.

4.1 CASE IN POINT: PROCESS AND RESULT NOMINALS

Nouns derived from verbs retain different aspects of the verb's original meaning. In Chapter 1, we saw that process nominals reflect the process referred to by the original verb while result nominals denote the resultant state referred to by the original verb's meaning. And we saw that this dichotomy regulates the co-occurrence of arguments with the nominals. The difference between the two types of nominals also regulates the potential co-occurrence of adjectives. As shown in (i) *swift* modifies the construction process, and leads to an unacceptable sentence if modification picks out a result meaning, as in (ii).

(i) The swift building ... of the house surprised me.
(ii) *The swift building ... is a pleasure to live in.

Looking cross-linguistically, we see that French and English exhibit subtle differences with respect to how these types of nominals compare when they occur in complex noun phrases. The result nominal *interpretation* in (iii) and (iv) allows the agent, Karajan, to be encoded in different ways: as a possessor using -'s or in a *by*-phrase in English. Similarly, in French, the possessive form (with post-verbal *de*) or a *by*-phrase (*par*) are possible, as in (iii) and (iv) (see Dekydtspotter et al., 1997).

(iii) **Karajan's** interpretation of the 9th symphony
l'interprétation de la 9ème symphonie **de Karajan**
(iv) the interpretation of the 9th symphony **by Karajan**
l'interprétation de la 9ème symphonie **par Karajan**

These grammatical patterns hold for process nominals in English, as seen with *destruction*, in (v). But the equivalent possessive construction in French is impossible. The agent of a process nominal in French is only possible in the form with *par* (vi).

(v) **Godzilla's** destruction of Tokyo
*la destruction de Tokyo de Godzilla
(vi) the destruction of Tokyo **by Godzilla**
la destruction de Tokyo **par Godzilla**

The fact that acquisition of such subtle and uninstructed properties is possible only really deepens the mystery of fundamental difference. Bley-Vroman's list of ten empirical observations about L2 learning seems reasonable. But if adult L2 learners are in principle capable of acquiring complex abstract grammatical properties, what prevents them doing this consistently? And, why do they struggle with seemingly simple properties of the target grammar if the difficult areas are in principle acquirable?

Explanations may lie in the fundamental differences that exist between child first and adult additional language learning contexts. Adults, whether as instructed learners in a classroom or as immigrants to an L2 speech community, are often under immediate pressure to communicate and cannot afford an extended **silent period** in which to simply hear instances of the L2 in use in a range of communicative settings. In addition, adults clearly have a much wider and more complex range of thoughts, opinions, motivations and emotions that they can seek to communicate. It is not inconceivable that communicative pressure may trump the development of linguistic properties. Typically, the communicatively relevant elements of any situation can be effectively conveyed by simply linking contentful words together, so why should one use morphosyntactically complicated parts of the grammar to convey meaning if it is not crucial to achieve one's communicative aims?

This point has been made by Klein and Perdue (1997), who point out that adult L2 learners often rely on a **Basic Variety** of the target language. This 'represents a particularly natural and transparent interplay between form and function in human language' (p. 304). In their study of forty adults learning a range of L2s naturalistically as immigrants, they find that a third of them do not progress beyond a basic variety, which is a form of grammar without inflectional morphology, conveying meaning through semantic and pragmatic mechanisms instead. The subtitle of Klein and Perdue's work, 'Couldn't Natural Languages Be Much Simpler?', illustrates that this basic variety is a perfectly functional and natural form which can be deployed in most everyday communicative settings. In naturalistic learning environments, where the L2 speaker has to use language to live and work and buy and sell and persuade and inform, there is clearly a premium to being able to convey necessary meanings effectively without the added grammatical embellishments of inflections for case, aspect, agreement and the other features which are often sticking points in acquisition and learning.

In addition to this communicative constraint, the other major difference between L1 and L2 acquisition is that L2 learners already have (at least one) entrenched linguistic system when they come to learn a foreign language. Babies' minds are equipped to handle any grammar, while adults have an instantiation of a specific grammar already etched in their minds. Some scholars, such as Klein and Perdue (1997), state that the influence of the existing L1 is minimal in comparison to

4.1 Additional Language Learning: Fundamentally Different? 125

the general communicative principles of the basic variety. Yet the task facing L2 learners is clearly different than for L1 children. More recent developments in cognitive research suggest shared neural mechanisms across languages. If one considers the degree to which one's language(s) from birth are mapped into one's neural network, it is perhaps not surprising if this set of neurons is not easily modified. We have seen how the same grammatical concept can have very different realisations in different languages. Being able to reconfigure for a new language is understandably difficult. In this way, it is not just a question of learning a language, but for particular grammatical phenomena, re-learning, or un-learning properties which differ between the languages. When appealing to one's full set of language knowledge, one would expect **transfer** of linguistic properties and cross-linguistic influence. And indeed, there is a large body of research showing transfer effects at all stages of L2 development.

From a more general cognitive point of view, the fact of having more than one linguistic system in one's mind means that the processing of linguistic data is itself potentially different compared to linguistic processing by monolinguals. Psycholinguistic and neurolinguistic research on multilinguals suggests that it is impossible to 'turn off' one grammatical system. Even if functioning in an L2 means that the L2 grammatical properties are activated, the L1 grammar also remains active, its resting levels never being driven completely to zero. This means that input from one language can be, in a sense, filtered through the grammar of another, and that implicit, subconscious translation between languages may be the norm (Sanoudaki & Thierry, 2014; Spalek et al., 2014; Vaughan-Evans et al., 2014). All this makes us question an approach that disallows recourse to the L1 in the L2 classroom, an issue we will return to when we discuss language education in Chapter 5. For now, the point is that the very existence of a prior linguistic system when trying to learn additional linguistic forms is one clear reason why we would expect differences.

Overall, it seems that the real, though messy, answer to the question of fundamental difference is: yes and no. There are indeed fundamental differences in the learning strategies and the starting point of learning, and there seem to be differences in the outcomes of L1 versus L2 learning. Adult L2 learners can exploit their skill-development abilities to attempt to master the L2 in a way that infants cannot. It remains unclear, however, whether they must necessarily rely solely on these mechanisms. There have been claims, in fact, that explicit rule learning can undermine language development. Research exploring the effect of rule teaching on adult language learning has suggested that learners may overgeneralise a 'grammar rule' typically taught in textbooks in a way that adult speakers who learn languages naturally do not, leading to what has been called the Competing Systems Hypothesis (Long & Rothman, 2013). While this might be controversial, what is emerging from empirical studies focusing on specific features of grammar is that aspects of language which are infrequent, untutored and complex are in principle acquirable, a finding which is attributed to language-specific acquisition abilities common in language acquisition of all types. However, these potential abilities clearly do not lead to the same outcomes; many L2 learners rely on communicatively effective options such as a grammatically simplified basic variety. But jumping to outcomes is getting ahead of ourselves. In the next section, we explore what the L2 research tells us about the typical course of L2 development and consider more specifically how and why it diverges or converges on target grammatical patterns.

4.2 LANDMARKS OF L2 GRAMMATICAL DEVELOPMENT

4.2.1 The Beginning

The starting point for L2 acquisition is, by definition, different than for children learning their first language. Yet understanding the nature of the L2 starting point is as difficult as it is crucial in SLA research. While much research has been devoted to studying the properties of the **initial state**, specifying what exactly is meant by initial state is fraught and opens up some chicken-and-egg problems for any theory of language acquisition. To illustrate, consider a language acquisition experiment where we test an L2 learner who has just one week's exposure to the L2. Our theory might say that we should find evidence of the existing L1 grammar in the learner's attempted L2 output. If we find no evidence of this, does this mean that the existing grammar doesn't actually play any role in L2 development? And can we say this is 'initial state' research? Is it possible that a one-week period is enough to have moved to some more advanced, though still elementary, stage of proficiency? This illustrates the practical problems in coming to a verifiable consensus in research, and one core challenge for those exploring the nature of L1 influence.

Most theories of L2 development assume that the L1 grammar has some influence on the L2, usually referred to as **L1 transfer**. The extent and nature of L1 influence will vary along factors such as the lexical or

4.2 Landmarks of L2 Grammatical Development

grammatical similarity of the L2 to the L1, how typologically close the languages are, and the relative complexity of L1 and L2 constructions, among other factors. It would, nevertheless, be logical to expect that, all else being equal, L1 influence on L2 knowledge and performance is stronger at the initial stages of L2 acquisition than at higher proficiency levels. One way of capturing this intuition is to assume that, in principle, the L1 grammar is the starting point of L2 grammatical learning. In effect, the grammatical structure of the L1 becomes the foundation which needs to be restructured to accommodate the second language (Schwartz & Sprouse's, 1996, Full Transfer Hypothesis).

While this is widely accepted in SLA study, some variations to the core idea have been proposed. It has been argued that the new grammar grows only from the core lexical categories to begin with. So, for example, verb phrases will initially only include lexically 'contentful' verbs and later, gradually develop functional elements such as auxiliary verbs, agreement and inflection (Vainikka & Young-Scholten's, 2011, Organic Grammar), a process argued to occur both in L1 child and L2 adult acquisition. This still predicts transfer in L2 acquisition, but in a much more restricted fashion. If learners at the L2 initial state only form utterances using lexical categories such as nouns and verbs, they can transfer the properties of these categories from L1 to L2, but not other more grammatical properties. As an illustration, languages vary as to whether an object noun comes before or after its verb (OV vs VO), which is a property that can be transferred as it involves the ordering of lexical nouns and verbs. But a property which involves other types of morphosyntactic category, e.g. tense or aspect, would not be transferred, and not produced at the initial state. This is supported by evidence that learners at the initial state do not produce verb endings or auxiliary verbs which indicate tense/aspect distinctions.

While this restricted initial state may seem reasonable when we consider the actual output of very beginning learners, there is evidence that seems to show that when there is transfer, everything transfers. But how can this be established, especially in those very early stages when learners struggle to express even the simplest of statements? The logic is this: if your grammar can only accommodate lexical categories, then producing or interpreting sentences which depend on more complicated syntactic architecture would be impossible. However, if you transfer all of the syntactic structure, you will be able to exploit the L1 grammar to interpret, and perhaps produce, more complex structures like questions. In this case, though, your performance will have the telltale signs of L1 influence. Of course, if our concern is to define what the initial state is, one needs to address the difficult question of how to actually capture data at the initial state. Recognising the difficulty that early learners have with producing language, Grüter (2006) and Grüter and Conradie (2006) investigated transfer properties on the basis of how learners of L2 German comprehend wh-questions. In order to be able to claim that the research covered the initial state period, the selection of learners was carefully controlled to ensure they had only twenty to thirty hours of exposure to German in the classroom. As the learners could not yet produce complex German sentences, they were deemed to be as close to the initial state as it is possible to test. The learners were tested on their interpretation of wh-questions such as in (1) and (2).

(1) Was beißt die Katze?
what bites the cat?
Meaning = EITHER what is biting the cat? OR what is the cat biting?

(2) Was hat die Katze gebissen?
what has the cat bitten?
Meaning = EITHER what has bitten the cat? OR what has the cat bitten?

As indicated by the word-by-word gloss, the English exact-word equivalent of (1) is a subject question, while in (2) it is an object question because English signals this meaning difference through word order. In German, by contrast, the word order difference is irrelevant for how to interpret the sentences, with case marking on subjects and objects indicating interpretation instead (see Case in Point 4.2). However, Grüter intentionally chose noun phrases which do not carry case because they have feminine or neuter determiners, which do not change form, making these questions completely ambiguous. For example, (1) can be understood to mean *which thing is the cat biting*, just as well as *which thing is biting the cat*. When German speakers were asked to answer such questions on the basis of pictures showing animals biting each other, their answers showed that they found the questions ambiguous. By contrast, the L1 English-speakers interpreted (1) as a subject question and (2) as an object question. An explanation for this would be that they use their full English grammar to attempt to comprehend German; the German input is filtered through the English grammar and so English-influenced answers are the result. Added to this for comparison, the same test was taken by L1 Afrikaans-speaking beginning learners of German because Afrikaans is the same as German in the relevant grammatical respects. As you might have guessed, Afrikaans-speaking learners behaved like the German speakers, allowing ambiguous interpretations.

4.2 CASE IN POINT: CASE AND WORD ORDER CUES

In earlier Cases in Point, we saw that languages exploit different strategies to indicate who does what to whom in terms of connections between arguments and verbs. One such strategy is case marking. English does not have cases on noun phrases and uses word order as a cue for sentence processing: a noun coming immediately before a verb is interpreted as the agent of the action, allowing (i) to mean something different to (ii).

(i) The dog bites the boy.
(ii) The boy bites the dog.

German, by contrast, uses case marking to indicate the function of nouns, and word order is highly flexible. Even though the word order in sentences (iii) and (iv) mirrors the English sentences, the interpretation in German does not change because the case marking differentiates the agent and patient no matter where in the sentence the noun phrases appear.

(iii) **Der Hund** beißt den Junge.
the.NOM dog bite.3PS the.ACC boy
'The dog bites the boy.'

(iv) Den Junge beißt **der Hund.**
the.ACC boy bite.3PS **the.NOM dog**
'The dog bites the boy.'

The use of case marking as a cue is not always completely straightforward in language. In German, while case is usually reliable as a cue, it is sometimes necessary to rely on word order. This happens in the following example because the feminine and neuter articles do not inflect for accusative or nominative case. Even though this makes a sentence like in (v) in principle ambiguous, German-speakers will strongly favour an interpretation of the first noun in the sentence as the agent.

(v) Das Kind grüsst die Mutter.
the.NEUT child greet.3PS the.FEM mother
'The child greets the mother.'

Semantic plausibility also actively affects interpretation, with our experience of the world leading to certain expectations about the prototypical agent of different actions. When 'real world' expectations and grammatical cues are in conflict, we can have difficulty in comprehension. In (vi) a first noun word order tendency combines with a real world expectation to cause conflict with the actual form which is case-marked as object. Such conflict may lead even a monolingual German-speaker to misinterpret this and assume that the dog bit the child.

(vi) Den Hund beißt das Kind.
 the.ACC dog bite.3PS the.NEUT child
 'The child bites the dog.'

When learning a new language, this difficulty can be made even more acute if the cues learners are used to relying on in their dominant language are different to the language being learned (see Bates & MacWhinney, 1987, and much subsequent work in the Competition Model; see also Case in Point 4.5 on garden path sentences).

4.2.2 The Middle Stages

It seems that, at least at the initial state, the L1 can act like a filter on the target language input, resulting in transfer errors. While we have illustrated this in terms of comprehension, this has been shown to hold for production as well (Klein & Perdue, 1997). Overcoming this filtering effect in subsequent stages of acquisition poses a more or less intricate problem depending on the grammatical structures and languages involved. As we have seen in a range of instances throughout this book, different languages express the same possible range of grammatical concepts by choosing differently from the palette of morphosyntactic or lexical features that a particular language makes available. Where the L1 and L2 express a similar concept using different features, or where a particular feature is present in one language but not in the other, restructuring the L2 grammar in response to patterns in the input, and overcoming the filtering effect of the L1 can prove difficult. Language acquisition researchers have cast this as a problem of 'feature reassembly' (Lardiere, 2009), an approach which relies on a technical term called a 'feature' within linguistics. For our purposes, a feature can be equated with our notion of grammatical concept, with difficulty arising when there is need for reassembly of grammatical concepts to form the patterns required by the target language (see Case in Point 4.3).

We can see then that the grammatical concepts of existence and interrogation are perfectly expressible in both Korean and English (and all other languages in some form or another). However, the way

4.3 CASE IN POINT: INTERROGATION AND EXISTENCE

English and Korean provide an interesting comparison, illustrating the potential complexity that can arise when grammatical concepts combine. English and Korean each uses a slightly different combination of lexical and grammatical properties to express existential versus interrogative concepts.

The languages share a similar paradigm of words which are used to form questions. Linguists have become used to calling these 'wh-words' due to the form that question words take in English: *who, what, when, where, why*. Many languages share this set of related words, in Korean these are *nwukwu, mues, encey, eti, ettehkey*, respectively. In both English and Korean, these question words are used to refer to the unknown person, thing, time, place, or reason being asked about, as illustrated with *what* / *mues* in (i) and (ii).

(i) What did Mary buy?
(ii) Mary-nun **mues**-ul sal-ass-umni-**ka**.
 Mary-TOP **what**-ACC buy-PST-POL-**Q** Korean
 'What did Mary buy?'

In English, an interrogative grammatical concept is an inherent property of these words; as such they always carry an interrogative force to do with seeking information. For example, in the declarative sentence (iii), the interrogative nature of *what* means that there is a reference to some entity, but we don't know what that entity is.

(iii) John knows **what** Mary bought.

In addition to having a word that means 'what', Korean forms questions by including an interrogative particle on the verb, *-ka* in (ii). But the word *mues* in Korean does not have inherent interrogative meaning by itself. We can know this because even though both sentences contain *mues*, the second sentence, (v) has an existential meaning. The interrogative force in (iv) is assumed to be a result of the question particle *ci*, not *mues*.

(iv) John-un Mary-ka **mues**-ul sassnun-**ci** an-ta.
 John-TOP Mary-NOM **'thing'**-ACC bought-**Q** know- DECL
 = John knows **what** Mary bought.
(v) John-un Mary-ka **mues**-ul sass-ta-ko an-**ta**.
 John-TOP Mary-NOM **'thing'**-ACC bought-DECL know-**DECL**
 = John knows that Mary bought **something**.

Notice in the English translation that existential meaning is encoded by a different grammatical structure and choice of word to refer to the unknown entity (*something* instead of *what*).

this difference is realised may cause potential problems for speakers of one language learning the other. For English speakers accustomed to interrogation being distinguished from declaration and existence by changes in word choice and order, the import of morphological difference in Korean may present a learnability issue. Choi and Lardiere (2006) tested this by investigating how intermediate-proficiency learners of Korean whose L1 was English comprehended sentences like (iv) versus (v). They found that learners could understand the meaning of (iv) better than (v). That is, their grammar treats the Korean term *mues* like the English *what* and so requires the question interpretation. The learners' grammars do not take into account the presence of the question versus declarative morpheme to create distinct meanings.

We can see a continued filtering effect of L1 grammatical and lexical properties in this case. In the learners' grammar, *mues* has been identified with *what* and thus it permits expression of only the grammatical concepts that *what* would allow. It has been suggested that issues of L2 grammatical restructuring are likely to be particularly acute in precisely these contexts which require knowledge and use of morphology to derive differences in meaning. Slabakova (2008) refers to this as the Bottleneck Hypothesis, noting that the bundling of complex grammatical concepts and meaning distinctions into morphemes seems to induce a bottleneck in L2 learning that is difficult to overcome. Everyone has access to the set of virtually possible grammatical concepts, but learning how these concepts are grammatically realised can be frustratingly difficult. Many studies have shown that mapping between concepts and their morphosyntactic expression is a persistent challenge for learners (see range of studies reviewed by Slabakova, 2008).

For some learners, this becomes an area of **fossilisation**, with no change for specific areas of grammar no matter how hard one tries. It appears as though fossilisation can occur at any point along the path of grammatical development, one clear fundamental difference between L1 and L2 development. The L1 child's ultimate attainment in grammatical competence reaches that of the ambient language speech community (though as explored in Chapter 3, there is also constrained variation in a range of ways). By contrast, adult learners of foreign languages will typically reach a plateau in their competence at a level which is more or less different from the norms of the target language speech community, and there is typically substantial variation in these levels between individual L2 learners. Klein and Perdue's view is that significant numbers of learners remain fossilised at the

4.2 Landmarks of L2 Grammatical Development

basic variety level. Whatever the level of the plateau, all L2 learners seem to experience 'a permanent cessation of … learning before [attaining target language] norms at all levels of linguistic structure' (Selinker & Lamendella, 1978, p. 187).

Turning now to the end point of acquisition, we see that it presents similar chicken-and-egg issues as the initial state. Just because a learner has not shown evidence of development for some time, should we completely rule out the possibility that there may be a change just around the corner? In practice, the end-state or point of ultimate attainment for L2 learning of particular grammatical properties is applied to learners who show no evidence of change in their knowledge/performance with respect to the property over an extended period of time. Other aspects of language will of course continue to change over an entire lifetime, both for L1 and L2 speakers. We can always learn new words and phrases and idioms or modify how we write or speak, learning to use new and unfamiliar genres.

4.2.3 The Advanced End-State

Since we have seen that L2 grammatical development may cease at any point during acquisition, the end-state cannot be automatically equated with advanced proficiency. That said, in the SLA literature, end-state research refers to research on speakers who, in their end-state of grammatical stability, are highly proficient, and seemingly L1-like. In common with the other concepts we have encountered, any conceptual definition of L1-like is not simple. In practice, researchers interested in studying this very advanced level of proficiency do so by choosing learners who achieve scores on standardised proficiency tests which fall within the range of those for whom the language is an L1. Additionally, there is sometimes a process of testing whether the speaker can 'pass' as an L1 speaker in interactions, as judged by interlocutors. However, what has been found is that even for those rare L2 learners who do make it to extremely advanced, L1-like levels of proficiency, there will still be areas of their linguistic knowledge and performance which diverge when compared to monolingual speakers of the target language.

What's interesting is that learners who achieve these measures still show linguistic traces which differ from L1 speakers in terms of both knowledge and performance. One such trace is the continued occurrence of types of **residual optionality** whereby speakers choose to use forms which are perfectly grammatical in the L2, but which just are not the way most L1 speakers would choose to express the same thing. This type of 'optionality' has been shown to be a common phenomenon amongst L2 speakers (Sorace, 2008). In other words, the grammatical mechanism used to express a particular grammatical concept is within the range of the morphosyntactic options provided by the L2, so not grammatically 'wrong', but when studied and measured by linguists, L2 speakers are found to use mechanisms that are much less frequently used by L1 speakers. One example comes from variation with respect to subject realisation and word order, which has been extensively studied within end-state research. We have already encountered the formal grammatical property of null subjects. The option to miss out the subject pronoun is a feature of a number of languages. Many null subject languages also allow overt subjects to occur either before or after the verb. Research shows that learners readily come to know that a subject pronoun does not have to be pronounced, and that overt subjects can be placed after the verb (Ayoun, 2005, ch. 5). However, even if learners quickly establish that this is possible, knowing when it is appropriate to include the subject pronoun or not, and when it is more natural for the subject to come before or after the verb, remains more elusive (see Case in Point 4.4).

Research on L2 Italian has shown that English speakers who have attained an L1-like level of Italian, including mastery of the grammar of null subjects, continue to use and comprehend subjects in ways that are pragmatically strange in Italian. L1 English speakers who are highly integrated, fully immersed members of the Italian community will tend to give the (a) answers to the sorts of questions outlined in Case in Point 4.4 – patterns which mirror English properties of including subject pronouns and placing subjects before verbs (Sorace, 2008, p. 140). This sort of variation on the part of the L2 speakers does not show any shortcoming in their Italian grammar in the 'form' sense. There is nothing grammatically wrong in their utterances in terms of the form of the sentence; it is just that these speakers have produced an utterance which sounds pragmatically odd to Italian ears. Interestingly, issues with subject production and placement also affect L1 Italian speakers who have lived in an English-speaking environment for extended periods and have attained very advanced proficiency in English as an L2. Their performance in their native, but less activated language, Italian, comes to resemble that of very advanced speakers of Italian as an L2 (Sorace, 2008).

The phenomenon of residual optionality and research at the end-state of L2 acquisition raise some interesting questions. For one thing, it takes us out of the realm of grammar and grammaticality in a strict sense. From a purely 'grammatical rule' perspective, we would say the speakers discussed here have fully acquired the grammar. But we can

4.4 CASE IN POINT: NULL SUBJECTS AND INFORMATION STRUCTURE

The null-subject phenomenon is a feature of grammar in which the morphosyntactic properties of the language allow sentences without subjects. In addition, these languages allow subjects, when they are pronounced, to occur before or after the verb. The choice between these options is regulated by pragmatics with discourse context and information-structure defining which types of subject are more or less appropriate in particular contexts. This is illustrated in Italian. In (i), the context of a question which names a specific agent allows the option of leaving the subject referring to this agent unspoken. In (ii), an open question which requires mention of a new referent allows the subject phrase to be placed after the verb (from Sorace, 2008, p. 140).

(i) Perchè Lucia non ha preso le chiavi?
    why   Lucia NEG has take her keys
    'Why didn't Lucia take her keys?'
    a. Perchè **lei** pensava di trovarti a casa.
       Because **she** thought she would find you at home.
    b. Perchè __ pensava di trovarti a casa.
       Because __ thought she would find you at home.

(ii) Che cosa è successo?
    'What happened?'
    a. Paola ha telefonato.
       Paola has telephoned.
    b. Ha telefonato Paola.
       Has telephoned Paola.

Even though both the (a) and (b) answers are *grammatically* possible, only the (b) answers without overtly stated subjects are pragmatically natural in Italian. The question in (i) establishes Lucia as the topic of conversation and the response does not require reference to any new topic, so including the pronoun *lei* sounds redundant to Italian speakers. An answer to question (ii) requires introducing a new referent. Italian most naturally does this by placing a new subject after the verb. The (a) answer would require some special context, such as the speaker expressing surprise that Paola should have phoned.

---

see that in the realm of context-dependent use of grammar, there are differences, and this is documented in a range of similar contexts where structures are found to be grammatically accurate but odd in context (e.g. Bohnacker & Rosén, 2008; Verheijen et al., 2013).

Additionally, we see that the two languages of L2 learners seem to have reached a status where they are affecting each other in both directions! This is all less surprising when one returns to contemporary understanding of cognitive processes. If there is a shared set of cognitive processes for Language, with ability to draw from one's cognitive store of Language depending on those aspects which are more entrenched and enjoy higher resting levels as a result of regular activation, then these findings are less surprising.

For language education, this tells us that at advanced levels, we are dealing very much in the realm of use, and not 'grammar' in the old-fashioned 'rule' sense. This is hardly news. But having empirical research to add specific examples is useful to illustrate those areas of L2 performance which are likely to remain stubbornly 'not wrong but not quite right' (Martinez Garcia & Wulff, 2012, p. 225). And perhaps more importantly, this tells us that even formal linguists say we should rethink both the ultimate aim of foreign language teaching and the nature of the target. In terms of the aim, this research endorses the move away from heavy focus on grammar at advanced levels, toward greater focus on use in context. Our experience is that teachers know this, but that many advanced level students keep asking for grammar, perhaps thinking that more 'rules' provide concrete answers when their interactions don't seem to be quite 'right'. We suggest that one way to combat this is if language education included more explicit understanding of the nature of language – from the beginning of learning a new language, as well as in L1 language education curricula. The grammatical realisation of meaning (i.e. grammatical concepts) and correct use of language is relevant in every grammar lesson even in beginner classes. And at all levels, we would hope that recognising the interplay between languages in our mind is embraced and celebrated in our increasingly interconnected world. But this is taking us away from our focus. We will return to these points in the next chapter, but move now to explore more ways in which we see L2 development as fundamentally similar to the L1.

4.3 ADDITIONAL LANGUAGE LEARNING: FUNDAMENTALLY SIMILAR?

In the previous discussion, we have seen that there are a number of ways in which L2 learning seems to be very different from L1 learning, not least because the starting point and social context for L2 learning are necessarily very different compared to infants acquiring their L1. This is the case whether the additional language learning is taking

4.3 Additional Language Learning: Fundamentally Similar?

place in a classroom or in some kind of immersion setting. In this section, we are not trying to deny or negate these obvious differences, but we want to explore some phenomena of first language acquisition to challenge any strong position that it is *totally* different because we want to show you how recognising parallels could be helpful. We are concerned that 'difference' and 'foreignness' itself creates an unhelpful barrier for the teaching and learning of language, especially with learner engagement if the language to be learned is assumed to be alien and difficult. Thus, we will try to convince you that consideration of the two contexts for language development reveals some useful points.

Research on child language acquisition has given rise to a rich body of literature from each of the form and function ends of the linguistics spectrum, as well as every point in between. We are not interested in reviewing that extensive literature, but rather to explore some of the core ideas from child first language acquisition research, in order to consider L1 and L2 development. A good starting point is the inherent ability for language which is unique to humans. As we have illustrated throughout, language allows humans an ability to go beyond the basic level of communication found amongst a range of animals. Our starting point here is that when considering L2 language development we should bear in mind the nature of language itself. The 'target' language is itself an idealisation, and as such doesn't change whether you are a first or additional speaker of it. We will explore this notion of Virtual Grammar more in this section.

Let's look at an example that illustrates some of these concepts. The example given in (3) shows a very well documented type of developmental, a so-called overgeneralisation 'error'.

(3) I maked it with water.   (Sarah 4 years 5months, from Brown, 1973)

You will immediately recognise what Sarah has done. We have put scare quotes around 'error' because it reveals a positive level of development in Sarah's grammar. From this example we know that at age four years and five months, Sarah can distinguish between verb forms as stems (e.g. *make*) and affixes that are attached to stems (*-ed*). She has very logically made use of the English grammatical past tense morpheme to indicate that the time reference of her action is in the past, and applied it to the verb stem *make* to create a past tense form. That this particular verb does not act in a logical way is not Sarah's fault. Irregular 'exceptions to the rule' are commonplace in language. While the utterance may be 'off-target', it is not an error if one is looking for evidence that Sarah has developed knowledge of the regular pattern for past tense marking in English.

Could Sarah's utterance be a product of input? While the mature speakers around her would not have said this, perhaps others in her playgroup have and she is just repeating it? The very large number of documented examples like this in the L1 acquisition literature, and the fact that Sarah will 'outgrow' this stage of development lead to the conclusion that there is more going on here. We will return to these points in the rest of this section, doing so with additional language learning in mind, to explore how, from a cognitive perspective, the nature of language and the ability for language development are both natural human phenomena, regardless of whether one is six months, six years or sixty years old.

4.3.1 The Language Instinct, Virtual Grammar and Language Learning

Infants do not learn language solely by memorising a store of utterances they have been exposed to and parroting them back (though young children can be impressively repetitive at times!). The example from Sarah illustrates that there is an element of creativity underlying language acquisition when some, but not all, of the constraints on a language have been acquired. While the idea that humans come pre-programmed for language remains controversial in some quarters (see Sampson, 2005), the fact that all children develop language is not, barring of course some pathological or excessively abusive barrier. In Steven Pinker's (1996) famous phrase, humans come equipped with a 'language instinct'. A Virtual Grammar perspective shares the spirit of the instinct idea. It sees all humans as having wants, intentions and needs, all of which can connect into Language. All languages express concepts through words. In addition, Language also contains a set of grammatical concepts, such as definiteness, association, politeness, among others. We have seen that there is a wonderfully wide range of ways any single language can use the core grammatical mechanisms of Language to express grammatical concepts. While some languages make extensive use of morphology with affixes expressing an array of grammatical concepts, others rely more on the ordering of words (i.e. syntax), while others make much heavier use of the immediate context (i.e. pragmatics). That all languages use all three of these grammatical mechanisms to express grammatical concepts is divorced from whether one is learning a language as an infant or an adult; as such, it is one fundamental similarity which you as a teacher may be able to exploit in your teaching.

4.3 Additional Language Learning: Fundamentally Similar?

One reason for the view of a preprogrammed instinct for language is research showing that tiny babies immediately key into aspects of the linguistic environment. As a number of findings from cognitive science research illustrate: newborn babies prefer listening to human speech over artificial speech analogues; babies can discriminate between the rhythms of unfamiliar languages; and they can detect word and phrase boundaries in speech. For details on this sort of research, see Gervain (2018), who writes that '[h]uman infants are born linguistic citizens of the world' (p. 62). The human instinct to perceive and pay attention to the rhythm of human language as distinct from other auditory stimuli means that babies and toddlers can use what is known as prosody, to start to analyse the speech stream into its lexical and grammatical components. The use of prosody to identify word/phrase boundaries, known as **prosodic bootstrapping**, allows young children to syntactically parse input. It has been shown, for example, that children use prosodic marking to differentiate between syntactically ambiguous phrases (de Carvalho et al., 2016).

Prosodic bootstrapping cannot explain the acquisition of the full range of grammatical properties that are eventually acquired. But one reason why a mechanism like prosody is useful is that a string of words may have different syntactic structures. This is illustrated in (4) and (5) in which one simple set of words in English, *the + baby + flies*, can add up to two very different grammatical structures, and thus meanings. Whether a young child, a teenager or elderly adult, when we hear language we have to incorporate – on a millisecond-by-millisecond basis – incoming sounds, and build them into morphemes, words, phrases, and ultimately as hierarchical syntactic structures. This is a formidable task which is subject to some margin of error as we have to rely on quite subtle cues in order to build appropriate structures. In the examples here, it is a prosodic break after *the baby* in (4) that marks this constituent as the subject of the sentence, in contrast to (5) where the subject is *flies*, which happen to be baby ones. While the difference is shown in the notation, if you say the two sentences out loud, you will notice the prosodic break and the point will be clear.

(4) [the baby]NP [flies]$_V$ his kite all day long.

(5) [the [baby]ADJ flies]] NP hide in the shadows.

The way this works is that as part of cognition, the language parser is primed to expect a verb. Because *flies* is ambiguous, potentially acting as

4.5 CASE IN POINT: GARDEN PATHS

Our minds have to segment and structure the stream of sounds which flood into our ears. The human mind includes a parser which is dedicated to the task of building a grammatical structure for the input stream. Usually the parser works so efficiently behind the scenes that we take it for granted. However, we have all experienced the feeling of misinterpreting a sentence because we have misparsed it, or misconstrued song lyrics, for example.

Psycholinguists can exploit this tendency in the lab to test how the human mind constructs a syntactic structure using what's known as garden path sentences, as in (i) and (ii)

(i) The horse raced past the barn fell.
(ii) The old man the boat.

You are likely to stumble over these sentences while reading. This is because in each case, the likely parse of the start of each sentence turns out to be the wrong one for the sentence as a whole. In (i), *the horse raced* is a likely noun–verb structure: *horses* are often the agent of the verb *to race*. On encountering the word *past*, the parser can continue to build a verb phrase, anticipating the noun indicating what the horse went past. *The barn* is a suitable complement and the parser can rest, having assigned a structure to the sentence. However, what to do with *fell*? This cannot be incorporated into the grammatical structure: the parser has been led up the garden path. In this case, the parser needs to send the sentence for **reanalysis** in order to discover the real structure, which is a reduced relative clause: *the horse **that was** raced past the barn fell.*

In a foreign language, we are faced with greater potential to be misled up the grammatical garden path. For example, as noted earlier, case in German is a cue for interpreting subject/object function, while word order is the relevant cue in English. English speakers learning German experience problems parsing sentences which rely on case, as in (iii).

(iii) Welche Ingeneurin hat der / den Chemiker gestern Nachmittag getroffen?
which-FEM engineer has the-NOM/ACC chemist yesterday afternoon met
'Which engineer did the chemist meet yesterday afternoon?' (NOM case)
'Which engineer met the chemist yesterday afternoon?' (ACC case)

4.3 Additional Language Learning: Fundamentally Similar?

> In line with the word order tendency in English, English-speakers learning German initially parse the first noun they encounter as the subject. Where they encounter nominative case later in the sentence, the parser needs to reanalyse the first noun as an object, a task which learners struggle with (see Jackson, 2007, 2008).

a verb or a noun, something else is needed to disambiguate it. A prosodic signal after *the baby* in (4) leads the language parser to assign the preceding phrase as the noun phrase subject. All of this happens almost instantaneously and without conscious awareness. Pre-school children who hear these sorts of prosodically differentiated strings can reliably make sense of the sentence in a grammatically appropriate way, recognising that what follows the subject in (4) is a verbal complement. Similarly, the absence of a prosodic break after *baby* will lead to a parse of the initial three words with *flies* as the head of the noun phrase as in (5), and the remaining words as the verbal predicate explaining what the baby flies did. Such perceptual abilities are understood to provide inroads into grammar for infants. As a teacher of a language like English which makes use of prosodic cues, you can appeal to the human ability for parsing, perhaps exaggerating the prosodic breaks in your speech to help your learners. We suspect that you do this naturally, as a responsive teacher. Knowing about it explicitly may encourage you to do it more intentionally with more explicitly useful effect.

A different suggestion in working with additional language learners has been to purposefully teach **formulaic sequences** or phrases without focussing on the grammatical material within (Myles, 2012; Wray, 2002). For example, a phrase taught very early like 'I'm a student', contains the auxiliary verb *to be* in its first person singular form, attached to the nominative pronoun so as to be pronounced /m/. The point from a 'formulaic sequences' point of view is that it would be inadvisable to explain all this to an early learner, but instead to encourage use of '*I'm a ...*' as a useful chunk which can be attached to a number of nouns in order for one to identify oneself. This way of thinking parallels the first language context, which also prioritises meaning and tends to focus on lexical items with young language users. Teaching chunks of language allows learners to immediately express themselves, and allows the grammatical detail within a chunk to be discounted until later when learners are at a stage when making sense of the grammar is more fruitful. However, it is important that learners do not get 'stuck' with formulaic sequences in a way that sees them over-applying them incorrectly. Myles et al. (1998) find that in L2 French classes, frequently taught chunks tend to be used in an unanalysed way in inappropriate contexts. For example, a chunk such as *j'aime*, the elided form of *je aime* (=*I like*), is retained when learners try to refer to second or third person subjects, as in (6), from Myles et al. (1998, p. 335). If you find teaching formulaic sequences useful in a particular context, you could make explicit use of prosody to indicate the boundaries of the chunk, and think about how the chunk will ultimately need to be decomposed in order to acquire the relevant grammatical properties which have been chunked together for phraseological ease.

(6) Richard j'aime le musée.
 Literally: Richard I like the museum.
 Intended: Richard likes museums = Richard aime le musée.

This discussion of language development leads us to suggest that there are interesting ways to exploit differences in oral versus literacy skills in L2 classrooms, to appeal to cognitive abilities for language which we know are robust in L1 acquisition. Providing useful set phrases and chunks will be helpful for speaking skills by allowing learners to communicate effectively in certain communicative situations. However, unlike children acquiring their L1, L2 learners might then over-rely on such set phrases, privileging communicative effectiveness over grammatical accuracy in context. Using written forms could prove useful in breaking the target language into its grammatical components, for example by highlighting the *j'* in the chunk *j'aime* discussed. The relevant point is that L2 learners will often have literacy skills that can be exploited in addition to simply listening to and speaking the target language. But this does not mean that one should rely too much on either oral or literacy skills; each will have a potentially useful role to play in L2 grammar learning.

Given the complexity of language, the ability of very young children to parse and produce any utterance in the language they are exposed to has led many experts to agree that there must be some genetic endowment in humans with some degree of underlying grammatical structure which allows them to develop language. This genetic endowment is the assumed biological basis for what we have designated as Virtual Grammar. Imagine an extra-terrestrial encounter with a hypothetical Martian linguist sent to study how Earthlings communicate. Virtual Grammar sees all languages of the Earth as dialects of a single universal 'Humanese', with commonalities which could be discerned by our ever-clever Martian linguist. One of these

4.3 Additional Language Learning: Fundamentally Similar?

commonalities is the hierarchical and structure-dependent nature of human language. If there were no hierarchical structure-dependent blueprint for the syntax of human language, the potential number of grammatical rules would proliferate and likely undermine the relatively effortless and swift acquisition of language by children. Indeed, research shows that children never entertain rules which violate structure-dependent hierarchies in language even if they are logically possible. An example of a logical rule independent of structure would be if the order of words was based on linear ordering instead of structure. A famous example, often cited in the research, is the problem of question formation in an English complex clause with two auxiliaries. In Chapter 2 we explored how question formation is structure dependent, and not based on a structure-independent rule such as logical linear ordering.

Similar subtleties can be seen to be at work in the acquisition of so-called floating numerals in Japanese (see Case in Point 4.6). A not-so-clever Martian faced with sentences such as (7) and (8), might appeal to a simple linear ordering rule rather than hierarchical structure, unlike Japanese children, and assume that the numeral associates with the closest noun. If this were the case, they would be mistaken, expecting that (8) means there are two frogs, when in fact both sentences have the same meaning, with two mice being the unfortunate target of frog-violence.

(7) Kaeru-ga **nezumi-o** **ni-hiki** tatakimasita.
 frog-NOM **mouse-ACC** **two-CL** hit
 'A frog hit two mice.'

(8) Nezumi-o **kaeru-ga** **ni-hiki** tatakimasita.
 mouse-ACC **frog-NOM** **two-CL** hit
 'A frog hit two mice.'

Studies of Japanese pre-school children's interpretation of such sentences on the basis of picture choices show that they are sensitive to the hierarchical distinctions, making appropriate interpretations using structure-dependent rules rather than linear order (Suzuki & Yoshinaga, 2013). And this is despite evidence in the form of the relevant distinctions being vanishingly rare in the utterances typically directed at children (Sugisaki, 2016, p. 86). (For explanation of how these examples rely on hierarchical distinctions, see Case in Point 4.6.)

Structure dependence aids the creative construction of grammar, and thus helps to explain how an infant builds an infinite system out of the finite and often messy language input s/he receives, and of course, this

4.6 CASE IN POINT: FLOATING QUANTIFIERS

A floating quantifier is one (like *all* in English) that is separated from the noun phrase which it modifies. The float metaphor implies that the quantifier is floating freely somewhere else in the clause detached from its noun.

(i) **All the children** are laughing.
(ii) **The children** are **all** laughing.

However, they aren't really floating free. They are subject to hierarchical grammatical structure which defines when and where they can occur. In Japanese, numeral quantifiers (two, three, four) may also float. The basic word order in Japanese means that a number phrase always comes after its noun, and the basic order of constituents in a clause is Subject-Object-Verb (SOV), as in (iii) and (iv).

(iii) **Gakusee-ga   san-nin**   hon-o   katta.
      student-NOM   three-CL   book-ACC   bought
      'Three students bought a book.'

(iv) Gakusee-ga   **hon-o**   **san-satu**   katta.
     student-NOM book-ACC   three-CL   bought
     'A student bought three books.'

But because Japanese word order is free, rearranging the constituents so that an object comes first can result in the numeral floating separately from the noun it modifies, as shown in (v). However, the numeral cannot float away from a subject in SOV structures, as illustrated by the ungrammaticality of (vi).

(v) **Hon-o**   gakusee-ga   **san-satu**   katta.
    book-ACC   student-NOM three-CL   bought
    'A student bought three books.'

(vi) *****Gakusee-ga**   hon-o   **san-nin**   katta.
     student-NOM   book-ACC   three-CL   bought
     'Three students bought a book.'

This asymmetry is the result of the rearrangement of subject and object from specific *hierarchical* positions, not just a linear rule that the numeral has to stay beside its NP.

applies to all languages, and a whole range of constructions, not just English questions and Japanese floating numerals (see Crain & Thornton, 1998). That structure dependence is a feature of language means that

4.3 Additional Language Learning: Fundamentally Similar?

structure violation is less likely by L2 learners as well. For example, as is true for young children acquiring English, it is not a normal feature or stage of language development for a learner of English to form a complex yes/no question by placing the wrong auxiliary at the front of the question to say, for example, *Is the lunch that on the table is yours?* To incorrectly retain the auxiliary in the main clause instead of the subordinate clause violates structure dependence in English in a way that makes this very unlikely. Of course, this sentence is pronounceable, and anyone is capable of a one-off slip, which is why we use the term **mistake** as opposed to error in language development. It is worth bearing in mind that mistakes happen to all speakers in writing and speech and in both their first and 'last' languages! We will return to the idea of targeted feedback in the next section, in the context of language input more generally. As a language teacher, it may be useful to make use of the distinction between errors and mistakes to help you be more focussed in your efforts, and in feedback and correction in particular.

4.3.2 Language Input

In line with much of the research in first language acquisition, we have emphasised the innate ability of very young children, but even the most nativist of research orientations recognise that there is a crucial role for 'nurture' as well. The advent of computational modelling has allowed an additional tool for considering distributions of linguistic properties in the input. The challenge is coming to grips with the intricate interplay between 'nature' and 'nurture' (see Yang, 2002, for a nativist perspective). Even if there are abstract in-built expectations for the possible structure of human language, ultimately arriving at a grammar which conforms to the parameters of the language found in the speech community requires exposure to and interaction within that community. Beyond the difficulty of weighing up nature and nurture, the study of 'nurture' is far from straightforward. Consider the fact that the actual set of input that an infant hears is going to vary by individual experience, as well as by social and cultural setting. There are, of course, also differences in linguistic performance amongst mature speakers who provide the input. Additionally, some children are more talkative and outgoing, and will seek differing amounts of input from their family and wider social environment. In sum, 'native' language development heavily depends on factors of context and input that exist outside of cognitive processes; and these external factors will vary widely from individual to individual. We note, however, that the wide range of variation of context and input is one area where there is core similarity in first, second and nth language development.

In child language acquisition research there is disagreement about the nature of what to count as input, as well as debate about thresholds for what is considered 'frequent' (see Legate & Yang, 2002; Pullum & Scholz, 2002). The challenge of characterising input is one more reason for the emphasis on the outcome in which (healthy) children develop the grammar of the ambient speech community despite divergent input experiences. While no child develops a grammar that cannot license a passive sentence, or which cannot produce case assignment, we saw earlier with the example of *maked*, that children do overgeneralise. When children learning English produce something like *I maked it with water* or *I catched the ball*, they are overgeneralising the past-tense rule to an irregular verb. This linguistically sophisticated 'error' is related to frequency in that the child will have met lots of examples of verbs that follow the regular rule for past tense. Of particular relevance to the phenomenon of overgeneralisation is the human predisposition to categorise and pattern match. Variation from the 'rule' by a single lexical item will require lots of occurrences of that single lexical item in the input in order to maintain its 'exceptional' status. It is logical to assume that if an exceptional rule only applies to a single word, and that word only occurs infrequently, then it will not remain exceptional over the course of language change. Because when a speaker wants to utter the word, they will match it with the pattern that applies to every other word, and this then becomes input for other speakers, who assume it is correct. This explains why a verb like *to be* can maintain highly exceptional paradigms – because it is used so often that its exceptional behaviour is reinforced. Despite these sorts of findings, it still remains somewhat unclear how retreating from overgeneralisation is possible, but the assumption is that in time there will be enough evidence in the input to force the learner to override the (very useful) general rule.

As a cognitively mature learner, the additional language learner will have a richer set of knowledge than the infant. We suggest that this can be seen as an advantage, especially for categorising and pattern matching. Indeed, traditional teaching methods have sometimes focused on patterns or 'grammar rules' to the exclusion of other aspects of language. Our perspective is not to suggest a return to traditional grammar teaching, especially since that has typically been done with a strong 'target language only' admonition. Instead, we suggest an increased recognition of the full capacity of your learners, appealing to the existing set of 'patterns' in the language(s) that they speak, and pushing learners to examine those patterns to see the abstract grammatical concepts that underlie the 'rules'. The ultimate aim is cognitive engagement which leads to forging of cognitive connections, and once linguistic connections are made, a strong reinforcement through activation which helps the connections to become cognitively stable. All this, however, must be done with a caution not to rely too heavily on apparent patterns. An impressively intricate example comes from plural formation with German nouns (see Case in Point 4.7). The absence of clear-cut rules for which noun takes which plural led Mark Twain to characterise the 'horrors of the German language' for L2 learners. Attempting simply to describe the patterns of plural formation results in ten grammatical rules with fifteen lists of exceptions (Marcus et al. 1995, appendix 2, based on Mugdan, 1977).

4.7 CASE IN POINT: NUMBER AND FORMS OF PLURAL

German instantiates only singular and plural forms of number as a grammatical concept, but the encoding of plural is highly complex. Five morphological endings can be added to nouns to form a plural, illustrated in (i) to (v). In the first three categories, the ending may be accompanied by a sound change in the noun stem (= umlaut), depending on the noun.

(i) der Apfel – die Äpfel   zero plural (with or without with umlaut)
(ii) die Hand – die Hände   -*e* plural (with or without umlaut)
(iii) das Kind – die Kind**er**   -*er* plural (with or without umlaut)
(iv) die Frau – die Frau**en**   -*(e)n* plural
(v) das Auto – die Auto**s**   -*s* plural

Interestingly, even though -*en* is the most frequently occurring plural, and thus often taught as the regular plural in German foreign language grammar, it does not seem to be the (psycho)linguistically regular rule. The -*s* plural is the one most readily applied to novel or borrowed words, as in *die Cafés*. It is characterised as the 'emergency' plural (Van Dam, 1940), which fits when others cannot apply for morphophonological reasons. It is also the default in a range of special grammatical circumstances, for instance when forming plurals from acronyms (vi), or onomatopoeic nouns (vii), among others (see Marcus et al., 1995, pp. 230–1).

(vi) GmbH – GmbH**s** (Plc's, as in 'public limited companies')
(vii) Wauwau**s** (bow-wows, as in 'doggies')

Thus, the most infrequent plural form seems nonetheless to be the regular one which can be applied most freely to new, unusual or phonologically distinct word classes, and which speakers rely on as default when other processes fail.

German plurals provide an interesting perspective on frequency, the status of rules and regularity in grammatical processes. Analysis of the different plural forms shows that more than half of nouns in German take the -*en* ending (Clahsen, 1999). It is therefore clearly the most regular plural, in the sense of frequency. But it is the much less frequent -*s* ending which is the psycholinguistically more regular plural for German speakers, a surprising finding considering that this plural marker applies to less than 7 per cent of nouns in German. We know this from speakers' performance in experimental settings. When German children are presented with rare words, the plural of which they might not know, such as (9), they tend to prefer the -*s* plural as the default. This is also the tendency both with adults and children who are presented with nonsense words (10) (Clahsen, 1999). This performance cannot simply be the case of relying on the most frequent patterns that one hears. Instead, the overgeneralisation is understood to be subject to default linguistic properties operating independently of frequency of occurrence. We see from this that even the most apparently unruly patterns of paradigms and rules are susceptible to a clear analysis when viewed from the appropriate perspective. Our contention has been that this applies to many more grammatical concepts in addition to just paradigmatic cases like plural formation.

(9) die Fassung 'the socket'
     Target plural: Most common response by children:
     Fassung**en**   Fassung**s**

(10) Fneik (nonsense   Plural preference by adults and children:
     word)   Fneik**s**

Overall, the message is that input and frequency do of course play crucial roles in language acquisition, but rarely in straightforward or simplistic ways. We should therefore not be surprised if input and frequency in the additional language context is not clear or straightforward. Having seen how wonderfully complex and varied Language is, one conclusion that some L2 researchers have come to is that some aspects of language may be more conducive to mastery through practice than others. The aforementioned Bottleneck Hypothesis, based on a large sample of L2 research argues that morphological affixes in particular pose a 'bottleneck' for L2 development. The researcher who proposed this theory has suggested that grammatical affixes are one area of language that would benefit from large amounts of targeted practice (Slabakova, 2008; 2014).

4.3 Additional Language Learning: Fundamentally Similar? 149

Another facet of language development to consider in addition to quantitative properties of the input is the qualitative nature of input. In the child first language context, adults tend to adopt a 'baby talk' register or what was originally called **motherese**. This speech register is characterised by a higher pitch, exaggerated rhythms and phonetic simplification. It also involves much repetition and relies on a degree of syntactic simplification. It might be assumed that this style of input is tailored specifically (though subconsciously) to teach language to infants. Yet well-known research examining motherese concluded that '[w]hatever constructional simplifications occur ... seem to arise for interactional reasons – as constraints on the kinds of things one talks about to children' (Newport et al., 1977, p. 145). In other words, to the extent that motherese has proscribed grammatical features, this is likely a side effect of the nature of interaction with infants rather than as a result of acting as grammar-teaching tool (though it no doubt facilitates comprehension and thus acquisition for infants).

But does this mean that caregivers cannot explicitly teach young children grammar? It has been argued that correction has some effect on recovering from errors (for evidence, see Saxton, 2000). But overall, the effect is minimal. It is worth bearing in mind that parents are themselves not conscious of their full range of complex grammatical knowledge, and so could hardly teach their toddler effectively even if inclined to. To add to the many examples of grammatical subtlety already given, consider the complexities of pronoun coreference in English: In a sentence like (11), the reflexive *himself* must refer to *Bill* and cannot refer to *John*, but in (12) the pronoun *him* may refer to *John*, or some other male referent in the discourse, but it cannot refer to *Bill*. (See also Case in Point 4.8).

(11) John said that Bill loves himself.

(12) John said that Bill loves him.

Patterns of interpretation like these pose particularly difficult acquisition problems because there is no obvious reason why this difference might exist. And use of the 'wrong' form is not ungrammatical. Instead, as a property of interpretation, if misused it is confusing or 'wrong' in terms of the validity of the statement rather than violating a grammatical rule. Adding to the complexity, sentences like (12) are ambiguous, allowing more than one 'correct' meaning, while ones like (11) are not. Imagine that caretakers know all this. You are a language teacher; did you know this? That someone will have pointed these linguistic properties out to a child in the course of their development is a bit absurd. While children seem to be able to comprehend reflexives quite easily from a very young age, there is a delay in their acquisition of the full range of pronoun interpretation, which has been attested in a range of languages. In a sentence such as (12), or equivalents in other languages, children will tend to allow *him* to refer to *Bill* roughly 50 per cent of the time. You won't be surprised to learn that careful comparisons between the properties of languages can predict areas of overlap and transfer (see Gürel, 2002, on Turkish/English bilinguals), nor that the difference in interpretation depends on hierarchical syntactic structure.

When caregivers do react to children's errors, this tends to involve semantic or pragmatic correction. In fact, concentration on meaning can easily cause one to ignore grammatically deviant forms, or even reinforce non-target grammatical patterns, as shown in the famous example given in (13) (Brown & Hanlon, 1970, p. 49).

(13) *Child*: Mama isn't boy, he a girl.
    Mother: That's right!

This does not mean caregivers don't sometimes correct their child's grammar. But another well-known facet of child development is that children often seem rather oblivious to this type of correction. The range of anecdotes in the literature include the dialogue in (14) (from McNeill, 1966, p. 69).

(14) *Child*: Nobody don't like me.
    Mother: No, say "nobody likes me."
    Child: Nobody don't like me.
    [... eight repetitions of this dialogue ...]
    Mother: No, now listen carefully, say "NOBODY LIKES ME."
    Child: Oh! Nobody don't likes me.

Because communication is the primary function of language, when corrections with young children do occur, instead of taking the form of grammatical corrections, they often come in the form of recasts or repetition (Marcus, 1993; Morgan et al., 1995). The communicative approach to adult language teaching has also meant that many language teachers opt to recast 'off-target' forms, repeating them back to the learner in a corrected form instead of interrupting an interaction in the classroom to make a grammatical correction. While the effectiveness of this approach in terms of grammatical development is difficult to measure, we would agree that when the priority is producing language and/or interaction in the classroom, a recast is more

4.8 CASE IN POINT: PRONOUN COREFERENCE

Pronouns and anaphors, such as reflexives (*themselves, oneself*) or reciprocals (*each other*), do not have independent reference. Instead, words such as *they* or *themselves* have to derive their meaning by linking to referring expressions somewhere in their linguistic vicinity (or from the context of an utterance). Linguists refer to this as coreference. Coreference may be pragmatic, linking referents in the discourse as in (i) with the pronoun *he* referring to *Bill*. Within sentences, there are grammatical constraints on coreference, which in linguistics is called binding. In (ii) *him* can only refer to *John*, while in (iii), *himself* refers to *Bill*. Notations using subscript letters (i, j, etc.) indicate these coreference facts.

(i) Mary gave Bill$_i$ a job. He$_i$ was very happy.
(ii) John$_i$ thought that Bill trusted him$_i$.
(iii) John thought that Bill$_i$ trusted himself$_i$.

The patterns in (ii) and (iii) indicate that pronouns like *him/her* behave differently compared to reflexives like *himself/herself*. In (ii), *him* cannot have coreference with the closest possible antecedent, while in (iii) *himself* must take its reference from the closest antecedent, *Bill* in each case. Together with other distributional evidence, this has led to two general principles for the distribution and interpretation of these elements across all languages:

PRINCIPLE A: a reflexive must have coreference with a local antecedent.
PRINCIPLE B: a pronoun must not have coreference with a local antecedent.

Unsurprisingly, there is constrained variability between languages. Depending on other properties in the language, defining how 'local' an antecedent is will vary and different types of interpretation will be permitted. To exemplify, Turkish has an overt third person pronoun 'o' as well as the option of a null pronoun, indicated by ___. These forms behave differently with respect to interpretation, as illustrated in the data from Gürel (2002).

(iv) Elif$_i$ Mehmet'in$_k$ o-nu$_{i/m}$ beğen-diğ-i-ni
    Elif$_i$ Mehmet-GEN$_k$ s/he-ACC$_{i/m}$ like-NOM-3SGPOSS-ACC
    söyle-di.
    say-PAST
    'Elif$_i$ said that Mehmet likes her$_i$ / him$_m$.'

(v) Elif$_i$ Mehmet'in$_k$ ___$_{i/k/m}$ beğen-diğ-i-ni   söyle-di.
    Elif$_i$ Mehmet-GEN$_k$ s/he-ACC$_{i/m}$ like-3NOM-SGPOSS-ACC   say-PAST
    'Elif$_i$ said that Mehmet likes her$_i$ / him$_{k/m}$.'

> The overt pronoun in (iv) shares similar properties to English him/her. In this case, it can only refer to Elif (=Mehmet likes Elif), or it can refer to some other third person referent not in the sentence. But 'o' cannot refer to Mehmet. By contrast, the null pronoun can.

appropriate than grammar correction. We would also point out, however, that occasionally diverting a learner's attention away from meaning to form might provide a meaningful learning experience precisely because you are redirecting the attention of the speaker. Of course, the importance of affective factors means that this, if done, should be done appropriately and not in a way that is going to demotivate the learner.

The bottom line is a need for cognitive engagement – whether implicit or explicit engagement is hotly debated with empirical support across the large body of existing research presenting a rather complex picture (see, for example, meta-analyses of published research by Norris & Ortega, 2000, and Spada & Tomita, 2010). From a linguist's point of view, this is unsurprising. A good proportion of the research seeking to determine whether explicit instruction is effective in grammar teaching has not given sufficient consideration to the linguistic properties being investigated. There is a tendency in this research to assume that different aspects of grammar are the same. This has led to claims made based on questionable assumptions, such as, for example, articles being considered equivalent to plural marking in terms of complexity (See Whong et al., 2014 for discussion). An example of a more linguistically informed piece of research on English articles has explored the role of perception for Japanese-speaking learners. Noting how difficult it is to hear articles in natural speech, Snape and Yusa (2013) trained learners to perceive them as part of article instruction, and found improvements in ways that have not previously been shown. Based both on this research, and our understanding of how language develops, we would urge you not be disheartened by the lack of clarity in current research, but instead to develop a clear pedagogical logic based on sound linguistic understanding to foster cognitive engagement with language amongst your learners – including at the level of grammar.

As the person responsible for providing input, it is worth a teacher thinking carefully both about what one takes time to correct as well as how one corrects. The increased understanding about language that you are developing as you work through this book will hopefully help you to make good decisions. There is a large and rich body of research on corrective feedback which explores the effectiveness of repetition vs clarification vs recasts. That there are no clear and directly useful results from this body of research may feel frustrating from the point of view of a teacher, but to us it is not surprising considering the rich complexity of Language which sees wonderful variation in languages, to say nothing of the level to which we currently understand the cognitive processes underlying language development and use. Our advice is that one should not be disheartened, but instead to make the most of what we do know. The best any of us can do is to modify our practices continuously based on what we know. After all, modification in light of the specific context of the particular learner(s) and teaching context is what all good teachers do all the time.

4.4 CAN LANGUAGE BE LEARNED LATER IN LIFE?

The first half of this chapter discussed the nature of L2 acquisition and whether it is fundamentally different compared to L1 acquisition. We then considered L1 acquisition in ways that allowed us to name some fundamental similarities. We will now move away from similarities and differences to consider whether language can be learned later in life. In the research literature, the answer to the question often depends on specific technical formulations of the nature of the language capacity and whether the same mechanisms are at work. We will generalise to say that some of the same mechanisms are at work, but that the different starting points for L1 and 'additional' language acquisition, as well as the different social context of each type of learning, result in outcomes which are different.

However, it will by now be clear that we do not think there are grounds to assume a total qualitative difference. Instances of difference in performance abound, but this does not mean that language learning is impossible in the sense of being fundamentally different. From an educational perspective, equating difference with a lack of success depends on our pedagogical beliefs and expectations. If our expectation is that foreign language learning should recapitulate primary language learning and result in the same sort of competence and performance, then clearly the answer is no – the same L1 development process cannot be repeated later in life. Even those learners who attain a very high level of proficiency will show continued evidence of variability in performance that is different from the (monolingual) speaker. But surely this isn't surprising given that the multilingual speaker has only one set of cognitive resources for language, regardless of how many languages and grammars s/he knows.

What makes things interesting for the researcher is that some grammatical features seemingly easy for the L1 learner, present persistent difficulties for L2 speakers, even where there is ample instruction and lots of exposure to the language. Lardiere (1998) presents evidence from intensive study of an individual Chinese-speaking user of English in an immersion setting in the USA. Lardiere collected data over a period of nine years, starting after the speaker had already lived, studied and worked in the USA for ten years. Thus, at the end of the research, the speaker had been immersed in English for almost twenty years. However, during the nine years of recording, certain apparently simple grammatical features showed little sign of change or improvement, in other words, they had fossilised. In up to 90 per cent of obligatory contexts, she did not provide agreement or tense marking on verbs in spontaneous production, as in (15).

(15) My mom also speak Mandarin.

Whether one views this as grammatically incorrect English, or as communicatively effective English, is a social or educational judgement. From a linguistic perspective, while utterances like (15) do not conform to the norms of (standard) English, it is certainly intelligible. Moreover it can be seen as a valid expression of natural language as many languages do not require the marking of tense and agreement on verbs, including some dialects of English. In other words, it is a legitimate realisation of the human language capacity.

What for us makes an interesting contrast is that some linguistically complex and far more subtle features of grammar are learnable, even without instruction. If adding third person –s to a verb in L2 English is tricky, consider the complexity involved in the potential ambiguity of sentences containing existentially quantified subject and universally quantified object phrases (see Case in Point 4.9).

Marsden (2008; 2009) studied how quantifier scope is acquired in L2 Japanese by learners with Chinese, English or Korean as their dominant L1. Ambiguity with respect to quantifier scope arises in Japanese and Korean when word-order changes lead to object-subject-verb (OSV) order, see (16a & b). By contrast, in English, the same ambiguity occurs in the basic SO word order (see Case in Point 4.9).

4.4 Can Language Be Learned Later in Life?

4.9 CASE IN POINT: QUANTIFIER SCOPE

Quantifiers are expressions which denote quantities, such as *all, every, each, some, no, many*, etc. with equivalents in other languages. The meanings of such words are difficult to define unequivocally without using logical symbols as they refer to abstract properties, but they are definable intuitively. For instance, *every* refers to all individual instances of some referent. *No* refers to the lack of some referent, as in (i) and (ii).

(i) I greeted **everyone** at the party.
(ii) There were **no** guests at the party.

Scope refers to how such expressions relate to each other. For example, (iii) is ambiguous with respect to the scope relationship between the quantified expressions. The interpretation along the lines of (a) is referred to as subject-wide scope while the (b) interpretation is known as object-wide scope.

(iii) **Someone** read **every** book.
   a. There is some person who read all the books.
   b. A different person read each of the books.

Quantification is a universal grammatical concept, but the grammar of different languages means that the scope of quantifiers and their interpretations may differ. For example, Japanese and Korean do not have the same ambiguity, with only the subject-wide scope a possible interpretation.

(iv) Dareka-ga   dono   hon-mo   yonda.   Japanese
(v) Nwukwunka-ka enu   chayk-ina ilkessta.   Korean
     Someone   every   book   read
     Interpretation: There is some person who read all the books.

(16) a. Japanese: Dono   hon-mo   dareka-ga   yonda.
     b. Korean: Enu   chayk-ina   nwukwunka-ka   ilkessta.
                  Every book   someone   read

   Possible Interpretations:
   There is some person who read all the books.
   A different person read each of the books.

Marsden wanted to know what difficulties subtle distinctions like this pose for learners of Japanese. Perhaps unsurprisingly given the similarities between Korean and Japanese, L1 Korean-speaking learners of

Japanese acquire the different interpretations quite readily. What's interesting is that even though L1 English speakers at lower proficiency levels do not seem to know the correct interpretations in Japanese, by intermediate to higher proficiency level, the English speakers grasp the interpretative differences in the different sentence types. The knowledge cannot have come from the L1, nor from the L2 input because we know that instruction in Japanese as a foreign language does not address this. What we have here instead is an example of linguistic development by L2 learners of Japanese that suggests that abstract properties of language can also be learned later in life.

In sum, we conclude that languages can indeed be learned later in life. That said, we recognise that additional language learning has distinct features. The ever-growing body of research is beginning to show that subtle meaning-based aspects of language seem to develop even without instruction, while a number of grammatical forms – which typically do form part of instruction – resist acquisition, including forms with meaning, such as tense morphology. Our view of language makes us feel quite relaxed about this. Taking tense as an example, a speaker who regularly misses out the associated morphology has a range of ways of making the meaning salient if necessary, whether by using the dedicated affix or by adding an adverbial to clarify, such as *today, after, yesterday* or *before*. As linguists, we'd encourage you to combine a sophisticated understanding of language with communicative priorities as you decide what to teach and assess in your language classroom.

4.5 CONCLUSIONS: THE SAME BUT DIFFERENT

A language learned later in life is qualitatively similar to other natural languages, at least in the sense that it is subject to the same sorts of grammatical constraints that any natural language must obey. This might come as small consolation to busy teachers faced with correcting an apparently never-ending array of non-target grammatical constructions, but rest assured that no L2 learner develops a 'wild' grammar; that is, a grammar which does not make use of the underlying grammatical concepts that the language faculty allows, or a grammar which does not rely on hierarchical structure or the properties made available from Virtual Grammar. Indeed, we have seen that extremely subtle properties of morphosyntax and semantic interpretation are apparently learnable even when they are never explicitly taught or addressed in the language classroom. Of course, the reason this is of little consolation is precisely because a language teacher is tasked with improving language performance; and a language learner is assessed and awarded qualifications on the basis of their performance. Even if all grammars, in the abstract sense, are equally valid expressions of the language faculty, linguistic performance may indeed be wild and changeable. Linguistic performance is more immediately subject to individual differences of memory capacity, personality, etc., as well as contextual constraints of the communicative situation. The relationship between language knowledge and language performance is extremely difficult to capture and not particularly well understood. The feeling is likely familiar to most language teachers: *We just spent a whole lesson explaining and working on this; they seemed to have understood. Why did they get it wrong?!*

The answer often resides in one of the three main learnability issues that emerge from research (and are likely familiar to teachers from practical experience): the role of the L1; the interaction of L1 filtering L2 input; and the use of grammatical properties in pragmatically appropriate ways. It is our contention that understanding something of the nature of the underlying properties and how they are implicated in acquisition problems may help to understand why particular patterns of usage are off-target. We also hope that seeing language development and cross-linguistic differences through the lens of a Virtual Grammar will facilitate greater understanding of the nature of grammatical properties and provide a different approach to questions of analysis, and recognition of underlying grammatical concepts. This in turn will potentially inform ways of attempting to address and improve performance by leveraging this knowledge about language. In the next chapter, we try to make connections between our linguistics-oriented perspective and the broader educational perspective.

4.6 EXERCISES AND QUESTIONS FOR DISCUSSION

1. Learning, Acquisition, Fundamental Difference

i) Consider the ten differences listed in the Fundamental Difference Hypothesis. Reflecting on your experience with language development, do you think that learning another language later in life is fundamentally different to learning one from birth?

ii) This chapter presented research which shows that there are aspects of additional language development that seem to contradict a view that learning language in later life is the same as general skills learning. To what extent has your own L2 language development seemed more like skills learning and to what extent has it seemed to involve more implicit development that you did not notice until you reflected on it?

iii) How would a view that L2 learning is fundamentally different to L1 development impact on choices you make with respect to teaching language in a classroom setting?

iv) If L2 learning mirrors L1 development, how would this impact on the choices you make in your teaching?

2. Cues and Language Processing

Bill VanPatten (1996; 2004) has formulated the idea of Processing Instruction as a way to address issues that arise from the way that cues for comprehension might differ in different languages. This technique aims to set up contexts in which learners have to use the cues that are relevant in the target language in order to understand input sentences.

i) One principle of Processing Instruction is the first noun principle, which states that when they are processing sentences, learners strongly tend to assume that the first noun phrase in the sentence is also the subject of the sentence. How might this lead to problems in learners' comprehension of a passive sentence like (a)?

(a) The frog was kissed by the princess.

ii) Consider how the first noun principle would also complicate comprehension of other types of sentence in English (questions, sentences that start with a meaningless 'it', sentences with relative clauses, etc.).

iii) Choose one of the types of sentences mentioned. Continuing to assume the first noun principle, what comprehension problems might learners face? Develop activities which require learners to process the input in a way that leads to the correct interpretation of the sentences you have chosen to explore in this exercise.

3. Morphology and the Bottleneck Hypothesis

i) Slabakova's (2008) Bottleneck Hypothesis suggests that the encoding of different types of meaning in particular morphemes

4.6 Exercises and Questions for Discussion

poses an acquisition problem for L2 learners. To what extent does this apply to the language(s) you know? How morphologically rich are they?

ii) A teaching suggestion resulting from the Bottleneck Hypothesis is that one needs to pay particular attention to inflectional morphology in grammar instruction such as suffixes for tense and agreement. Consult some language teaching materials to consider the focus on morphology. To what extent is inflectional morphology presented with respect to its associated meaning?

iii) Pick one grammatical structure to focus on. Consider the extent to which meaning is implicated in the structure you have chosen. Now think about different contexts which might influence the use of the grammatical structure. Can you create an exercise that requires learners to make connections between meaning and the grammatical structure you have chosen to focus on?

4. Advanced Proficiency and Residual Optionality

i) Can you think of a point of grammar which might give rise to residual optionality? Remember that this is when a grammatical pattern is accurate in terms of form, but used in non-standard ways (i.e. where the context would not naturally require the form).

ii) Consider whether you think this presents a crucial issue for your learners in terms of priority for teaching. Does your view change when considering teaching at different proficiency levels? Would the type of teaching context make a difference?

iii) If you wanted to raise awareness of the tendency for L2 speakers to optionally use unnecessary forms, how might you do this in a way that was effective for learning?

5. Information Structure and Grammatical Patterns

i) In this chapter, we saw that information structure is an important element in regulating subject placement in languages like Italian and Spanish. Consider the language(s) that you know. Do they seem to make use of topics at the sentence level? Or are they more like English, which relies heavily on subjects? (Note: some languages use different grammatical morphemes for subjects and topics.)

ii) Our discussion of topics and information structure has been limited to the level of the sentence. What is the role of a topic in larger texts?

iii) Develop an exercise that focuses on topic and focus at the sentence level, and an exercise that focuses on topic and focus at the text level. Are there commonalities that span these two levels of focus on language?

6. Garden Paths and Grammar

We saw that garden-path sentences are ones which raise a reader's or listener's expectations for a particular type of grammatical structure, only to indicate later that the sentence relies on a different structure (e.g. *The horse raced past the barn fell*).

i) Try to construct further such sentences for English. Can you also construct garden-path sentences for the language you teach? (Searching the Internet will deliver some examples for a range of languages.)

ii) Do you think you could use such sentences to raise learners' awareness for different types of grammatical structure? For example, to highlight the use of reduced relative clauses in the *horse raced* sentence.

iii) Consider how such ambiguity or unexpected interpretations of grammatical structures might occur in jokes in the language you teach. How might you use this in illustrating points of grammar?

5 Language Education

Much controversy in the teaching of language (and foreign language teaching in particular) has centred on the role of grammar. Chapter 1 outlined how some of this controversy has played out in the history of language teaching trends in moves from grammar-translation to communicative teaching methods, and various other approaches. Many of the issues seem to rest on binary choices with respect to teaching: *either* one takes a grammar-translation approach *or* a communicative approach; *either* one fosters explicit knowledge about language *or* one develops communicative abilities to use language. While a particular teacher might be more oriented towards one end of these continua than the other, they are surely continua rather than discrete concepts. Teachers' decisions about what and how to teach are circumscribed by cultural norms for education in particular settings, complex policy regulations, abstract overarching educational ideals, and the social and didactic dynamics of particular classrooms. Teachers will therefore necessarily have to exercise flexibility, drawing on different types of approach as appropriate for the aims of specific lessons or learner groups.

The dichotomies mentioned here are not expected to be consistently represented in actual teaching practice. Where a more communicative approach might be mandated by a curriculum or educational policy, a teacher is likely to explicitly discuss and address certain aspects of grammar. Where materials might present grammar points in explicit isolation, teachers are likely to embed the relevant features into the context of communication. What's more, various non-linguistic questions of cultural education are also expected to be bundled with language teaching. So, while decision-making in classroom teaching does not lend itself to simple dichotomous choices, it is nevertheless useful to juxtapose these apparently contradictory discrete ideas and notions in order to interrogate the underlying fuzzy concepts in the middle in terms of how they are relevant for questions of language education. This is what we seek to do in this chapter, against the background of the notion of language and grammar we have developed so far. We start by considering what the purposes of foreign language education are, before looking in turn at issues of 'nativeness' versus foreignness, awareness versus ability and grammar acquisition versus grammar skills. Unlike in previous chapters, we will not use Cases in Point to illustrate different grammatical concepts. For each of the dichotomies discussed, we illustrate with a discussion of findings from the literature which highlight some relevant pedagogical issues.

Finally, we explore the idea of applying linguistics. There has been much academic discussion about the value of applying insights from linguistics and language acquisition to language education. Different schools of linguistics and applied linguistics might question the validity or applicability of concepts from academia to questions of pedagogy. For this reason, we conclude by situating our approach in the field of applied linguistics.

5.1 WHAT IS FOREIGN LANGUAGE TEACHING FOR?

There is no simple answer to this question, and the lack of a straightforward answer is not confined to issues of language education. In this question, 'foreign language' could be replaced by any subject that is taught on educational curricula, and it would give rise to the same philosophical questions: What is mathematics teaching for? What is history teaching for? In many ways, it is useful to view language as a teaching subject alongside others. From the perspective of pupils and students, language is likely to be seen as another subject on the curriculum that they have to study alongside mathematics, history, art, etc. However, language does of course pose its own unique complexities because it is the vehicle for all education as well as a topic of education. In addition, language is a natural human phenomenon in ways that other educational subjects are not. From a linguistic perspective, children are implicit masters of grammar before they ever get to school (and even if they never get to school at all). This is not the case for mathematics, history and the rest. The differences between language as a phenomenon in comparison to (and perhaps in conflict with) language as a subject of study contribute to the multifarious particularities associated with defining the purpose of foreign language teaching.

5.1 What Is Foreign Language Teaching For?

Sato and Loewen (2019, p. 11) have said that 'researchers generally agree that the goal of instruction is to help learners achieve the ability to use the L2 accurately and fluently for meaningful purposes, during either written or oral communication'. While reasonable as a generality, there are several points worth considering. Firstly, the idea that researchers agree on the goals of instruction is problematic. The constraints and motivations of researchers (including applied linguistics researchers) are inevitably different from the aims and constraints of the teaching profession. We will consider applied linguistics research later in this chapter. A second issue is to do with how we understand notions of accuracy and fluency in language education. How is 'accurate' to be defined? We see here potential issues of prescriptive versus descriptive norms of usage (see Chapter 3). Prescriptively accurate usage might be descriptively unusual. Grammatically accurate usage might be contextually out of place (see Chapter 4). The nature of the language taught in the foreign language classroom is necessarily very different from the nature of that same language in the speech community where it is the vehicle of communication and culture (Widdowson, 2000a; 2002). And research on bilinguals and advanced language learners has shown that bilingual performance in certain areas is simply going to be different from monolingual L1 performance. It is thus problematic to take norms of monolingual usage of the target language as the point of reference from which to measure accurate usage for bilingual speakers.

Despite these criticisms, we would not wish to imply that the goals summarised by Sato and Loewen are misguided. As teachers ourselves, we would consider our teaching successful if our students achieved the ability to use their L2 (English in our case) accurately and fluently for meaningful purposes. Instead we seek to highlight the tension between clear ideals and messy reality – as a facet of both language research and language education. There are many ways in which teaching could be defined as successful and having reached its objectives even if learners do not attain the ideal of fluent and accurate L2 usage (however fluent and accurate are to be defined). Language teaching is embedded in much broader educational goals beyond just communicative ability in a foreign language.

Kramsch (2008) highlights a distinction between purely communicative competence and broader educational goals by differentiating between language learning and language education. Language learning involves proficiency development oriented towards communicative language use, and language training for transactional or professional contexts. Language education as it is 'inscribed within the schooling career of adolescents and young adults' (Kramsch, 2008, p. 6) aims to facilitate foreign language communicative proficiency, but it also seeks to provide 'an aesthetic education that links taste and moral value and expands learners' notion of the good and the beautiful' (Kramsch, 2008, p. 7). Thus, the teaching of foreign languages is in practice often a vehicle for achieving wider educational goals beyond just language proficiency, and becoming a fluent speaker of a foreign language becomes simply one facet of educationally successful language teaching.

We see this reflected in curricula and policy goals for foreign language teaching.[1] For example, in the European context, Beacco and Byram (2007, p. 34) propose that language education policies should 'enhance the value of and develop the linguistic repertoires of social agents through education for plurilingualism ... and education for plurilingual awareness, as education for linguistic tolerance'. While the conceptualisation of plurilingualism is perhaps particular to the European context, teachers in any context will no doubt recognise ideals of intercultural understanding and intercultural communication as typical aims of foreign language education. Byram and Wagner (2018) highlight intercultural issues as a key feature of language teaching and propose greater integration of language learning with other subjects related to citizenship education across the curriculum.

Returning to the question of what language teaching is for, we have the aims of developing accurate and fluent usage, facilitating intercultural understanding and international dialogue, as well as the intention to contribute to general aesthetic and moral edification. We would argue that understanding of the properties of language itself is a further fundamental aim for teachers and learners. Arguably, linguistic expertise is basic to the development of language proficiency. From our Virtual Grammar orientation, we assert that it can help in delivering aesthetic edification and intercultural understanding. We saw in Chapter 1 that, in linguistics, language is studied from a range of perspectives. This underpins the diversity in language education goals: language can be seen as formal and

---

[1] At the risk of Eurocentrism, we cite here EU language education policy goals as examples of readily available documentation with extensive discussion (see www.coe.int/en/web/language-policy/). While these are obviously not globally applicable, they do represent the result of wide cross-national consultation on language education policy and are intended as surpranational guidelines. We invite readers to compare their local policies and curricula with these. Our search for available documentation indicates that broadly comparable goals are a typical feature of curricula for foreign language education in other jurisdictions.

5.1 What Is Foreign Language Teaching For?

functional; it is cultural and cognitive, etc. We saw also that trends and fashions in language education are liable to change, emphasising at different times different facets of our understanding of language.

Just as foreign language education encompasses a range of potential aims, there is scope for fostering linguistic understanding as a key element of language awareness and 'knowledge about language' as equally crucial elements of language education alongside cultural learning, communication training, etc. The remainder of this chapter is devoted to fleshing this out. As a prelude, we note that it is not novel. Hudson (2008) proposes that formal linguistics can contribute to knowledge about language as a valuable component of general language education. He states:

> [A] deeper understanding of language deserves a place in any liberal curriculum because of its long-term intellectual benefits; if it is important for children to understand their bodies and their social environment, it is at least as important for them to understand the faculty which makes social life possible. (Hudson, 2008, p. 55)

Widdowson (2002, p. 67) outlines similar logic extended to foreign language teaching to say that 'understanding the nature of language is something which should be central in education, and not just something left to be randomly and imperfectly inferred from the learning of particular languages'. However, the subjects offered on school curricula *are* particular languages and Widdowson notes that, within this constraint, teaching for language awareness is one way of addressing wider educational aims during the learning of particular foreign languages. But, crucially, he also observes that awareness has tended to be influenced by critical approaches and 'has become socio-political awareness, nurtured by expedient interpretation often based on a very limited knowledge of the nature of language' (Widdowson, 2002, p. 67). Sociopolitical awareness and linguistic awareness are not mutually exclusive. Language is used to influence and persuade for social and political ends and education should seek to enable citizens to navigate political and social discourses. Our concern is that even though an understanding of the nature of language is intellectually and culturally valuable, the socio/political/cultural seems often to crowd out the linguistic nature of language awareness. We believe that a clearer understanding of the specifically linguistic is beneficial for educators tasked with delivering language education and all its related educational goals. We would call for emphasis on the linguistic to be a key goal of education for language awareness.

5.2 NATIVENESS AND FOREIGNNESS

In the discussion in Section 5.1, we mentioned the idea of plurilingualism. This is one instantiation of frameworks, in addition to translanguaging or multicompetence (Cook, 1992), which call into question traditional discrete notions of native versus non-native, or L1 versus L2, which are increasingly problematic as labels for types of language knowledge and ability in ever-more 'superdiverse' contexts in contemporary society (see Blommaert & Rampton, 2011; see also Blommaert's definition of multilingualism below). By promoting a notion of a Virtual Grammar we highlight the grammatical nature of language, with an emphasis on the idea that there is a shared set of grammatical concepts which are instantiated differently from language to language, thus we all share the same core linguistic knowledge. Another facet of our notion of Virtual Grammar, however, is explicitly directed at more socioculturally oriented questions of language in society and language in schools. As an enrichment and addition to the teaching of individual discrete foreign languages, we follow Widdowson and Seidlhofer in calling for addition of the study of language – i.e. Language with a capital 'L' – in schools, as a subject (see also work in Denham & Lobeck, 2010), or as a more important part of individual language subjects. But in doing so we are not advocating any position of linguistic purism which continues to drive educational policies in many countries (Lin, 2013). An understanding of Language, as a shared, unified phenomenon, directly challenges the notions of nativeness and foreignness, breaking down unhelpful psychological and cultural barriers within language education.

Given the nature of our modern, globalised world, chances are that each of us has competence in a range of registers and dialects within our most dominant language(s). Statistically, it is also likely that we each also know (at least one) lingua franca variety, whether that is English, Chinese, Spanish, Swahili or Arabic, to name the largest. It is well known that monolingualism itself is the exception, and not the norm in the world's population. While traditionally, multilingualism was understood to refer the ability to speak a number of languages, according to Blommaert:

> Multilingualism should not be seen as a collection of languages that a speaker controls, but rather as a complex of *specific* semiotic resources, some of which belong to a conventionally defined 'language', while others belong to another 'language'. The resources are concrete accents, language varieties, register, genres, modalities such as writing – ways of using language in particular communicative settings and spheres of life. (Blommaert, 2010, p. 102)

5.2 Nativeness and Foreignness

One sees here that contemporary understanding of multilingualism, or plurilingualism, does not assume that this means a person can speak a set of discrete individual languages in the sense of national or well-defined standard varieties. This conceptualisation of multilingualism finds expression in the notion of translanguaging, which has been used to refer to what we do with the languages that we know. One definition characterises translanguaging as 'the strategic deployment of multiple semiotic resources, e.g. languages, modalities, sensory cues, to create a socio-interactional space for learning and understanding, knowledge construction and identity negotiation'. (Li Wei, 2015, p. 32). Translanguaging uses all the resources in one's linguistic repertoire, not just scaffolding, but also identity, interest, world view, etc. (García & Lin, 2017). The idea of Virtual Grammar takes a particularly grammatical perspective on these issues. We are equipped with a facility for grammar we exploit using the various overt linguistic resources at our disposal to create meaning and form as necessary for our needs. While the resulting linguistic forms might not conform to any particular idea of a putative native speaker 'norm' of the language, such forms are constrained and licit expressions of grammatical concepts.

The extent to which ideas of plurilingualism or translanguaging have trickled down into actual foreign language teaching practice is debatable. Take, for example, the case of foreign language proficiency assessment. Even if we know that language knowledge is a fluid and dynamic phenomenon, there is often a comparison (at least implicitly) to assumed native speaker norms when foreign language proficiency is tested. This is in many ways understandable as a practical solution to difficult testing challenges – the 'native speaker norm', no matter how conceptually and socially problematic, at least provides some standard against which learner performance can be measured. Nevertheless, we can see that theoretical rethinking of the native/non-native concept in applied linguistics has had some impact on understanding in teaching and assessment. This is reflected, for example, in the influential Common European Framework of Reference (CEFR) project: 'the aim of language education is profoundly modified. It is no longer seen as simply to achieve "mastery" of one or two, or even three languages ... with the "*ideal native speaker*" as the ultimate model. Instead, the aim is to develop a linguistic repertoire, in which all linguistic abilities have a place.' Of course, how to actually test any and all linguistic abilities in terms of 'standardised' proficiency measures remains extremely tricky.

What does all this mean for the notion of grammar and acquisition we have been developing? Breaking down strict binary distinctions between L1 and L2, native and foreign, provides scope for using any and all existing linguistic knowledge that is available among language learners in order to promote learning of properties in unfamiliar languages or new language varieties. In one sense, this is a completely mundane and uncontroversial educational idea. We acquire new knowledge by relating to, building on and refining what is familiar. In education research, there has been a great deal of attention to the specific notion of scaffolding, which is a more technical understanding of similar ideas of supporting new learning based on existing knowledge (see Reiser & Tabak, 2014). However, given the traditional native/foreign, L1/L2 dichotomy, and strong beliefs about the best way to teach language, such notions are potentially controversial when applied to language teaching (see Turnbull & Dailey-O'Cain, 2009). Prodromou (2002, p. 6, cited in Butzkamm, 2003) notes that for teachers of foreign languages, the issue of use of the learners' mother tongue in instruction is 'a skeleton in the cupboard ... a taboo subject, a source of embarrassment'.

Quite apart from the uneasiness associated with the use or non-use of the L1, a strict distinction between L1 and L2 can be seen as a barrier to effective learning. In the context of bilingual education programmes, Cummins has promoted 'teaching for transfer' because 'learning efficiencies can be achieved if teachers explicitly draw students' attention to similarities and differences between their languages and reinforce effective learning strategies in a coordinated way across languages' (Cummins, 2007, p. 233, and see Cummins, 2008). In the context of foreign language teaching, Butzkamm (2003) has developed a similar approach, which seeks to use known, mother-tongue language knowledge in effective ways in order to promote foreign language development. Known as 'bilingualisation' (see also Butzkamm & Caldwell, 2009), this framework has much to recommend it and is amenable to the notion of grammatical concepts that we have been developing so far. Rather than seeing the L1 as a skeleton in the cupboard, Butzkamm (2003, p. 29) points out that 'the mother tongue is ... the greatest asset people bring to the task of foreign language learning'. This is because a full implicit understanding of grammar has already been acquired and this can be leveraged effectively in order to promote L2 learning, an insight which has received recent empirical support in acquisition research (see for example; McManus, 2019; McManus & Marsden, 2017). As an example, Butzkamm (2003, p. 34) discusses issues of grammatical progression in

5.2 Nativeness and Foreignness

textbooks and teaching materials and questions why the subjunctive, for example, is introduced late as something difficult for learners to grasp. He notes that English speakers who are learning German could quite readily handle a subjunctive form such as (1) in their first week of lessons if it is related to the pattern they know from English. This kind of thinking means that a wider range of input materials are potentially available because understanding of what might be grammatically 'difficult' reading texts or listening materials can be revised.

(1) Ich hätte   gern eine Cola.
    I   have(SBJV) gladly a cola
    'I would like a cola.'

This is precisely the sort of approach that we have been outlining in previous chapters. If all actual instantiations of languages are simply encoded variants of a universal abstract Virtual Grammar, then by exploring the underlying concepts we can relate more effectively between existing knowledge from our native language(s) and dialects to the new variants to be learned. Seen from this perspective, we can think of the idea of acquiring or learning a 'foreign' language not as something new and strange, divorced from our existing linguistic knowledge; rather, we can see it as scaffolding different variants of existing knowledge by extension, adaption or reformulation. Most of us can move quite naturally from register to register, and many of us are able to navigate smoothly from one dialectal variety to another. In the same way, adding a new language to our repertoire can be seen as similar to adding a variety or register of a language that we already know, and something that can be achieved more effectively by building on existing knowledge. What's more, we know from the acquisition literature that this happens anyway: learners will inevitably transfer knowledge from their previous language experience to the learning of a new language. It would be advisable to work with this where it can be used positively rather than seeing L1 knowledge or use as a taboo subject to be avoided or suppressed in a classroom setting.

Let's look at an example from language acquisition which illustrates the issues. We saw in Chapter 1 that aspectual distinctions such as telicity, habituality, etc. are universal. Virtual Grammar allows a range of aspectual properties, but specific languages differ with respect to how such distinctions are grammatically encoded. Slabakova (2000) studied the acquisition of the aspectual property of telicity (see Case in Point 1.8, Chapter 1) in English by learners whose primary languages were either Spanish or Bulgarian. The aim was to investigate whether learners of English had different ideas about the acceptability of sentences such as (2) compared to (3).

(2) Antonia worked in a bakery and made a cake.

(3) Sharon worked in a bakery and made cakes.

Recall that one way in which English encodes a telic interpretation is in the form of objects of transitive verbs, rather than in the form of the verb itself. An object which is interpreted as specific, or which is marked with a particular number value results in the verb phrase also being interpreted as telic (2), while a bare plural without a particular quantification is interpreted as atelic (i.e. part of an open-ended activity), as in (3). Thus, while both these sentences are grammatical, (2) is markedly less natural. This is because in the context of being employed in a bakery, one would expect an open-ended activity, as denoted in (3), that the worker is generally engaged in the making of cakes, rather than making just one cake. Learner interpretations of these types of sentences are interesting with respect to L1 transfer because Bulgarian typically marks telicity directly on the verb with prefixes (4) while Spanish works similarly to English in the relevant respects (5).

(4) a. Tja govti jadene 3 časa.   ATELIC
       She cook-3PS/AOR food for 3 hours
       'She cooked food for 3 hours.'
    b. Tja **z**-govti jadene za 3 časa.   TELIC
       She **PV**-cook-3PS/AOR food in 3 hours
       'She cooked some food in 3 hours.'

(5) a Juan comió manzanas.   ATELIC
       Juan eat-3PS/PRET ten apples
       'Juan ate ten apples.'
    b. Juan comió diez manzanas.   TELIC
       Juan eat-3PS/PRET ten apples
       'Juan ate apples.'

If the L1 has an influence on L2 learning, it would therefore be expected that the Spanish and Bulgarian learner groups would perform differently. And this is what Slabakova (2000) found. Bulgarian-speaking learners of English tended to judge sentences like (2) to be more acceptable than English speakers or Spanish-speaking learners of English. We can interpret this as showing that the Bulgarian speakers look to the verb as the site for aspectual encoding and because the verb form does not change in these English sentences, they do not

5.2 Nativeness and Foreignness

detect the aspectual distinction. They have not (yet) acquired the calculation of verb form plus object noun phrase form that gives rise to the aspectual distinction in English. However, the good news is that despite the potential influence of their dominant language, L1 Bulgarian speakers at higher proficiency levels can come to reliably make the aspectual distinctions based on English forms which do not have a clear counterpart in Bulgarian, for the types of sentences illustrated in (2) and (3) as well as for other related phenomena (see Slabakova, 2003).

What can we take away from these types of findings for our discussion of nativeness and foreignness? Firstly, we see that foreignness in the sense of a language encoding some foreign (i.e. strange or unusual) meaning is relative. From the perspective of Virtual Grammar, telicity is a universal potential concept, which in itself is not particularly difficult to grasp. There is nothing inherently problematic or foreign about acquiring or using this property; we have all done so quite readily in the language(s) that we have mastered. However, when the concept is encoded in L2 forms which are not available in the L1, or differ from the L1, this can lead to learnability issues. Mapping between a familiar meaning and unfamiliar forms is difficult. For the Bulgarian learners of English, telicity is not the problem; encoding telicity in the form of objects rather than on the verb is the issue. Taking the bilingualisation approach, it would seem perfectly reasonable to use existing linguistic knowledge available in the classroom in order to provide inroads into the L2 system. For example, in the case of teaching English in Bulgaria, one could imagine contrasting Bulgarian aspectual distinctions and thinking about how these map onto English forms as a way of raising awareness for what the languages have in common (a telic/atelic distinction) as well as how this is distributed differently in each of the languages (verbal morphology versus the form of noun phrases).

We return below to the question of awareness and seek to make the case for grammatical awareness as a useful facet of language learning. For now, we will simply assume that awareness is useful and point out that existing language competence is a rich potential source of grammatical awareness if it is exploited cleverly and effectively. This depends on pitching the sort of grammatical awareness we are seeking at an appropriate level in order to be able to make comparisons which are relevant for particular learning contexts. We suggest that drawing on the idea of grammatical concepts as part of a Virtual Grammar is a potentially useful way of doing this. We break down any notion of a strict 'native' versus foreign dichotomy in this way and can see any language or variety as choosing from the range of virtual options that language provides. We have all acquired a version of Virtual Grammar, and the task of learning a new language can be seen as learning a different form of this grammar, rather than something foreign, new and strange.

Finally, let's return to the question of the purposes of teaching with this discussion in mind. We noted that fluent and accurate L2 use is a laudable learning goal and we noted that language awareness is a useful educational goal. We can see that comparing properties of L1 and L2 can relativise notions of foreignness and heighten language awareness. This could be used to promote accurate L2 use from early stages of learning. However, we would emphasise the 'bilingual' part of the bilingualisation framework in order to temper any strict ideas of L2 accuracy. The end result of teaching a foreign language is bilingual competence, and as has been noted several times, this is different from monolingual competence/performance. If we assume that foreign language learners should end up with language abilities and language awareness that mirror monolingual 'native speaker norms', we are setting ourselves up for failure. A more cogent aim is to foster bilingual ability and awareness, and part of being a bilingual is cross-fertilisation of knowledge between the language systems. Fostering such knowledge is a worthwhile educational goal in and of itself.

5.3 AWARENESS AND ABILITY

We have already mentioned language awareness as a valuable aspect of language education. Here we discuss this further with respect to the notion of language ability. The aim is to explore where explicit awareness can be useful in the service of fostering language ability. But beyond that, and continuing the theme we have outlined above, we seek to illustrate that linguistic awareness is a legitimate goal in itself and that one way of exploring this is via the notion of Virtual Grammar. Though we all have access to the same core Virtual Grammar, the underlying properties can only be brought to light via awareness raising. Awareness raising is particularly valuable where it includes exploration of the non-obvious properties of our language knowledge which link into interesting abstract features that constrain any language.

Our suggestion that focus on grammatical points in teaching can be implemented with explicit reference to grammatical and semantic

5.3 Awareness and Ability

patterns in learners' previously acquired languages is likely to bring to mind the large body of second language classroom research which seeks to explore implicit versus explicit forms of grammar instruction. Unfortunately, it seems that there are very few definitive conclusions that can be drawn from this research. The well-known meta-analysis by Norris and Ortega (2000) is often cited as confirming the effectiveness of explicit instruction in language education, but as is the nature of a meta-analysis, much depends on the details of the original studies and how particular grammar points had been conceptualised and how instruction was delivered. What's more, evidence in favour of explicit instruction does not entail that implicit exposure is ineffective. As we saw in the previous chapter, there are features of grammar that learners come to know despite not being explicitly taught and despite there being little input evidence at all to motivate acquisition. And, frustratingly, we also know that there are features which are repeatedly taught and drilled but which learners never seem to come to master completely. The absence of clarity in classroom-based acquisition research may be one reason why there are so many different approaches to language teaching which are endorsed in teacher training courses, taking their cues from different studies with differing findings.

While the lack of clarity might seem frustrating, it can also be viewed as positive as it potentially allows a range of approaches as long as a clear pedagogical rationale can be provided for specific choices. The most reasonable position to take is an assumption that all approaches enjoy some level of effectiveness, and that some aspects of language are more effectively taught through one method than another. We seek to emphasise the potential role of awareness in the sense of forms of explicit knowledge about language, but not at the expense of implicit knowledge. The aim is not to favour one type of knowledge or instruction over the other, but rather to provide an educational rationale for the use of explicit awareness as an antidote to any potential feelings of unease a teacher might feel with respect to providing instruction about grammar. As Ur (2011, p. 507) notes, 'in spite of the current promotion of communicative and task-based methodologies by ministries of education worldwide, grammatical explanations and exercises continue to be prominent both in course books and in the classroom practice of teachers in school-based foreign-language courses'. Rather than seeing explicit grammar instruction as something to be avoided at all costs, we suggest consideration of the potential logic for its use – in particular contexts within specific moments of instruction – instead of simply as a failure to abide by prevalent communicative or task-based techniques. Otherwise, 'grammar' risks joining the skeleton of L1 use in teachers' cupboards of taboo.

Some of the difficulties surrounding implicit versus explicit language knowledge presumably derive from the fact that language is a natural human ability that we usually don't have to consciously think about or reflect on at all. One can have perfect ability in a language with next-to-no explicit awareness of its grammatical properties. This is the typical state of affairs for 'naive' speakers with respect to their mother tongue. By contrast, it is also possible to have a very high level of awareness of a language with next-to-no ability in it. Scholars who have studied an ancient or classical language might be able to analyse sentences and inscriptions and explain the complexities of grammatical rules and paradigms, but they are unlikely to be able to carry on a conversation in colloquial Akkadian, or Gothic, etc.

You might object to this last characterisation as representing a lack of 'ability'; analysing text and understanding the grammatical nature of language is surely a worthwhile, albeit different sort of, ability. And this is the fundamental point which we seek to emphasise by thinking in terms of awareness and ability rather than alternative either/or dichotomies like the many that seem to exist in language education. From the point of view of education more broadly, we see reason in calling for both awareness AND ability as fundamental to education in any field. Even though language is 'special' in the sense that humans have an innate capacity to develop language, once we include language as a subject on a school curriculum, it is perfectly valid to see it as one facet of what it means to gain an education. After all, it is the norm in all the subjects included within educational curricula to develop awareness and ability. Setting up an opposition between these ideas is not useful, and we run the risk of thinking in terms of oppositions if we exclusively rely on distinctions between implicit versus explicit, or communication versus grammar.

If we apply the dichotomous thinking which has sometimes characterised language education to other subjects, the absurdity of binary thinking becomes clear. What would you think of an approach to teaching music in which learners were simply exposed to melodies and were expected to develop from this an implicit musical ability? Music is taught so that pupils develop the ability to play music, but it is also taught in order to foster aesthetic awareness and appreciation, and to encourage reflection on the cultural importance of music. All of this (and more besides) are perfectly valid and important aspects of music education. A successful student of music might be one who is

5.3 Awareness and Ability

a virtuoso in some instrument, or they might be one who develops a rich aesthetic appreciation of different genres of music even if they cannot play music particularly well themselves. Ideally, they have developed some aspects of playing ability and music appreciation. We propose that defining successful language education exclusively in terms of implicit fluent communicative ability is akin to assuming that music teachers should be churning out virtuosi. In addition, the inclusion of study of literature, media and culture in foreign language curricula illustrates that the educational goals stretch far beyond just communicative language ability.

Education means developing awareness. And we have seen that the goals that are set for language education often include aspects of awareness, even if this is typically defined in terms of intercultural awareness and sensitivity. We agree with Hudson (2008) and Widdowson (2002) that awareness of the nature of language itself is also a key aspect of language education that should be addressed in teaching and can subsequently be used to illuminate questions of culture and literature. If we assume that this sort of awareness is educationally beneficial, and given findings that explicit linguistic knowledge can be useful in promoting foreign language learning, we are in the happy position of being able to tick both language education and language learning boxes by drawing explicitly on aspects of grammatical awareness. We have suggested that using grammatical concepts is one useful way of implementing this. Let's look at an example of how this might be done.

German and Swedish are grammatically very similar, especially with respect to syntactic properties. They are closely related members of the Germanic language family and each has the typical Germanic 'verb second' property. This means that a finite verb must appear as the second constituent of a main clause. Other phrases are relatively free to move to different positions in the sentence. However, while the languages are grammatically very similar, the uses of these grammatical patterns are subtly different. Bohnacker and Rosén (2008) show that patterns of information structure in verb-second clauses are different in German and Swedish, as illustrated in (6) and (7). Note that only one constituent can come before the verb, and that while all of the sentences are grammatically possible, there are differences in how frequently they are used and in monolingual speakers' reaction to how natural they sound (see also Case in Point 4.4 on Null Subjects and Information Structure).

(6) a. Det bor många studenter här.   Swedish – preferred order
       it live many students here
    b. Många studenter bor här.   Swedish – dispreferred order
       many students live here
       'Many students live here.'

(7) a. Es wohnen viele StudentInnen hier.   German – dispreferred order
       it live many students here.
    b. Viele StudenInnen wohnen hier.   German – preferred order
       many students live here
       'Many students live here.'

Drawing on the discussion in Chapter 4, you might be able to predict what happens when speakers of Swedish learn German, or vice-versa. Bohnacker and Rosén (2008) found that in written production and when asked to rate or rewrite German sentences, Swedish-speaking learners overgeneralised to produce patterns such as (7a). While these are grammatically possible in German, the use of the expletive pronoun *es* is less frequent and less natural than placing the grammatical subject in first position. In Swedish, the preferences are reversed: it is more natural to start the sentence with the expletive pronoun *det*. And this L1 information structure pattern carries over from Swedish into L2 German.

We have seen that in precisely these sorts of subtle areas, even advanced proficiency learners who have mastered the grammatical patterns of the target language will tend to have difficulties getting to grips with the information structural patterns (i.e. the use of grammar in context). In this sort of area, awareness raising based on underlying shared concepts of information structure might be advisable as a way of exploring the nature of the problem and highlighting where learners' grammatical abilities do not always match contextual expectations. It might not 'solve' the problem, and indeed you might not consider this sort of thing a problem at all, after all the learner production is grammatically accurate. Either way, it would surely be educationally useful to explore the nature of how grammar is exploited in the service of information structure, and how information structure is a universal underlying concept contributing to acceptability of grammatical patterns in context.

One might consider the nature of Swedish *det* compared to German *es* (= *it*) as a way of exploring how these apparently equivalent words actually have functionally different properties. In Swedish, it more often occurs as a placeholder in first position to allow new information to be introduced later in the clause. Although this can happen in German, it sounds relatively less natural in context. Such an exploration introduces ideas of information structure which are relevant for writing skills in any language. This sort of explicit knowledge can then be used to think about aspects of literacy in addition to grammar. To repeat, this might not 'solve' any acquisition problems or increase 'ability' in the sense of fluent accurate production, but it would make educational sense to use awareness raising nevertheless, at the very least to provide a way to reflect on learners' own production and to highlight input patterns which might be useful in learning but which would otherwise not be easily noticeable without having attention drawn to them.

We all have language ability in a specific cognitive sense that we have naturally acquired at least one language. This means that even without training, each of us has a large body of implicit knowledge about a range of subtle and complex features in at least one language. We ideally want learners of foreign languages to develop a similar rich implicit body of knowledge, and as we saw in Chapter 4, this can indeed happen. Ability to master subtle grammatical properties can be acquired without conscious attention. Even if this is the case for certain properties, making hidden, unfamiliar aspects of the world clearer and bringing them into conscious awareness is fundamental to formal education, and there is little justification for assuming that this should not apply to language education. For this reason, expertise in language as an object of study is as important for language teaching as a well-developed ability to do language is. We have suggested that this this can be thought of as knowledge about specific languages as well as knowledge about Language, developing the notion of Virtual Grammar to characterise the way our grammatical system captures the impulses we all share as humans with thought, feelings and intentions. The ability to provide explanation about language and raise awareness of relevant properties compared to existing linguistic knowledge depends on the expertise that comes with linguistic training.

5.4 GRAMMAR ACQUISITION AND GRAMMATICAL SKILLS

The expertise that comes with linguistic training raises further interesting issues with respect to applications for language education. A different distinction that cuts across ideas of awareness and ability is that between acquisition and learning. In the last chapter we talked about post-critical-period learners using their skill-development and problem-solving abilities in order to develop an new grammar, and it was mentioned that this may result in a general lack of success because these sorts of problem-solving abilities are ill-suited to the task of language acquisition. Indeed, colleagues who hold a strict nativist approach to language acquisition will probably not view this as 'real' acquisition but rather as 'learning', in the sense of learning *about* language. An axiom of the nativist approach is a strict distinction between true subconscious linguistic ability, with its own dedicated module in the mind, and explicit development of language skills, which is the result of general problem-solving abilities that can be applied to any cognitive puzzle we are confronted with. As we have hinted previously, the fact that it is possible to make such a distinction for language as opposed to other subjects in education results in a certain tension. As well as awareness in different fields of knowledge, education seeks to develop skills relevant to those fields. If we now explore questions of acquisition and learning from the perspective of grammar acquisition and grammatical skills, we seek to show how the notion of grammatical concepts embedded in a virtual grammar can further underpin the proposals here to use explicit grammatical information from L1, L2 or Lx in order to promote fruitful development of language skills and abilities.

If we see language learning as a problem to be solved in the classroom by the application of skills, our argument has been that teachers' having knowledge of grammatical concepts would be beneficial as this provides a fresh perspective and some additional clarity on the nature of the learning problem to be solved by their learners. We have seen that underlying grammatical concepts – properties such as telicity, unaccusativity, etc. – are at play in the acquisition of language and can be used to explicate language learning, both where it happens successfully and where there are learnability issues. If teachers are aware of these issues, they are equipped to think in different ways about the issues their learners encounter and develop alternative ways to address them. Teachers would then be equipped to think about pedagogical rules and surface patterns of language structure in potentially more productive ways. Of course, surface-level pattern matching and pedagogical rules of thumb as a solution to the language learning puzzle must happen to some extent. But this cannot be the whole story; poverty of the stimulus phenomena show that grammar acquisition also involves much more subtle 'below the surface'

5.4 Grammar Acquisition and Grammatical Skills

grammatical properties. Where necessary, having the option as a teacher to dive below the surface is a productive tool.

Additionally, while we can descriptively group linguistic phenomena according to surface patterns, this provides little in the way of explanation of why grammatical structures are as they are, for which we need to dig deeper. Consider the data on articles or verb classes discussed in Chapter 1 as an example. While we can easily classify articles as definite/indefinite, or assign certain types of verbs to classes based on their surface distribution or obvious facets of meaning, explaining the grammatical behaviour of these words requires recourse to less obvious virtual notions of specificity and genericity for articles, or the inherent semantics of manner versus result for verb classes. These concepts are pertinent for the acquisition of any language, even where the concept has no obvious surface linguistic encoding. For example, there is no 'specific article' or no 'generic morpheme' to be acquired in English, but these concepts nevertheless explain patterns of development in L2 English (e.g. Ionin et al. 2004, Snape, 2008).

Those semantic and grammatical ideas which are familiar to linguists but typically don't find their way into pedagogical grammar are used in linguistics in order to be able to develop explanations for phenomena rather than just descriptions. There are few phenomena in language which adhere to a logically discernible surface 'pattern'. Many teachers will recognise the frustrating experience of presenting a rule or paradigm only to be confronted in short order by some exception that seems to contradict the rule or flout the established paradigm. Given the vagaries of historical development, cultural exchange and language borrowing, there are inevitably going to be corners of irregularity in any grammar which defy simple accounts, but if an approach allows deeper levels of analysis, we can have a different perspective on exceptions or more subtle properties that are pertinent to learnability. Think, for instance, of the Swedish/German example above, or the idea of learner production that is 'not wrong but not quite right' (see Chapter 4). These become more amenable to analysis when thought of in light of linguistic notions like topic/focus rather than any account of obvious morphosyntactic properties.

So far in this section, we have concentrated on how deeper grammatical knowledge might be useful for teachers. Obviously, it should also prove useful ultimately for learners. We have already noted that this thinking should contribute to language awareness in general, and bilingual awareness in particular, and how these are crucial educational goals. But beyond awareness, exploiting deeper grammatical concepts in the classroom should also aid language learning/acquisition. This relies again on distinctions between learning/acquisition and explicit/implicit. Rothman's (2008; 2010; Long & Rothman, 2013) work on Competing Systems identifies differences in competence and performance between advanced naturalistic L2 learners and advanced tutored L2 learners. It is suggested that the differences can be traced back to competition between different cognitive processes. As discussed in Chapter 4, we can acquire linguistic knowledge naturally from the input but we can also know meta-linguistic facts about language. These two systems of knowledge compete in language learners who have access to taught input. When tested on features of linguistic knowledge (e.g. performance on aspect in L2 Spanish in Rothman, 2008), learners who have developed a grammatical system based mainly on naturalistic exposure (i.e. immersion and interaction in the L2 community), perform in more accurate ways than tutored learners who are similarly advanced in terms of general proficiency. The competing systems model traces this back to the fact that 'oversimplification in classroom instruction can lead to the formation of a static system of learned rules that are imprecise in their description of how the actual target grammar operates' (Long & Rothman, 2013, p. 67).

A connection to the grammatical viruses idea (see Chapter 3) is obvious here. Simplified rules of thumb can become over- and under-generalised in different ways to produce patterns which do not reflect the way that underlying grammar works. This connection to viruses also illustrates that these issues are not confined to foreign or second language learners. If monolingual speakers of a language are exposed to explicitly learned 'prestige' rules for usage which do not conform to their implicit grammatical system, they too will produce inconsistent patterns of usage, for example sometimes saying *it is I* and sometimes *it is me*. Long & Rothman (2013, p. 76) propose that one solution to problems of simplified pedagogical rules is to 'provide [teachers] with linguistically precise rules of the target grammar, as well as tangible proof that they are not presently armed with such precise tools without some training in linguistics'. We agree with the spirit of this but note that precise rules are also difficult to come by in linguistics: analyses are liable to change and as we discussed in Chapter 1, different schools of linguistics will have very different takes on the nature of rules. We therefore suggest that a more useful solution is to provide a way to think linguistically so that teachers can navigate areas where rules are not standardly provided in pedagogical materials, or develop

5.4 Grammar Acquisition and Grammatical Skills

their own informed rules based on the nature of the target language they teach as well as the source languages of their learners. In addition to aiding teachers, this sort of thinking could also aid learners in the classroom setting. Let's look at one example of how this could work.

The distribution and properties of the English quantifier *any* are linguistically quite complex and, unsurprisingly, learners can be faced with problems acquiring these. This is also typically an element that is taught in EFL settings. Do the pedagogical rules reflect the deeper linguistic and conceptual rules? Could we perhaps revise the former in light of the latter to provide clearer instruction and richer grammatical explanation for learners? Marsden et al. (2018) compare the pedagogical analysis typically represented in textbooks and teaching materials with the semantic/grammatical analysis that is to be found in linguistic research. Their analysis reveals that pedagogical materials for English tend in the main to illustrate that *any* is used in questions and after negation and this is contrasted with the use of *some*, which can be used in declarative, positive contexts (see (8) and (9)).

(8) Do you want any cake? / Jenny doesn't want any cake.

(9) Jenny wants some cake. / *Jenny wants any cake.

However, while useful as a rule of thumb, this does not cover the full range of more subtle contexts where *any* occurs. Consider the sentences in (10) and (11). Even though they are all declarative sentences without negation, there are differences in acceptability of *any*.

(10) a. Jenny denies that she ate any cake. (cf. *Jenny ate any cake.)
     b. *Jenny thinks that she ate any cake.

(11) a. Jenny hardly ate any cake.
     b. *Jenny probably ate any cake.[2]

Marsden et al. (2018) tested L2 English learners with L1 Arabic on their knowledge of the acceptability of *any* in a range of different contexts. They find that learners have the most robust knowledge in areas that are typically taught (i.e. questions and negation), but that they can also come to know about more subtle properties of accept-

---

[2] You might wonder about this and object that this is a possible sentence in English. It is possible if *any* is interpreted as a free-choice quantifier rather than with the existential quantifier meaning that Marsden et al. (2018) focussed on. We set this issue aside here to minimise the complexity involved. But we note in passing that the fact there are really two *any*s in English is in itself an interesting linguistic fact that is also not always outlined in pedagogical materials but that could be useful.

ability in areas that are not taught, even if this knowledge does not appear to be as robust. This is established on the basis of statistical differences in learners' ability to reject ungrammatical sentences in different contexts or accept grammatical sentences.

How can we leverage this information for teaching? You might have noticed that acceptability of *any* relies crucially on the concept of negation, even if negation is not present in the sentence in the form of the negator *not*. For example, *Jenny denies* . . . implies that *Jenny claimed she did not* . . . . Similar ideas extend to other contexts we have not yet discussed. For instance, *any* can occur in conditionals or after *without*, as illustrated in (12) and (13). These are also amenable to a negation-type analysis. A conditional structure is used to refer to a situation that has not yet happened; *without* implies a conceptual sense of negation – *I am without ideas* is semantically equivalent to *I have no ideas*.

(12) If you hear anything, let me know.

(13) He left without any breakfast.

Thus, rather than thinking in terms of discrete rules, or summaries of particular contexts for *any*, we come to have a grammatical skill in the sense of an ability to analyse distribution which allows us to develop a more subtle and fuller account than simplified pedagogical rules. What emerges from this kind of approach is recognition that use of *any* in English seems to correspond to negation, as a grammatical concept. Thinking in terms of the Competing Systems model, appealing to relevant grammatical concepts should provide more appropriate input for learners. The association between *any* and negation emerges when samples of language are considered together, but not if we concentrate on summary rules of thumb (useful though these may be in certain contexts).

Collecting samples of language as a way of dealing with tricky questions about grammar has the added bonus of enhancing the linguistic expertise of teachers. Thinking in terms of abstract virtual concepts is likely to allow for wider application than discrete individual pedagogical rules. For example, many languages have words, phrases or grammatical patterns that are associated with underlying notions of negation (known in formal linguistics as polarity sensitivity or negative polarity items). Thinking more broadly in terms of such concepts may provide new and productive ways to approach what might otherwise seem like idiosyncratic behaviour in language. If we think not just in terms of acquisition of grammar, but developing of grammatical skills based on sound linguistic thinking, we can contribute to learning and educational goals.

5.5 PRELIMINARY CONCLUSION

Education and teaching are complex phenomena no matter what the subject matter is, with Language particularly difficult given its nature. But precisely because so many points of view are licensed by different goals for language education, we can justify taking an eclectic approach which frees us from binary constraints of L1 versus L2, explicit versus implicit or learning versus acquisition. All of these facets of language will inevitably be represented in the language classroom and rather than confining some to 'skeletons in the cupboard', we have reflected on how they can be used proactively and appropriately to attain educational goals. We have suggested that thinking linguistically in terms of grammatical concepts as elements of a Virtual Grammar is a useful way to do this, for teachers in particular, but ultimately also for learners if teachers can develop this idea and use it productively.

This does not mean that teachers are expected to become academic linguists. Linguistics researchers are responsible for becoming experts in a precise area of grammar. They can and do write entire books devoted specifically to in-depth analysis of a small spectrum of grammar. Teachers must be generalists: becoming a leading expert on the properties of a particular feature in a particular language will serve no one well. Developing a way to think about the complexity, but underlying unity, of grammatical properties, no matter the language variety, is a useful grammatical skill that can be exploited to enhance awareness via any of the language varieties that are already present in a classroom. Such awareness should then contribute to different ways to think about learning/acquiring the grammatical properties of language. Developing this facility in learners equips them with a way to reflect on rules that they might encounter for their target languages, and thus to go beyond simplified rules of thumb and make connections between different areas of knowledge.

5.6 CONCLUSION: APPLYING LINGUISTICS

This entire book has been predicated on the assumption that the academic field of linguistics has potential use for language pedagogy and language education. We would like to end by devoting a few words to this assumption. The relationship between linguistics as an academic discipline and the field of language teaching/education has not been a straightforward one.[3] This may come as something as a surprise to the layperson who would perhaps naturally assume that the aims of linguistics, that is language description and explanation of descriptive patterns, would lend themselves to insights for the teaching and learning of languages. Historically, there have been close connections between ideas in linguistics and language acquisition research and trends in language teaching (see, Howatt & Widdowson, 2004 on historical trends in English language teaching; Thomas, 2013 on history of SLA research). One issue that has given rise to some controversy is whether these trends have always been beneficial for language teaching. We have talked about dichotomous choices between ideas such as explicit teaching, communicative teaching, the direct method, etc. These changing trends in teaching reflect, to some extent, trends in linguistic thinking, from behaviourism to the generative enterprise, and so on. The absence of any single 'solution' for successful language learning from the fields of linguistics and language acquisition research is perhaps one reason why there has been a certain level of scepticism with respect to the latest ideas emanating from linguistics and whether they should occasion different approaches to teaching.

In the opening chapter of this book, we provided an overview of the field of linguistics showing how 'formal' and 'functional' theoretical frameworks approach language in fundamentally different ways. The difference in orientation means that each of these research paradigms reaches conclusions that also differ. Seen in this way, it is not surprising that these contrasting theoretical approaches find differences when applied to questions of language education and do little to clarify the potential relevance of linguistics for language education. If language is (only) form, than it makes sense that language teaching would be the teaching of (only) grammar. While if language is (only) function, then teaching (only) communicative use makes good sense. Attempts to directly apply ideas from one theory sets up either–or choices for both language education policy and the actual delivery of language teaching in the classroom. Application of theory in language education based on the theory of the day can see the pendulum swing between the extremes of explicit grammar teaching and communicative language teaching.

---

[3] The theme and subsequent Proceedings of two British Association for Applied Linguistics (BAAL) conferences illustrate the debate. See Blue and Mitchell (1996) on language and education, and Trappes-Lomax (2000) on change and continuity in applied linguistics.

5.6 Conclusion: Applying Linguistics

All of this makes it unsurprising if there is now a deep suspicion of research and theory on the part of practitioners. Medgyes provides an arresting image of the perceived relationship between research and language teaching practice:

> [Researchers'] insistence on providing assistance reminds me of the situation when, seeing an old man standing round the corner, a young man walks up to him, grabs him by the arm and helps him cross the street, despite the old man's protest that he actually wants to stay on this side of the street. (Medgyes 2017, p. 492)

Henry Widdowson has also been an influential voice interrogating the connections between linguistics as an academic field and language teaching practice. He observes that the teaching profession often considered linguistics to be 'an abstruse field of enquiry at several removes from the reality of the language classroom' (Widdowson, 2003, p. 4). However, this represents a more nuanced perspective than one might initially assume. Widdowson is not endorsing a blanket rejection of any utility for linguistics. The aim is rather to formulate what can be usefully considered applied linguistics, as opposed to what Widdowson (2000a; 2000b) terms 'linguistics applied'. This is itself a research-oriented perspective, seeking to differentiate independent fields of inquiry and to carve out what characterises applied linguistics as its own academic field distinct from linguistics. For Widdowson, a key difference is 'mediation'. Applied linguistics as an area of inquiry involves mediation by taking into account social, cultural and educational perspectives as part of the research paradigm that are not crucial for linguistics as a distinct field. Linguistics applied can be seen as the more direct application of linguistic description by equating this with the language that is to be taught in the classroom. A language classroom is its own social reality; the language that linguists describe as an object of study and the languages that pupils are exposed to as a subject on an educational curriculum are not the same thing. Linguistic research is carried out on its own terms with its own constraints and motivations, distinct from the nature of the language as taught and used in the foreign language classroom. It is therefore not surprising that linguistic research may not have direct unmediated application to the classroom. Widdowson summarises the point concisely:

> [I]t is not within the brief of linguists to make useful theories. On the contrary, as soon as they start doing that, they lose their scholarly independence and with it their value to the non-scholarly world. This

> value depends not on making useful theories, but making theories useful. (Widdowson 2003, pp. 10–11)

A clear distinction between research and practice is not particularly controversial. Most would surely agree that there is little direct application between academic fields of inquiry and the teaching of academic subjects, at least at the school level. It is useful to reflect on whether cutting edge mathematics research could or should find application in maths classrooms, and so on. But as Widdowson observes, there must be some, albeit mediated, connection between the two. One crux of the issue in discussions of research–practice interaction seems to be who could or should act as mediators between academic research and teaching practice. Our reading of the field is that 'linguistics applied' is sometimes used as a charge against any attempt to apply more theoretically oriented research in order to exclude it from discussion of application. This seems contrary to Widdowson's intention. As we noted, he observes that theories and ideas can be made useful, but suggests that linguists themselves cannot judge what use might be made of linguistic theory and that this is for others to decide (Widdowson, 2003, p. 11).

We take issue with the idea that discussing applications of theory is automatically linguistics applied, and we take issue with the idea that linguists cannot themselves judge the use that might be made of linguistic theory. There can be no a priori definition of linguistics applied as it depends on mediation and the way that any particular suggestions are framed. It is noteworthy that Widdowson's (2000a; 2000b) criticisms were levelled at, among other things, corpus linguistics and task-based language learning. Researchers in these areas would likely more readily define themselves as applied linguists as opposed to theoreticians in formal and functional linguistics. The key point is that no particular area of linguistic research is necessarily more applied, or inherently more applicable compared to others. How the research is mediated is the defining feature.

This brings us to the suggestion that academic linguists cannot themselves engage in mediation and application. There are two issues here. Firstly, even if academic linguists typically work within a framework that is not immediately applicable to educational questions, they can surely step outside of their frameworks and reflect critically on what might be useful for pedagogy, and how that usefulness might be formulated. Secondly, if one assumes that linguists cannot themselves act as mediators, it leaves a gap which is in practical terms impossible to fill. One cannot expect practitioners to want

5.6 Conclusion: Applying Linguistics

or need to develop the necessary expertise in facets of linguistic research in order to consider how it might be relevant to practice. And applied linguists are not 'applicators' looking around for linguistic theories to mediate. Applied linguists interested in language pedagogy inevitably have their own conceptual baggage with respect to views of language and the way that language is acquired or learned. Given the diversity in linguistic research paradigms, it is also unrealistic to expect even the most ecumenical of applied linguists to know the details of all frameworks and potential areas of application. Thus, applied linguistics is also defined in and on its own terms, with inevitable blind spots with respect to areas of linguistic theory and language acquisition research.

If linguists do not themselves attempt to fill this gap, it means a wealth of interesting and potentially relevant research will remain unavailable for research in pedagogy or teacher training. Many years ago, Chomsky proposed that:

> It is possible – even likely – that principles of psychology and linguistics, and research in these disciplines, may supply insights useful to the language teacher. But this must be demonstrated, and cannot be presumed. It is the language teacher himself who must validate or refute any specific proposal. There is very little in psychology or linguistics that he can accept on faith. (Chomsky, 1971 [1965], p. 155)

Of course educators cannot accept any proposal on faith, but before they can interrogate proposals, they have to have heard them in the first place. If scholars from linguistics and language acquisition research don't attempt to make their research paradigms accessible, or if they are barred by charges of linguistics applied from doing so, an unhelpful disconnect will remain.

Seeking to close this gap also comes with risks from the theoretical direction. Mediation of theoretical linguistics will inevitably mean that concepts that are seen as axiomatic in research will be relaxed, reformulated and repackaged for a new audience with no particular theoretical axe to grind. For example, our idea of Virtual Grammar has clear connections to the idea of Universal Grammar, but we hope without any theoretical or conceptual baggage which might hinder engagement from education. The risk here is that researchers themselves take issue, perhaps taking exception to repackaging and reformulation as a distortion or caricature of the key ideas of the research paradigm. Our response to any such criticism would depend on the exact nature of the supposed problem. If the criticism is that ideas have been changed, well yes, they have. Mediation requires this, and any overly strict adherence to theoretical concepts and their undiluted application to questions of education will simply result in continuing apprehension and misunderstandings between linguistics, applied linguistics and language education. If the criticism is that some theoretical notion or empirical evidence has not been mediated appropriately or usefully, then we see this simply as an invitation to further refine the ideas and adjust the rationale for formulating our claims. It would be extremely surprising, indeed disappointing, if the ideas outlined here are the last word in applications of linguistics to language pedagogy. It is to be expected that certain ideas will be challenged and revised and that some will be useful and others not. Surely this is in the nature of mediation and engaging across disciplines and paradigms.

Ultimately, the result of any such engagement will hopefully be an enrichment of teacher training and teachers' knowledge, not some 'new' or 'better' methodology. As we have emphasised throughout, there are more than enough suggestions for methods of language teaching. We do not assume that the latest empirical results are going to be immediately useful for teaching. Indeed, we agree with Larsen-Freeman (2015, p. 274) that thinking exclusively in terms of applicability is not necessarily the most useful way to engage between research and practice. The suggestion is that maybe 'the most important contribution of research to practice is to challenge teachers to think differently, to experiment with new practices, and to help them make the tacit explicit by cultivating new ways of talking about their practice' (Larsen-Freeman, 2015, p. 274). We hope that the ideas presented in this book provide opportunities to think differently about grammar.

5.7 EXERCISES AND QUESTIONS FOR DISCUSSION

1. Purposes of Language Teaching

What is the purpose, value and role of language in education as outlined in education policy or syllabus guidelines you are familiar with? What is your own understanding of what language teaching is for? How does your own opinion differ from ideas outlined in education policy?
   i) How does the purpose differ for teaching of the national language and teaching of additional languages for you? Where is it the same?

5.7 Exercises and Questions for Discussion

ii) Does the purpose differ if included at primary school level as opposed to middle or secondary school teaching? How about adult language teaching, for example, to recently arrived migrants?

iii) Is purpose dependent on national context? Or type of school? Or does it depend on the socioeconomic status of the students in question?

iv) Consider the answers to these questions in terms of the Virtual Grammar view of Language we have presented in this book. How does a Virtual Grammar approach relate to your thinking about why we teach language? Is there variation in your response based on the different contexts listed here?

2. Language Subjects

This chapter contrasts the teaching of language with the teaching of other subjects in school.

i) Brainstorm to list six to ten subjects typically taught in a school system you are familiar with. Then consider each in relation to language. In what ways is a language as a school subject different or similar to the subjects you have listed? Do you find that your list of subjects can be subdivided into any types based on your discussion?

ii) Given your discussion of language as a subject in school, now consider the content matter and the learning outcomes in a language class as opposed to other subjects. Does consideration of this more specific aspect of the question change or modify any of the points you considered? If you teach a non-language subject as well as a language subject, how does your approach to teaching and learning change?

iii) Now think about methods and approaches to teaching. Does the teaching of language require particular pedagogical methods that are distinct from teaching for other subjects?

3. Language Acquisition and Learning

There are many things about language learning and language development that we still do not understand. List three questions about language development that you have.

i) Now consider each question in terms of whether or not it could be used as a Research Question for empirical or theoretical study? Do so by thinking about how you could go about finding the answer to the question. Is it something that is 'research-able'?

ii) Now consider each question you came up with in terms of teaching. What effect does each question have on classroom pedagogy? In other words, if you don't know the answer to the question you have posed, then what does this mean you might do (or not do) in your teaching?
iii) Think about where your questions came from. Do they stem from your own experiences as a language teacher? Or perhaps your experience as a language learner? Do any of them find some clarification from ideas presented in this book? To what extent do the ideas in this book raise additional questions for you?

4. Previous Language Knowledge

We have argued throughout that (an) existing language(s) is an advantage to be valued and exploited in the teaching of a new language.
i) To what extent do you agree with this view?
ii) Reflect on your own experience learning a language. Do you remember drawing from your knowledge and ability in your existing dominant/primary language(s) as you were learning the new language? What was the approach your teachers and/or language learning materials took with respect L1 knowledge?
iii) What would you do as a teacher of language with regard to the existing language knowledge amongst your learners? If you agree that it is a resource to be exploited, what ways can you think of to exploit it? If you disagree and feel that the 'target language only' approach is correct, how can you account for the generally accepted precept in education that there is value in building on existing knowledge?

5. Nativeness

The term 'native' language has become very controversial in applied linguistics. What is your view on the use of this term?
i) To what extent do you think the language(s) you learned from birth differs from the language(s) you learned later in life? Are there any clear differences? Are there differences that you think could disappear under any circumstances or do you think they would persist no matter what?
ii) What is your view on the difference between learning a language and acquiring a language? In other words, do you think some language development happens through 'natural' implicit development while other aspects of linguistic development depend on conscious explicit learning? To what extent does your view

5.7 Exercises and Questions for Discussion

change when you consider language development in the context of an infant and development later on in life?

iii) Our Virtual Grammar orientation has led us to suggest that knowing another language is much like knowing another dialect, and even like knowing another register within the same dialect of a language. This approach can be seen to remove the objection to 'native' as a term because all forms of all languages, in this view, are equally valuable. To what extent do you agree or disagree with this?

6. Linguistics and Language Teaching

What is the role of linguistics in language education? How relevant is linguistics research to language teaching itself?

i) To what extent should linguists be expected to 'translate' their research to ensure that developments in thinking are known and understood within language education? Should language teachers be expected to keep abreast of developments in linguistic research?

ii) How about language acquisition research? Should second language acquisition researchers be expected to 'translate' their research to ensure that developments in thinking are known and understood within language education? Should language teachers be expected to keep abreast of developments in second language acquisition research?

iii) What is your view on theory and practice in general? How does the practice of teaching relate to theory? Does the answer vary if considering theory in different domains such as: linguistic theory? cognitive theory? education theory?

References

Aboh, E. O. (2015). *The Emergence of Hybrid Grammars: Language Contact and Change*. Cambridge: Cambridge University Press.
Aijmer, K. (ed.) (2009). *Corpora and Language Teaching*. Amsterdam: John Benjamins.
Aikhenvald, A. (2004). *Evidentiality*. Oxford: Oxford University Press.
Ambridge, B., & Lieven, E. (2011). *Child Language Acquisition: Contrasting Theoretical Approaches*. Cambridge: Cambridge University Press.
Armstrong, N., & MacKenzie, I. E. (2013). *Standardization, Ideology and Linguistics*. Basingstoke: Palgrave Macmillan.
Ayoun, D. (2005). *Parameter Setting in Language Acquisition*. London: Continuum.
Baker, M. (2002). *The Atoms of Language*. Oxford: Oxford University Press.
Balcom, P. (1997). Why is this happened? Passive morphology and unaccusativity. *Second Language Research*, 13, 1–9.
Bates, E., & MacWhinney, B. (1987). Competition, variation, and language learning. In B. MacWhinney, ed., *Mechanisms of Language Acquisition*. Hillsdale, NJ: Erlbaum, pp. 157–94.
Beacco, J.-C., & Byram, M. (2007). *Guide for the development of language education policies in Europe: From linguistic diversity to plurilingual education*. Language Policy Division, Council of Europe, www.coe.int/t/dg4/linguistic/Source/FullGuide_EN.pdf.
Bernstein, T. M. (1965). *The Careful Writer: A Modern Guide to English Usage*. New York: Atheneum.
Biber, D., & Conrad, S. (2009). *Register, Genre, and Style*. Cambridge: Cambridge University Press.
Bley-Vroman, R. (1990). The logical problem of foreign language learning. *Linguistic Analysis*, 20, 3–49.
Bley-Vroman, R. (2009). The evolving context of the fundamental difference hypothesis. *Studies in Second Language Acquisition*, 31(2), 175–98.
Blommaert, J. (2010). *The Sociolinguistics of Globalisation*. Cambridge: Cambridge University Press.
Blommaert, J., & Rampton, B. (2011). Language and superdiversity. *Diversities*, 13(2), www.unesco.org/shs/diversities/vol13/issue2/art1.
Blue, G., & Mitchell, R. (eds.) (1996). *Language and Education: Selected Papers from the Annual Meeting of the British Association for Applied Linguistics*. Clevedon: Multilingual Matters.

Boas, F. (1938). Language. In F. Boas, ed., *General Anthropology*. Boston, New York: D.C. Heath and Company, pp. 124–45.
Boers, F., & Lindstromberg, S. (eds.). (2008). *Cognitive Linguistic Approaches to Teaching Vocabulary and Phraseology*. Berlin: Mouton de Gruyter.
Bohnacker, U., & Rosén, C. (2008). The clause-initial position in L2 German declaratives: Transfer of information structure. *Studies in Second Language Acquisition*, 30(4), 511–38.
Brown, C. (2000). The interrelation between speech perception and phonological acquisition from infant to adult. In J. Archibald, ed., *Second Language Acquisition and Linguistic Theory*. Oxford: Blackwell Publishing, pp. 4–63.
Brown, R. (1973). *A First Language: The Early Stages*. Cambridge, MA: Harvard University Press.
Brown, R., & Hanlon, C. (1970). Derivational complexity and order of acquisition in child speech. In J. R. Hayes, *Cognition and the development of language*. New York: Wiley, pp. 11–53.
Brumfit, C. (2001). *Individual Freedom in Language Teaching: Helping Learners to Develop a Dialect of Their Own*. Oxford: Oxford University Press.
Butzkamm, W. (2003). We only learn language once: The role of the mother tongue in FL classrooms: Death of a dogma. *The Language Learning Journal*, 28(1), 29–39.
Butzkamm, W., & Caldwell, J. (2009). *The Bilingual Reform: A Paradigm Shift in Foreign Language Teaching*. Tübingen: Narr-Studienbücher.
Byram, M., & Wagner, M. (2018). Making a difference: Language teaching for intercultural and international dialogue. *Foreign Language Annals*, 51 (1), 140–51.
Camden, W. G. (1979). Parallels in structure of lexicon and syntax between New Hebrides Bislama and the South Santo language as spoken at Tangoa. In P. Mühlhäusler et al., eds., *Papers in Pidgin and Creole Linguistics No. 2*. Canberra: Australian National University (Pacific Linguistics A-57), pp. 51–117.
Campbell, L., & Mixco, M. (2007). *A Glossary of Historical Linguistics*. Edinburgh: Edinburgh University Press.
Candelier, M. (2008). "Awakening to Languages" and educational language policy. In J. Cenoz & N. H. Hornberger, eds., *Encyclopaedia of Language and Education, Vol. 6: Knowledge about Language* (2nd ed.). Berlin: Springer, pp. 219–32.
Carlson, G., & Pelletier, F. J. (eds.) (1995). *The Generic Book*. Chicago: University of Chicago Press.
Choi, M.-H., & Lardiere, D. (2006). The interpretation of wh-in-situ in Korean second language acquisition. In A. Belletti, E. Bennati, C. Chesi, E. DiDomenico & I. Ferrari, eds., *Language Acquisition and Development: Proceedings of GALA 2005*. Cambridge: Cambridge Scholars Press, pp. 125–35.
Chomsky, N. (1959). A review of B. F. Skinner's *Verbal Behavior*. *Language*, 35, 26–57.

Chomsky, N. (1971[1965]). Language Teaching. In J. Allen & P. van Buren, eds., *Chomsky: Selected Readings*. Oxford: Oxford University Press, pp. 148–59.

Clahsen, H. (1999). Lexical entries and rules of language: A multidisciplinary study of German inflection. *Behavioral and Brain Sciences*, 22(6), 991–1013.

Clahsen, H., & Felser, C. (2006). Grammatical processing in language learners. *Applied Psycholinguistics*, 27(1), 3–42.

Cochrane, J. (2003). *Between You and I: A Little Book of Bad English*. London: Icon Books.

Collins, C., & Postal, P. (2012). *Imposters: A Study of Pronominal Agreement*. Cambridge, MA: MIT Press.

Comrie, B. (1989). *Language Universals and Linguistic Typology* (2nd ed.). Chicago: University of Chicago Press.

Cook, G. (2010). *Translation in Language Teaching*. Oxford: Oxford University Press.

Cook, V. J. (1992). Evidence for multi-competence. *Language Learning*, 42(4), 557–91.

Corbett, G. (2000). *Number*. Cambridge: Cambridge University Press.

Cowan, R. (2008). *The Teacher's Grammar of English: A Course Book and Reference Guide*. Cambridge: Cambridge University Press.

Craig, C. (1987). Jacaltec: Field work in Guatemala. In T. Schopen, ed., *Languages and Their Speakers*. Philadelphia: University of Pennsylvania Press, pp. 3–58.

Crain, S., & Thornton, R. (1998). *Investigations in Universal Grammar: A Guide to Experiments on the Acquisition of Syntax and Semantics*. Cambridge, MA: MIT Press.

Cummins, J. (2007). Rethinking monolingual instructional strategies in multilingual classrooms. *Canadian Journal of Applied Linguistics*, 10, 221–41.

Cummins, J. (2008). Teaching for transfer: Challenging the two solitudes assumption in bilingual Education. In J. Cummins & N. H. Hornberger, eds., *Encyclopedia of Language and Education, Vol. 5: Bilingual Education*. Berlin: Springer, pp. 65–75.

Cutts, M. (2009). *Oxford Guide to Plain English* (3rd ed.). Oxford: Oxford University Press.

Cysouw, M. (2013). Inclusive/exclusive distinction in verbal inflection. In M. Dryer, S. Matthew & M. Haspelmath, eds., *The World Atlas of Language Structures Online*. Leipzig: Max Planck Institute for Evolutionary Anthropology, http://wals.info/chapter/40.

de Carvalho, A., Lidz, J., Tieu, L., Bleam, T., & Christophe, A. (2016). English-speaking preschoolers can use phrasal prosody for syntactic parsing. *The Journal of the Acoustical Society of America*, 139, EL216–EL222.

Deal, A. R. (2015). Ergativity. In T. Kiss & A. Alexiadou, eds., *Syntax – Theory and Analysis: An International Handbook, Vol. 1*. Berlin: Walter de Gruyter, pp. 654–708.

Dekydtspotter, L., Sprouse, R., & Anderson, B. (1997). The interpretive interface in L2 acquisition: The process-result distinction in English-French interlanguage grammars. *Language Acquisition*, 6(4), 297–332.

Denham, K., & Lobeck, A. (eds.) (2010). *Linguistics at School: Language Awareness in Primary and Secondary Education*. Cambridge: Cambridge University Press.

Dickey, E. (2016). *Learning Latin the ancient way: Latin textbooks from the Ancient World*. Cambridge: Cambridge University Press.

Dulay, H. C., & Burt, M. K. (1974). Natural sequences in child second language acquisition. *Language Learning*, 24, 37–53.

Dulay, H. C., Burt, M. K., & Krashen, S. D. (1982). *Language Two*. New York: Oxford University Press.

Dussias, P., & Sagarra, N. (2007). The effect of exposure on syntactic parsing in Spanish–English bilinguals. *Bilingualism: Language and Cognition*, 10(1), 101–16.

Evans, N., & Sasse, H.-J. (2002). Introduction. In N. Evans & H.-J. Sasse, eds., *Problems of Polysynthesis*. Berlin: Akademie Verlag, pp. 1–13.

Fanselow, G., & Cavar, D. (2002). Distributed deletion. In A. Alexiadou, ed., *Theoretical Approaches to Universals*. Amsterdam: John Benjamins, pp. 65–109.

Fillmore, C. J. (1970). The grammar of *hitting* and *breaking*. In R. Jacobs & P. Rosenbaum, eds., *Readings in English Transformational Grammar*. Waltham, MA: Ginn, pp. 12033.

Friedman, V. (2007). Balkanising the Balkan Sprachbund: A closer look at grammatical permeability and feature distribution. In A. Aikhenvald & R. M. W. Dixon, eds., *Grammars in Contact: A Cross-Linguistic Typology*. Oxford: Oxford University Press, pp. 201–19.

García, O., & Lin, A. (2017). Extending understandings of bilingual and multilingual education. In O. García, A. M. Y. Lin & S. May, eds., *Bilingual and Multilingual Education*. Springer, pp. 1–20.

Garcia, O., & Wei, L. (2014). *Translanguaging: Language, Bilingualism and Education*. New York: Palgrave Macmillan.

Gervain, J. (2018). The role of prenatal experience in language development. *Current Opinion in Behavioral Sciences*, 21, 62–7.

Goldschneider, J. M., & DeKeyser, R. M. (2001). Explaining the 'natural order of L2 morpheme acquisition' in English: A meta-analysis of multiple determinants. *Language Learning*, 51, 1–50.

Götz, S., & Mukherjee, J. (eds.) (2019). *Learner Corpora and Language Teaching*. Amsterdam: John Benjamins.

Greenberg, J. (1963). Some universals of grammar with particular reference to the order of meaningful elements. In J. Greenberg, ed., *Universals of Language*. Cambridge, MA: MIT Press, pp. 73–113.

Grüter, T. (2006). Another take on the L2 initial state: Evidence from comprehension in L2 German. *Language Acquisition*, 13(4), 287–317.

Grüter, T., & Conradie, S. (2006). Investigating the L2 initial state: Additional evidence from the production and comprehension of Afrikaans-speaking learners of German. In R. Slabakova, S. A. Montrul, & P. Prévost, eds., *Inquiries in Linguistic Development: In Honor of Lydia White*. Amsterdam: John Benjamins, pp. 89–114.

Gürel, A. (2002). Linguistic Characteristics of Second Language Acquisition and First Language Attrition: Turkish Overt and Null Pronouns. PhD Dissertation, McGill University, Montreal.

Haegeman, L. (2017). Unspeakable sentences: Subject omission in written registers: A cartographic analysis. *Linguistic Variation*, 17(2), 229–50.

Haegeman, L., & Gueron, J. (1999). *English Grammar: A Generative Perspective*. Oxford: Blackwell Publishing.

Haegeman, L., & Ihsane, T. (2001). Adult null subjects in the non-pro-drop languages: Two diary dialects. *Language Acquisition*, 9(4), 329–46.

Hale, K. (1983). Warlpiri and the grammar of non-configurational languages. *Natural Language & Linguistic Theory*, 1(1), 5–47.

Halliday, M., & Webster, J. (2009). *Continuum Companion to Systemic Functional Linguistics*. London; New York: Continuum.

Harley, B. (1993). Instructional strategies and SLA in early French immersion. *Studies in Second Language Acquisition*, 15(2), 245–70.

Hawkins, E. (1984). *Awareness of Language: An Introduction*. Cambridge: Cambridge University Press.

Hirakawa, M. (2013). Alternations and argument structure in second language English: Knowledge of two types of intransitive verbs. In M. Whong, K. H. Gil, H. Marsden, eds., *Universal Grammar and the Second Language Classroom*. Dordrecht: Springer, pp. 117–38.

Hockett, C. F. (1960). The origin of speech. *Scientific American*, 203, 88–111.

Holes, C. (1995). *Modern Arabic: Structures, Functions, and Varieties*. London: Longman.

Howatt, A. P. R., & Widdowson, H. G. (2004). *A History of English Language Teaching*. Oxford: Oxford University Press.

Huddleston, R. D., & Pullum, G. K. (2002). *The Cambridge Grammar of the English Language*. Cambridge: Cambridge University Press.

Hudson, R. (2008). Linguistic theory. In B. Spolsky & F. Hult, eds., *The Handbook of Educational Linguistics*. Malden, MA: Blackwell Publishing, pp. 53–65.

Hyland, K. (2004). *Disciplinary Discourses: Social Interactions in Academic Writing*. Ann Arbor, MI: University of Michigan Press.

Hymes, D. (1972). On communicative competence. In J. B. Pride & J. Holmes, eds., *Sociolinguistics: Selected Readings*. Harmondsworth: Penguin, pp. 269–93.

Ionin, T., Ko, H., & Wexler, K. (2004). Article semantics in L2 acquisition: The role of specificity. *Language Acquisition*, 12(1), 3–69.

Ionin, T., Montrul, S., Kim, J., & Philippov, V. (2011). Genericity distinctions and the interpretation of determiners in second language acquisition. *Language Acquisition*, 18(4), 242–80.

Jackson, C. N. (2007). The use and non-use of semantic information, word order, and case markings during comprehension by L2 learners of German. *Modern Language Journal*, 91(3), 418–32.

Jackson, C. N. (2008). Proficiency level and the interaction of lexical and morphosyntactic information during L2 sentence processing. *Language Learning*, 58(4), 875–909.

Jean, G., & Simard, D. (2011). Grammar teaching and learning in L2: Necessary, but boring? *Foreign Language Annals*, 44, 467–94.

Keck, C., & Kim, Y.-J. (2014). *Pedagogical Grammar*. Amsterdam: John Benjamins.

Kegl, J. (1994). The Nicaraguan sign language project: An overview. *Signpost*, 7(1), 24–31.

Keesing, R. M. (1988). *Melanesian Pidgin and the Oceanic Substrate*. Stanford: Stanford University Press.

Khamis-Dakwar, R., & Froud, K. (2007). Lexical processing in two language varieties: An event-related brain potential study of Arabic native speakers. In M. Mughazy, ed., *Perspectives on Arabic linguistics XX*. Amsterdam & Philadelphia: John Benjamins, pp. 153–68.

Khamis-Dakwar, R., Froud, K., & Gordon, P. (2012). Acquiring diglossia: Mutual influences of formal and colloquial Arabic on children's grammaticality judgments. *Journal of Child Language*, 39, 61–89.

Kiparsky, P. (1998). Partitive case and aspect. In M. Butt and W. Geuder, eds., *The Projection of Arguments: Lexical and Compositional Factors*. Stanford: CSLI Publication, pp. 265–308.

Kiss, K. (2002). *The Syntax of Hungarian*. Cambridge: Cambridge University Press.

Klein, W., & Perdue, C. (1997). The Basic Variety (or: Couldn't natural languages be much simpler?). *Second Language Research*, 13(4), 301–47.

Kramsch, C. (2008). Applied linguistic theory and second/foreign language education. In N. Van Deusen-Scholl & N. H. Hornberger, eds., *Encyclopedia of Language and Education, Vol. 4: Second and Foreign Language Education*. Berlin: Springer, pp. 3–15.

Krifka, M., Pelletier, J. M., Carlson, G. N., ter Meulen, A., Chierchia, G., & Link, G. (1995). Generictiy: An introduction. In G. Carlson & F. J. Pelletier, eds., *The Generic Book*. Chicago: University of Chicago Press, pp. 1–124.

Kroeger, P. (2010). The grammar of *hitting* and *breaking* (and *cutting*) in Kimaragang Dusun. *Oceanic Linguistics*, 49, 2–20.

Kumaravadivelu, B. (2001). Toward a postmethod pedagogy. *TESOL Quarterly*, 35, 537–60.

Langer, N. (2001). *Linguistic Purism in Action: How Auxiliary tun Was Stigmatized in Early New High German*. Berlin: Walter de Gruyter.

Lardiere, D. (1998). Case and tense in the 'fossilized' steady-state. *Second Language Research*, 14(1), 1–26.

Lardiere, D. (2009). Some thoughts on the contrastive analysis of features in second language acquisition. *Second Language Research*, 25(2), 173–227.

Larsen-Freeman, D. (2003). *Teaching Language: From grammar to Grammaring.* Boston: Heinle & Heinle.

Larsen-Freeman, D. (2008). Does TESOL share theories with other disciplines? *TESOL Quarterly,* 42(2), 291–4.

Larsen-Freeman, D. (2011). Teaching and testing grammar. In M. Long and C. Doughty, eds., *The Handbook of Language Teaching.* Oxford: Blackwell Publishers, pp. 518–42.

Larsen-Freeman, D. (2015). Research into practice: Grammar learning and teaching. *Language Teaching,* 48(2), 263–80.

Larsen-Freeman, D., & Anderson, M. (2011). *Techniques and Principles in Language Teaching.* Oxford: Oxford University Press.

Lasnik, H., & Sobin, N. (2000). The *who / whom* puzzle: On the preservation of an archaic feature. *Natural Language and Linguistic Theory,* 18, 343–71.

Lee, I., & Ramsey, S. R. (2000). *The Korean Language.* New York: State University of New York Press.

Lefebvre, C., White, L., & Jourdan, C. (eds.) (2006). *L2 Acquisition and Creole Genesis: Dialogues.* Amsterdam: John Benjamins.

Legate, J. A., & Yang, C. (2002). Empirical re-assessment of stimulus poverty arguments. *Linguistic Review,* 19, 151–62.

Levin, B., & Rappaport Hovav, M. (2005). *Argument Realization.* Cambridge: Cambridge University Press.

Lewis, M. (1993). *The Lexical Approach.* London: Language Teaching Publications.

Li, C. N., & Thompson, S. A. (1976). Subject and Topic: A New Typology of Language. In C. N. Li, ed., *Subject and Topic.* New York: Academic Press, pp. 457–89.

Li, Wei. (2015). New Chinglish: Bad, uncivilised and ugly, or creatively subversive? *Babel: The Language Magazine,* 10.

Lin, A. (2013). Toward paradigmatic change in TESOL methodologies: Building Plurilingual pedagogies from the ground up. *TESOL Quarterly,* 47(3), 521–45.

Loewen, S., Li, S., Fei, F., Thompson, A., Nakatsukasa, K., & Ahn, S. (2009). Second language learners' beliefs about error instruction and error correction. *Modern Language Journal,* 93, 91–104.

Long, M. (1991). Focus on form: A design feature in language teaching methodology. In K. De Bot, R. Ginsberg, & C. Kramsch, eds., *Foreign Language Research in Cross-Cultural Perspective.* Amsterdam: John Benjamins, pp. 39–52.

Long, D., & Rothman, J. (2013). Generative approaches and the competing systems hypothesis: Formal acquisition to pedagogical application. In J. W. Schwieter, ed., *Innovative Research and Practices in Second Language Acquisition and Bilingualism.* John Benjamins, Amsterdam, pp. 63–84.

Lopez, E., & Sabir, M. (2019). Article pedagogy: Encouraging links between linguistic theory and teaching practice. *RELC Journal,* 50(1), 188–201.

Lyons, C. (1999). *Definiteness.* Cambridge: Cambridge University Press.

Mackenzie, I. E. (2013). Participle-object agreement in French and the theory of grammatical viruses. *Journal of Romance Studies*, 13(1), 19–33.

Maddieson, I. (1984). *Patterns of Sounds*. Cambridge: Cambridge University Press.

Makoni, S., & Pennycook, A. (eds.) (2007). *Disinventing and Reconstituting Languages*. Clevedon: Multilingual Matters.

Marcus, G. F. (1992). Negative evidence in language acquisition. *Cognition*, 46(1), 53–85.

Marcus, G. F., Brinkmann, U., Clahsen, H., Wiese, R., & Pinker, S. (1995). German inflection: The exception that proves the rule. *Cognitive Psychology*, 29, 189–256.

Marr, T., & English, F. (2019). *Rethinking TESOL in Diverse Global Settings*. Oxford: Bloomsbury Academic.

Marsden, H. (2008). Pair-list readings in Korean-Japanese, Chinese-Japanese and English-Japanese interlanguage. *Second Language Research*, 24(2), 189–226.

Marsden, H. (2009). Distributive quantifier scope in English-Japanese and Korean-Japanese interlanguage. *Language Acquisition*, 16(3), 135–77.

Marsden, H., Whong, M., & Gil, K-H. (2018). What's in the textbook and what's in the mind. *Studies in Second Language Acquisition*, 40(1), 91–118.

Martinez-Garcia, M. T., & Wulff, S. (2012). Not wrong, yet not quite right: Spanish ESL students' use of gerundial and infinitival complementation. *International Journal of Applied Linguistics*, 22(2), 225–44.

Massam, D. (ed.) (2012). *Count and Mass across Languages*. Oxford: Oxford University Press.

McArthur, T. (1988). *Worlds of Reference: Lexicography, Learning and Language from the Clay Tablet to the Computer*. Cambridge: Cambridge University Press.

McManus, K. (2019). Awareness of L1 form-meaning mappings can reduce crosslinguistic effects in L2 grammatical learning. *Language Awareness*, 28(2), 114–38.

McManus, K. & Marsden, E. (2017). L1 explicit instruction can improve L2 online and offline performance. *Studies in Second Language Acquisition*, 39(3), 459–92.

McNeill, D. (1966). Developmental psycholinguistics. In F. Smith & G. A. Miller, eds., *The Genesis of Language: A Psycholinguistic Approach*. Cambridge, MA: MIT Press, pp. 15–84.

McWhorter, J. (2007). *Language Interrupted: Signs of Non-native Acquisition in Standard Language Grammars*. Oxford: Oxford University Press.

Medgyes, P. (2017). The (ir)relevance of academic research for the language teacher. *ELT Journal*, 71(4), 491–98.

Milroy, J., & Milroy, L. (1999). *Authority in Language: Investigating Language Prescription and Standardisation*. 3rd ed. London: Routledge.

Mitchell, R., Brumfit, C., & Hooper, J. (1994). 'Knowledge about Language': policy, rationales and practices. *Research Papers in Education*, 9(2), 183–205.

Morgan, J., Bonamo, K., & Travis, L. (1995). Negative evidence on negative evidence. *Developmental Psychology*, 31(2), 180-97.
Mugdan, J. (1977). *Flexionsmorphologie und Psycholinguistik*. [Inflectional Morphology and Psycholinguistics]. Tübingen: Narr.
Myles, F. (2012). Complexity, accuracy and fluency: The role played by formulaic sequences in early interlanguage development. In A. Housen, F. Kuiken, & I. Vedder, eds., *Dimensions of L2 Performance and Proficiency: Complexity, Accuracy and Fluency in SLA*. Amsterdam: John Benjamins, pp. 71-94.
Myles, F., Hooper, J., & Mitchell, R. (1998). Rote or rule? Exploring the role of formulaic language in classroom foreign language learning. *Language Learning*, 48(3), 323-64.
Newmeyer, F. (1998). *Language Form and Language Function*. Cambridge, MA: MIT Press.
Newport, E., Gleitman, H., & Gleitman, L. (1977). Mother, I'd rather do it myself: Some effects and non-effects of maternal speech style. In C. E. Snow & C. A. Ferguson, eds., *Talking to Children*. Cambridge: Cambridge University Press, pp. 109-49.
Norris, J. M., & Ortega, L. (2000). Effectiveness of L2 Instruction: A research synthesis and quantitative meta-analysis. *Language Learning*, 50(3), 417-528.
Notes. (1997). *Language in Society*, 26(3), 469-70. doi:10.1017/S00 47404500019679.
Olson, G., & Faigley, L. (1991). Language, politics and composition: A conversation with Noam Chomsky. *Journal of Advanced Composition*, 11, 1-35.
Oshita, H. (2000). What is happened may not be what appears to be happening: A corpus study of 'passive' unaccusatives in L2 English. *Second Language Research*, 16(4), 293-324.
Oshita, H. (2001). The unaccusative trap in second language acquisition. *Studies in Second Language Acquisition*, 23, 279-304.
Paltridge, B. (2001). *Genre and the Language Learning Classroom*. Ann Arbor: University of Michigan Press.
Parrott, M. (2010). *Grammar for English Language Teachers*. Cambridge: Cambridge University Press.
Pelletier, J. F. (2012). Lexical nouns are both +MASS and +COUNT, but they are neither +MASS nor +COUNT. In D. Massam, ed., *Count and Mass across Languages*. Oxford: Oxford University Press, pp. 9-26.
Pereltsvaig, A. (2012). *Languages of the World: An Introduction*. Cambridge: Cambridge University Press.
Pérez-Llantada, M. C., & Larsen-Freeman, D. (2007). New trends in grammar teaching: Issues and applications: An interview with Prof. Diane Larsen-Freeman. *Atlantis*, 29(1),157-63.
Picallo, M. (1991). Nominals and nominalizations in Catalan. *Probus*, 3(3), 279-316.

Pinker, S. (1996). *The Language Instinct*. New York: Harper Perennial.
Polinsky, M. (2001). Grammatical voice. In N. J. Smelser & P. B. Baltes, eds., *International Encyclopedia of Social & Behavioral Sciences*. Elsevier Science, pp. 6348-53.
Prodromou, L. (2002). The role of the mother tongue in the classroom. *International Association of Teachers of English as a Foreign Language Issues*, 166, 6-8.
Pullum, G. K. (2018). The usage game: Catering for perverts. In I. Tieken-Boon van Ostade, ed., *English Usage Guides. History, Advice, Attitudes*. Oxford: Oxford University Press, pp. 177-96.
Pullum, G. K., & Scholz, B. (2002). Empirical assessment of stimulus poverty arguments. *Linguistic Review*, 19, 9-50.
Radford, A., & Felser, C. (2011). On preposition copying and preposition pruning in wh-clauses in English. *Essex Research Reports in Linguistics*, 60 (4), www.essex.ac.uk/linguistics/publications/errl/errl60-4.pdf.
Rappaport Hovav, M., & Levin, B. (2010). Reflections on manner/result complementarity. In M. Rappaport Hovav, E. Doron & I. Sichel, eds., *Syntax, Lexical Semantics, and Event Structure*. Oxford: Oxford University Press, pp. 21-38.
Reiser, B., & Tabak, I. (2014). Scaffolding. In R. Sawyer, ed., *The Cambridge Handbook of the Learning Sciences*. Cambridge: Cambridge University Press, pp. 44-62.
Rothman, J. (2008). Aspectual selection in adult L2 Spanish and the competing systems hypothesis: When pedagogical and linguistic rules conflict. *Languages in Contrast*, 8(1), 74-106.
Rothman, J. (2010). Theoretical linguistics meets pedagogical practice: Pronominal subject use in Spanish as a second language (L2) as an example. *Hispania*, 93(1), 52-65.
Sampson, G. (2005). *The 'Language Instinct' Debate*. London: Continuum.
Sanoudaki, E., & Thierry, G. (2014). Bigrammatism: When the bilingual mind juggles with two grammars. In E. M. Thomas & I. Mennen, eds., *Advances in the Study of Bilingualism*. Bristol: Multilingual Matters, pp. 214-30.
Sato, M., & Loewen, S. (2019). Towards evidence-based second language pedagogy: Research proposals and pedagogical recommendations. In M. Sato & S. Loewen, eds., *Evidence-based Second Language Pedagogy: A Collection of Instructed Second Language Acquisition Studies*. New York: Routledge, pp. 1-24.
Saxton, M. (2000). Negative evidence and negative feedback: Immediate effects on the grammaticality of child speech. *First Language*, 20(60), 221-52.
Schwartz, B. D., & Sprouse, R. A. (1996). L2 cognitive states and the Full Transfer/Full Access model. *Second Language Research*, 12(1), 40-72.
Schwartz, B. D., & Sprouse, R. A. (2013). Generative approaches and the poverty of the stimulus. In J. Herschensohn & M. Young-Scholten, eds., *The Cambridge Handbook of Second Language Acquisition*. Cambridge: Cambridge University Press, pp. 137-58.

Selinker, L. (1972). Interlanguage. *International Review of Applied Linguistics*, 10, 209-31.
Selinker, L. (1992). *Rediscovering Interlanguage*. London: Longman.
Selinker, L., & Lamendella, J. T. (1978). Two perspectives on fossilization in interlanguage learning. *Interlanguage Studies Bulletin*, 3(2), 143-91.
Sharwood Smith, M. (2017). *Introducing Language and Cognition: A Map of the Mind*. Cambridge: Cambridge University Press.
Sharwood Smith, M., & Truscott, J. (2014). *The Multilingual Mind: A Modular Processing Perspective*. Cambridge: Cambridge University Press.
Sick, B. (2004). *Der Dativ ist dem Genitiv sein Tod – Ein Wegweiser durch den Irrgarten der deutschen Sprache*. [The Dative is to the Genitive its Death – A guide through the maze of the German language]. Cologne: Kiepenheuer und Witsch.
Siegel, J. (2008). *The Emergence of Pidgin and Creole Languages*. Oxford: Oxford University Press.
Siewierska, A. (2013). Passive Constructions. In M. Dryer, S. Matthew, & M. Haspelmath, eds., *The World Atlas of Language Structures Online*. Leipzig: Max Planck Institute for Evolutionary Anthropology. http://wals.info/chapter/107.
Simons, G. F., & Fennig, C. D. (eds.) (2018). *Ethnologue: Languages of the World* (21st ed.). Dallas, TX: SIL International. Online version: www.ethnologue.com, accessed July 2018.
Singler, J., & Kouwenberg, S. (eds.) (2008). *The Handbook of Pidgin and Creole Studies*. London: Blackwell Publishing.
Slabakova, R. (2000). L1 transfer revisited: The L2 acquisition of telicity marking in English by Spanish and Bulgarian native speakers. *Linguistics*, 38(368), 739-70.
Slabakova, R. (2003). Semantic evidence for functional categories in interlanguage grammars. *Second Language Research*, 19(1), 42-75.
Slabakova, R. (2008). *Meaning in the Second Language*. Berlin: Springer.
Slabakova, R. (2014). The bottleneck of second language acquisition. *Foreign Language Teaching and Research*, 46(4), 543-59.
Snape, N. (2008). Resetting the nominal mapping [parameter in L2 English: Definite article use and the count-mass distinction. *Bilingualism: Language and Cognition*, 11(1), 63-79.
Snape, N., & Yusa, N. (2013). Explicit article instruction in definiteness, specificity, genericity and perception. In M. Whong, K. H. Gil, & H. Marsden, eds., *Universal Grammar and the Second Language Classroom*. Dordrecht: Springer, pp. 161-83.
Sobin, N. (1994). An acceptable ungrammatical construction. In S. D. Lima, R. Corrigan, & G. Iverson, eds., *The Reality of Linguistic Rules*. Amsterdam: John Benjamins, pp. 51-66.
Sobin, N. (1997). Agreement, default rules, and grammatical viruses. *Linguistic Inquiry*, 28, 318-43.

References

Sohn, H.-M. (1999). *The Korean Language*. Cambridge: Cambridge University Press.

Sorace, A. (2000). Gradients in auxiliary selection with intransitive verbs. *Language*, 76(4), 859–90.

Sorace, A. (2008). Near-nativeness. In C. J. Doughty & M. H. Long, eds., *The Handbook of Second Language Acquisition*. Oxford: Blackwell Publishing, pp. 130–51.

Spada, N., & Tomita, Y. (2010). Interactions between type of instruction and type of language feature: A meta-analysis. *Language Learning*, 60(2), 263–308.

Spalek, K., Hoshino, N., Wu, Y. J., Damian, M., & Thierry, G. (2014). Speaking two languages at once: Unconscious native word form access in second language production. *Cognition*, 133(1), 226–31.

Sugisaki, K. (2016). Quantifier float and structure dependence in child Japanese. *Language Acquisition*, 23(1), 75–88.

Sundquist, J. D. (2011). Negative movement in the history of Norwegian: The evolution of a grammatical virus. In D. Jonas, J. Whitman & A. Garret, eds., *Grammatical Change: Origins, Nature, Outcomes*. Oxford: Oxford University Press, pp. 293–312.

Suzuki, T., & Yoshinaga, N. (2013). Children's knowledge of hierarchical phrase structure: Quantifier floating in Japanese. *Journal of Child Language*, 40, 628–55.

Swales, J., & Feak, C. (1994). *Academic Writing for Graduate Students*. Ann Arbor: University of Michigan Press.

Talmy, L. (1985). Lexicalisation patterns: Semantic structure in lexical forms. In T. Shopen, ed., *Language Typology and Syntactic Description. Vol. 3: Grammatical Categories and the Lexicon*. Cambridge: Cambridge University Press, pp. 57–149.

Talmy, L. (1991). Paths to realization: A typology of event conflation. In *Proceedings of the Berkeley Linguistics Society*. Berkeley: Berkeley Linguistics Society, pp. 480–519.

Thomas, M. (2013). History of the study of second language acquisition. In J. Herschensohn & M. Young-Scholten, eds., *The Cambridge Handbook of Second Language Acquisition*. Cambridge: Cambridge University Press, pp. 26–45.

Trappes-Lomax, H. (ed.) (2000). *Change and Continuity in Applied Linguistics: Selected Papers from the Annual Meeting of the British Association for Applied Linguistics*. Clevedon: Multilingual Matters.

Truss, L. (2003). *Eats, Shoots and Leaves: The Zero Tolerance Approach to Punctuation*. London: Profile Books.

Turnbull, M., & Dailey-O'Cain, J. (2009). Introduction. In M. Turnbull & J. Dailey-O'Cain, eds., *First Language Use in Second and Foreign Language Learning*. Bristol: Multilingual Matters, pp. 1–14.

Ur, P. (2011). Grammar teaching: research, theory and practice. In E. Hinkel, ed., *Handbook of Research in Second Language Teaching and Learning*. Abingdon: Routledge, pp. 507-22.

Vainikka, A., & Young-Scholten, M. (2011). *The Acquisition of German: Introducing Organic Grammar*. Berlin: De Gruyter.

Van Dam, J. (1940). *Handbuch der deutschen Sprache: 2 Wortlehre*. [Handbook of the German Language 2: Lexicology]. Groningen: Wolters-Noordhoff.

Van Lier, L. (1996). *Interaction in the Language Curriculum: Awareness, Autonomy, and Authenticity*. London: Longman.

VanPatten, B. (1996). *Input Processing and Grammar Instruction: Theory and Research*. Norwood, NJ: Ablex.

VanPatten, B. (ed.) (2004). *Processing Instruction: Theory, Research and Commentary*. Mahway, NJ: Erlbaum.

Vaughan-Evans, A. H., Kuipers, J. R., Thierry, G., & Jones, M. W. (2014). Anomalous transfer of syntax between languages. *Journal of Neuroscience*, 34(24), 8333-5.

Verheijen, L., Los, B., & de Haan, P. (2013). Information structure: The final hurdle?: The development of syntactic structures in (very) advanced Dutch EFL writing. *Dutch Journal of Applied Linguistics*, 2, 92-107.

Whong, M. (2013). A linguistic perspective on communicative language teaching. *Language Learning Journal*, 41, 115-28.

Whong, M., Gil, K. H., & Marsden, H. (2014). Beyond paradigm: The 'what' and the 'how' of classroom research. *Second Language Research*, 30(4), 551-68.

Widdowson, H. G. (2000a). Object language and the language subject: On the mediating role of applied linguistics. *Annual Review of Applied Linguistics*, 20, 21-33.

Widdowson, H. G. (2000b). On the limitations of linguistics applied. *Applied Linguistics*, 21(1), 3-25.

Widdowson, H. G. (2002). Language teaching: Defining the subject. In H. R. Trappes-Lomax & G. Ferguson, eds., *Language in Language Teacher Education*. Amsterdam: John Benjamins, pp. 68-81.

Widdowson, H. G. (2003). *Defining Issues in English Language Teaching*. Oxford: Oxford University Press.

Widdowson, H. G. (2016). ELF, adaptive variability and virtual language. In M. L. Pitzl, & R. Osimk-Teasdale, eds., *English as a Lingua Franca: Perspectives and Prospects: Contributions in Honour of Barbara Seidlhofer*. Berlin: Mouton de Gruyter, pp. 31-7.

Widdowson, H. G., & Seidlhofer, B. (2008). Visions and delusions: Language proficiency and educational failure. In S. Doff, F. Klippel, & W. Huellen, eds., *Visions of Languages in Education – Visionen der Bildung durch Sprachen*. Berlin: Langenscheidt Verlag, pp. 207-13.

Wray, A. (2002). *Formulaic Language and the Lexicon*. Cambridge: Cambridge University Press.

Yang, C. (2002). *Knowledge and Learning in Natural Language*. Oxford: Oxford University Press.

Yip, V. (1995). *Interlanguage and Learnability: From Chinese to English*. Amsterdam, Philadephia: John Benjamins.

Yip, V., & Matthews, S. (2017). *Basic Cantonese: A Grammar and a Workbook*. (2nd ed.) London: Routledge.

Zobl, H. (1989). Canonical typological structures and ergativity in English L2 acquisition. In S. M. Gass & J. Schachter, eds., *Linguistic Perspectives on Second Language Acquisition*. Cambridge: Cambridge University Press, pp. 203–21.

Index

accent, 62
acquisition/learning distinction, 178, 180, 183
activation, 22
Afrikaans, 82, 128
agglutinative languages, 58
agreement, 6, 8, 29, 44, 47, 51, 65, 76, 86, 89, 105, 106, 124, 127, 154, 159
Albanian, 55
alignment, 8, 15
ambient language, 117
Arabic, 48, 64, 65, 70, 82, 89
Arawak, 18
arbitrariness, 44
areal features, 55
argument alternations, 15
aspect, 25, 29, 31, 59, 108, 109, 112, 124, 127, 169, 170
aspectual, 29, 31
associativity, 41, 42, 45, 48, 55, 70, 71
Attachment Ambiguity, 81, 82
Audiolingual Approach, 34

Basic Variety, 124, 133
Bayso, 47, 54
Berlitz Method, 34
bilingualization, 168
Bininj Gunwok, 58, 59
Bislama, 71
Bottleneck Hypothesis, 132, 148
Breton, 62
Bulgarian, 169, 170, 171, 202

Cantonese, 46
case marking, 8, 27, 29, 31, 102, 103, 124, 129
causative, 16
Cayuga, 58, 59, 83
Central Eastern Oceanic, 70, 71
Chechen, 42
Chinese, 42, 45, 46, 50, 51, 57, 58, 59, 67, 154

classifiers, 51. *See also* noun classification
Cognitive Linguistics, 11, 14
communicative language teaching, 34, 161
competence, 9, 166
  communicative competence, 14, 163
Competing Systems Hypothesis, 126, 180, 182
conditional, 182
constituents, 17, 84, 106, 139, 144, 175
Constructivists, 9
co-reference, 151
corpus linguistics, 17
Creoles, 70, 71, 72
critical period, 120, 178
Croatian, 85

definiteness, 2, 18, 20, 76, 92, 93, 95, 96, 107, 138
derivational, 18
descriptive grammar, 7, 90, 93, 105
Deverbal Nouns, 12
dialect, 61, 62, 66, 108
diglossia, 64
Direct Method, 33
discontinuity, 85, 87
discourse analysis, 14
discreteness, 44
displacement, 85, 87
domain, 22, 26, 68, 120
dual, 47, 48, 50, 53, 64, 65, 71, 89
duality of structure, 44
Dutch, 55, 62, 63, 82

error, 137
evidentiality, 18, 107
existential, 28, 29, 30, 32, 131

feature reassembly, 130
Finnish, 29, 30, 31, 67
floating quantifiers, 144
Formalists, 4, 15

206

Index

formulaic sequences, 141
fossilisation, 117, 132
French, 30, 31, 55, 56, 58, 62, 82, 83, 86, 102, 106, 109, 111, 122, 123, 142
Full Transfer Hypothesis, 127
Functionalists, 4
Fundamental Difference Hypothesis, 120

gender, 6, 18, 50–3, 106
genericity, 28, 29, 30, 31, 54, 94, 95, 179
German, 51, 55, 56, 62, 63, 82, 83, 100, 103, 104, 128, 129, 130, 140, 141, 147, 148
grammar, 88
  descriptive grammar, 58, 79, 80, 81, 88, 89, 116, 163, 184
  pedagogical grammar, 90, 179
  prescriptive grammar, 63, 79, 80, 81, 83, 84, 86, 87, 88, 89, 100, 102, 104, 105, 116, 163
  reference grammar, 79, 88, 89, 90
Grammar Translation, 33, 34
grammar-translation, 161
grammatical concepts, 3, 5, 18, 20, 26, 27, 29, 30, 32, 45, 48, 54, 70, 88, 91, 92, 95, 98, 107, 112, 113, 130, 131, 132, 136, 138, 146, 148, 156, 157, 175, 182
grammatical virus, 101, 102, 105, 106, 180
Greek, 55, 82
Greenberg's language universals, 46
Gujarati, 42

Hungarian, 31, 36, 57

inchoative, 16
inflection, 18, 19, 124, 127, 159
inflectional languages, 58
information structure, 35, 135, 176
initial state, 126
interlanguage, 26, 95, 96, 97, 98
International Phonetic Alphabet (IPA), 19, 33
isolating languages, 58
Italian, 48, 58, 89, 99, 134, 135

Jacaltec, 51, 52
Japanese, 18, 45, 48, 69, 79, 107, 143, 144, 152, 154, 155

Korean, 1, 18, 20, 53, 69, 107, 130, 131, 154, 155

L1 transfer. *See* transfer
Language, 43, 61, 162, 166, 177, 183
language contact, 55
Latin, 42, 58, 83
lexical, 15

Malay, 42, 53
Mandarin, 23, 36, 42, 46, 154
marked, 36, 59, 170
mass/count distinction, 54, 93, 94
medium, 66
metafunctions, 13
meta-knowledge, 121
mistake, 145
mode, 66
Modular Cognition Framework (MCF), 21
modularity, 21, 22, 178
Morphology, 18, 25, 58, 59, 83, 97, 156
motherese, 149
motion events, 57
multicompetence, 166

nativist, 9, 145, 178
Natural Method, 33
Navajo, 58
negation, 182
negative evidence, 121
Ngiti, 42
Noun Classification, 6, 51
Null Subjects, 135
Number, 46, 47, 48, 50, 54, 65, 71, 86, 89, 94, 106, 107, 144, 147

Oral Approach, 34
Organic Grammar, 127
overgeneralisation, 97, 104, 119, 126, 137, 146, 148, 176, 180

Partitivity, 27, 31
Passive, 5, 10, 98
paucal, 47, 48, 50, 54
pedagogical grammar, 79, 88, 89, 90, 91, 93, 95, 98, 105
performance, 9
person, 6, 41, 44, 45, 47, 53, 67, 71, 141, 151, 154
phoneme, 44
Phonetics, 19
phonology, 58
Pidgins, 70, 72

plural, 42, 44, 47, 48, 50, 53, 54, 64, 65, 70, 71, 76, 84, 89, 94, 106, 118, 147, 148, 152, 170
plurilingualism, 164, 166
politeness, 68, 69
polysynthesis, 58
Post-methods' era, 37
poverty of the stimulus, 9, 121, 178
pragmatics, 14, 35, 138
preposition stranding 88
prescriptive grammar, 84, 86
process and result nominals, 123
productive, 11
property theory, 21
prosodic bootstrapping, 139
proto-language, 55

quantifier scope, 155
quantifiers, 181
Question Formation, 49, 143

reference grammar, 80
register, 66, 86, 108, 149, 166, 169
residual optionality, 133
resting level, 22, 23
Russian, 25, 50

Samoan, 92, 93
satellite-framed, 56, 57
Semantics, 20, 58
Singular, 29, 47, 48, 50, 54, 65, 71, 76, 89, 141, 147
Situational Approach, 34
Spanish, 43, 55, 57, 58, 67, 81, 82, 83, 102, 108, 170
Specificity, 1, 2, 54, 91, 92, 179

Structure Dependence, 48, 49, 60, 77, 82, 143, 144
Swahili, 5, 6, 96
syntax, 17, 22, 58, 82, 90, 138
Systemic Functional Linguistics, 13

Tamil, 79
Tariana, 18, 107
Telicity, 25, 169, 171
tenor, 68
tense, 31, 59, 109, 127
Tok Pisin, 71
Tones, 46
transfer, 24, 125, 127, 130, 150, 170
translanguaging, 24, 110, 166, 167
Turkish, 43, 55, 58, 150, 151
typology, 57, 58, 59, 61

unaccusativity, 97, 99, 111
unergative, 98
Universal Grammar, 9, 21, 111, 187
universals, 53, 60, 61, 98, 171
Upper Sorbian, 47
Usage-based approaches, 11

Verb Classes, 12, 15
verb-framed, 56, 57
Vietnamese, 42, 45
Virtual Grammar, 3, 26, 28, 29, 37, 43, 48, 53, 59, 64, 73, 78, 81, 91, 95, 107, 108, 110, 111, 112, 113, 118, 137, 138, 142, 156, 157, 164, 166, 167, 169, 171, 172
voice, 9

Welsh, 62